BUILDING A .... SOCIETY:
NEW PRIORITIES FOR PUBLIC POLICY

Contributors

Dr Michael Argyle	Emeritus Professor of Psychology, Oxford Brookes University
Dr Dick Atkinson	Director, The Phoenix Centre, Birmingham and Co-ordinator, The Building Sustainable Communities Agenda
Nicola Baker	Editor and Freelance Researcher
Dr Andrew Briggs	Lecturer, Department of Materials, University of Oxford
Dr Martin Clark	Research Associate, Centre for Training Policy & Research, University of Sheffield
Gabrielle Cox	Co-ordinator, Greater Manchester Low Pay Unit
Rev. Graham Cray	Principal, Ridley Hall, Cambridge
Professor Shirley Dex	Economist and Lecturer in Management Studies, Judge Institute for Management Studies, University of Cambridge
David French	Director, RELATE 1987–95
Timothy M. Green	Chief Executive, Switch Card Services Ltd
Professor A.H. Halsey	Emeritus Fellow, Nuffield College, Oxford
Wally Harbert OBE	Director of Planning & Development, Help the Aged 1990–96
Professor Nathaniel Lichfield and Dalia Lichfield	Partners of Dalia and Nathaniel Lichfield Associates, Urban Environmental Development Planning
Clive Mather	Head of Information and Computing, Shell International BV
John Monks	General Secretary, Trades Union Congress
Ceridwen Roberts	Director, Family Policy Studies Centre
Dr Helen Roberts	Co-ordinator, Research and Development, Barnardo's
Dr Michael Schluter	Director, The Relationships Foundation

Building a Relational Society

New priorities for public policy

edited by
Nicola Baker

arena

© Nicola Baker 1996

All rights reserved. No part of this publication may be reproduced, stored in a retrieval system, or transmitted in any form or by any means, electronic, mechanical, photocopying, recording or otherwise without the prior permission of the publisher.

Published by
Arena
Ashgate Publishing Limited
Gower House
Croft Road
Aldershot
Hants GU11 3HR
England

Ashgate Publishing Company
Old Post Road
Brookfield
Vermont 05036
USA

British Library Cataloguing in Publication Data

Building a relational society: new priorities
  for public policy
  1. Community development – Great Britain
  2. Social planning – Great Britain 3. Great Britain –
  Social policy
  I. Baker, Nicola
  361.6'1'0941

Library of Congress Catalog Card Number: 96-85247

ISBN 1 85742 349 6 (paperback)
ISBN 1 85742 348 8 (hardback)

Typeset by Raven Typesetters, Chester and printed in Great Britain by Hartnolls Ltd, Bodmin

Contents

Biographical details ix

Acknowledgements xv

Preface xvii

Part I Introduction: Relationships matter

1 Making relationships a priority for public policy 3
   Michael Schluter

2 Committed relationships: Current trends 17
   Ceridwen Roberts

3 The effects of relationships on well-being 33
   Michael Argyle

4 Short-term relationships: Reaping the liberal whirlwind 49
   A.H. Halsey

5 Postmodernism: Mutual society in crisis 65
   Graham Cray

Part II Vulnerable relationships

6 Till death do us part? 83
   David French

7	Children in need *Helen Roberts*	93
8	From generation to generation *Wally Harbert*	107

Part III Sources of pressure on relationships: Work versus family dilemmas

9	Stakeholders in the workplace *John Monks*	121
10	Developing corporate responsibility *Clive Mather*	135
11	Employment and caring within households *Shirley Dex*	151

Part IV Sources of pressure on relationships: The wider context

12	Science and technology: Profit or loss? *Andrew Briggs*	167
13	Fiscal and welfare policy: Why families lose out *Gabrielle Cox*	183
14	Banking and finance: The importance of relationships *Timothy M. Green*	201
15	Urban relationships: A challenge in town planning *Dalia and Nathaniel Lichfield*	217

Part V The way forward

16	The common sense of community *Dick Atkinson*	233
17	Relational impact statements: Measuring the effect of public policy on personal relationships *Martin Clark*	249
18	Changed priorities ahead: Rebuilding the relational base *Nicola Baker*	267

Further reading	287
The Relationships Foundation	289

Biographical details

Michael Argyle is Emeritus Professor of Psychology at Oxford Brookes University, Reader in Social Psychology at Oxford University and a Fellow of Wolfson College. He has been a visiting professor at several universities in the USA, Canada, Australia, Africa, Israel and Continental Europe. Dr Argyle pioneered the use of social skills training in Britain, helped to found the *British Journal of Social and Clinical Psychology* and was its social psychology editor (1961–7). He has edited series of social psychology books for Penguin Books and Pergamon Press and has published extensively on social psychology issues, including: *The Psychology of Interpersonal Behaviour* (Penguin, 1967, 1972, 1978, 1983), *The Social Psychology of Religion* (with B. Beit-Hallahmi, Routledge & Kegan Paul, 1975), *The Anatomy of Relationships* (with M. Henderson, Penguin, 1985) and *The Psychology of Happiness* (Methuen, 1987). He is married with four children and eight grandchildren.

Dick Atkinson is Director of the Phoenix Centre in Birmingham, which encourages and disseminates good practice in urban regeneration. He is also Co-ordinator of the new Building Sustainable Communities Agenda. Previously, he lectured at Manchester and Birmingham Universities in Social Sciences before setting up the St Paul's community education and development agency in Balsall Heath and working with Birmingham Education Authority to plan their education and development policy. He is the author of *Orthodox Consensus, Radical Alternative: A Study in Sociological Theory* (Heinemann, 1973), *Radical Urban Solutions* (Cassell, 1994) and *Cities of Pride* (Cassell, 1995). He is married with two children.

Nicola Baker now works as an editor and researcher on current political and social issues. Until 1995, she co-ordinated the research work of the Jubilee Policy Group, which specialised in public policy analysis from a Christian perspective. Previously, she has worked in political research, public relations and international finance. She (with J. Burnside, Waterside Press, 1994) jointly edited an earlier series of papers, *Relational Justice: Repairing the Breach*, which advocated a new approach to criminal justice that puts restoring relationships at the heart of the justice system. She is married with two (part-time) stepchildren.

Andrew Briggs is Lecturer in Materials at Oxford University. He read physics as an undergraduate, did a PhD at the Cavendish Laboratory, University of Cambridge, where he also completed a degree in theology. His current area of research involves studying surfaces over a logarithmic range of depth scales, from a fraction of a millimetre to the top layers of atoms and molecules, using acoustic microscopes and scanning tunnelling microscopes. Dr Briggs's recent publications include the Clarendon Press Monograph, *Acoustic Microscopy* (Oxford University Press, 1992), *The Science of New Materials* (Blackwell, 1992) and the new series 'Advances in Acoustic Microscopy' (Plenum, 1995), acting as editor for these latter two. In addition, he has written 160 articles and scientific papers with colleagues in Oxford and elsewhere. He is married with two children.

Martin Clark has been Research Associate at the Centre for Training Policy Studies at the University of Sheffield, where he developed an evaluation strategy for Sheffield's Single Regeneration Budget programme. He has a PhD in geography at Sheffield, where he analysed the experiences of long-term unemployed young people on government training schemes. He is currently working for the Relationships Foundation to develop a 'civic identity' strategy to address unemployment. He and his wife live in Nottingham.

Gabrielle Cox is Co-ordinator of the Greater Manchester Low Pay Unit and author of a number of reports on employment issues. She is founder and secretary of the Campaign Against Poverty, a voluntary national network, and also has particular interests in inner-city issues through involvement in a range of community groups in Moss Side, Manchester. She is married with two children.

Graham Cray is Principal of Ridley Hall Theological College, Cambridge. For 14 years, he was Vicar of St Michael-le-Belfry in York, with a regular congregation of 800. He has chaired the annual Christian Greenbelt Arts Festival, and his particular areas of interest are communicating Christian teaching and ethics within modern culture, and contemporary music. Recent publications include: *The Gospel and Tomorrow's Culture* (CPAS, 1994), 'A Gospel for our Culture' in *To Proclaim Afresh* (SPCK, 1995) and 'Cultures and Worldviews: 25 years of change' in *All Things to all People: Mission Beyond 2000* (St John's College, Nottingham, 1995). He and his wife have two daughters.

Shirley Dex is Economist and Lecturer in Management Studies at the Judge Institute, University of Cambridge. For the last five years she has been Research Professor (part-time) at the ESRC Research Centre on Micro Social Change, University of Essex. Previously, she has held posts in economics at the Universities of Keele and Aston. Her publications include: *French and British Mothers at Work* (with P. Walter and D. Alden, Macmillan, 1993), *Flexible Employment in Britain: A Statistical Analysis* (Equal Opportunities Commission, 1995) and *Caring and Employment* (Employment Department Research Series No. 39, 1994). She is married with two children.

David French was Director of RELATE (formerly the National Marriage Guidance Council) from 1987 to 1995. During that time, he oversaw a 100% increase in the volume of the agency's work. He began his career in the brewing industry but moved into the voluntary sector in 1971, where he worked for the National Council for Voluntary Organisations. In 1974, he became Head of the Social Services Department at the Royal National Institute for the Deaf, until, in 1978, he became Director of Services at the Children's Society. David is married with four sons and lives in St Albans.

Timothy M. Green started his career in banking with NatWest in the North of England and has held a number of positions both at home and abroad. In 1988, while still with NatWest, he launched the Switch Card Scheme, and he is currently Chief Executive of the company. He is also a Fellow of the Chartered Institute of Bankers and Freeman of the City of London. For many years, Tim Green was Chairman of NatWest's Christian Fellowship, and he is a member of the City Ethics Forum, Churchwarden at St Margaret's Lothbury in the City of London, as well as an elder in his local church in Danbury. He is married and has two children.

A.H. Halsey is Emeritus Fellow, Nuffield College, Oxford, having been Professor of Social and Administrative Studies at Oxford University from 1977 to 1990. His academic career started at the London School of Economics and included studies at the Universities of Liverpool and Birmingham, as well as at the Center for Advanced Study of the Behavioural Sciences, Palo Alto, USA, and also a year as Visiting Professor, University of Chicago. Among his extensive range of publications and monographs are: *Change in British Society* (Oxford University Press, 1978, 1981, 1986, Open University foundation text, 1995), *English Ethical Socialism: From Thomas More to R H Tawney* (with N. Dennis, Oxford University Press, 1988), and 'The Present State of Sociology in Britain' in *British Journal of Sociology* (September 1989, editor of whole issue). Professor Halsey lives in Oxford and is married with five children.

Wally Harbert, OBE trained as a psychiatric social worker and worked in community mental health services for eight years. After serving as General Secretary of the Liverpool Personal Service Society, he became Director of Social Services, first for Hackney and then for 17 years for Avon. He was President of the Association of Directors of Social Services in 1978/79. He joined Help the Aged in 1990 as Director of UK Operations and later became Director of Planning and Development. Wally Harbert has published on social policy and management issues, served on several government committees and carried out assignments in Europe for the United Nations, the World Health Organisation and the European Union. He is married with five grown-up children and lives in the West Country.

Dalia and Nathaniel Lichfield are Partners in Dalia and Nathaniel Lichfield Associates, Urban Environmental Development Planning. Nathaniel and Dalia are a husband-and-wife team who enjoy the pleasures and tribulations of the dual-career family. They share four children and three grandchildren.

Dalia Lichfield studied Architecture and Planning at the Technion University, Haifa, Israel, where she holds a BA and MSc. Her publications include: 'Alternative Strategies for Redistribution' in *Habitat International* (1982, Vol.8, No.3/4), 'Assessing Project Impacts as though People Mattered, a method for enhancing public involvement and planning accountability' in *Planning* (1994, No.1058) and 'The Integration of Environmental Assessment and Development Planning, Prospect Park, Hillingdon' (with Nathaniel Lichfield) in *Project Appraisal* (1992, Vol.7, No.3).

Nathaniel Lichfield is Professor Emeritus of the Economics of Environmental Planning, University of London, and a Past President of the Royal Town Planning Institute. He is internationally renowned for his work on development planning, conservation, and in particular on Community Impact Evaluation (1996, University College Press). Other publications include *Economics in Urban Conservation* (Cambridge University Press, 1988), *Land Policy in Planning* (with H. Darin-Drabkin, Allen & Unwin, 1980) and *Evaluation in the Planning Process* (with P. Kettle and M. Whitbread, Pergamon Press, 1975).

Clive Mather was Director of Personnel and Administration for Shell UK Ltd when asked to contribute to this volume. He has now taken up a new post with Shell International BV as Head of Information and Computing. His long career with Shell has involved management positions in human resources and marketing and many international assignments. He is a trustee of the Windsor Leadership Trust and, until recently, an Equal Opportunities Commissioner. He is married with three children and a dog.

John Monks became General Secretary of the TUC in 1993 after having been

Deputy General Secretary for six years and previously Head, Organisation and Industrial Relations Department, for ten years. He was a member of ACAS until 1995 and continues to be a member of the National Advisory Council for Education and Training Targets. His other concerns include being a trustee of the National Museum of Labour History, membership of the governing bodies of both Goldsmith's College and the London School of Economics, and also of the Council of the Policy Studies Institute. John Monks lives in south-east London, where he is also governor of a large comprehensive school and supports the Goldsmith's Youth Orchestra. He is married with three children.

Ceridwen Roberts has been Director of the Family Policy Studies Centre since October 1992. A sociologist, she worked previously in the Employment Department and Trent Polytechnic. She has a long-standing interest in the interaction between family life and employment and, together with Jean Martin, wrote *Women and Employment: a lifetime perspective* (HMSO, 1984). She leads the centre's work analysing family trends and family policy and is currently involved in research projects on 'Kinship and Friendship Networks', 'Childlessness in Britain' and 'The Changing Role of Fathers'.

Helen Roberts co-ordinates research and development at Barnardo's, the largest childcare charity in the UK and is Visiting Senior Fellow with the Social Statistics Research Unit, City University, London. Her research interests include the evidence basis for social welfare interventions, and the ways in which we can effectively listen to children in research. Her most recent publications are: *Young People's Social Attitudes* (ed. with D. Sachev, Barnardo's, 1996), *Children at Risk: Safety as a Social Value* (with S.J. Smith, Open University Press, 1995) and *What Works in the Early Years?* (with G. Macdonald, Barnardo's, 1995).

Michael Schluter is the founder and Director of the Relationships Foundation, part of the Jubilee Centre in Cambridge. The foundation was set up to develop responses to public policy issues from the perspective of their impact on human relationships. He trained as an economist and worked in East Africa with the World Bank and the International Food Policy Research Institute. He is joint author of *The R Factor* (with D. Lee, Hodder and Stoughton, 1993), which advocates a relational approach to public policy. He is married with three children.

Acknowledgements

Readers of this collection of papers may express surprise at the range and variety of the contributors. You may wonder what could possibly have brought them together, given their different professional disciplines, diverse expertise and divergent political views.

This volume is a testimony to the breadth of relationships which Dr Michael Schluter and others at the Relationships Foundation have within the academic community, the worlds of business and commerce and with public, private and voluntary agencies of all kinds. Some contributors are old friends; some new. Some are active supporters and some are only respectful and partial endorsers of the Foundation's aims and objectives.

As editor of this collection and charged with the task of drawing together the contributions, my chief thanks go to all our authors for sparing their time so generously towards this project. Their experience and expertise has vastly extended the understanding of how our family, work and social relationships are impacted by public policies and corporate strategies at many levels.

I would also acknowledge my gratitude to those who have lent me moral, intellectual and practical support during the editorial process. In particular, I would like to thank Michael Schluter whose vision has been the major source of inspiration behind this project; also David Lee, John Ashcroft and Andrew Crook who have provided background research and data; and especially to Tina Kempson who patiently co-ordinated 18 different scripts. The Relationships Foundation is extremely grateful to Mr and Mrs Gideon Hudson, Mr and Mrs Paddy Marsh and Mr and Mrs William Norris for their generous donations towards this project. Finally, I want to thank my husband Iain who last year married not only me, but also a partially-completed book.

Nicola Baker
May 1996

Preface

A long-term programme of research and initiatives has been undertaken by the Relationships Foundation since the publication of *The R Factor* in 1993. The goal has been to demonstrate how decisions made in public life by corporates and government impact on the way individuals and groups relate to one another, both in an organisational context and in the domestic environment.

The first book to flow from this work, *Relational Justice*, analysed the criminal justice system from a relational perspective. If crime is defined as a breakdown in the relationship between offender and victim, or offender and local community, policy changes are demanded in sentencing practice, in crime prevention strategies and in the place of the victim in the judicial process. One practical application has been a method to measure and benchmark the quality of relationships in the prison system. Further research is now in progress on 'relational healthcare' within the NHS, and into relational values in civic life with particular emphasis on issues surrounding unemployment.

Building a Relational Society is the second book in this series. It grew out of work by Nicola Baker over several years on issues of family policy. An important point of consensus across caring agencies, as well as political parties, was that long-term, stable, committed relationships are the key to personal well-being. This priority applied however 'family' was defined. External factors which impact on the quality of these relationships are thus a legitimate source of public concern.

The various contributors to this book have made valuable progress in staking out the ground which needs to be covered if, as a society, we are to address the relational breakdown so much in evidence around us. Widespread policy changes will be required if society is to provide a framework conducive to strengthening our relational base. We hope that this volume will give rise to a lively debate across the political spectrum as to how relational priorities in public life can be promoted in the future.

Michael Schluter
The Relationships Foundation
Cambridge, July 1996

Part I

Introduction: Relationships matter

1 Making relationships a priority for public policy

Michael Schluter

A friend of mine visiting from Africa was not convinced Britain was a better place to live. Yes, we agreed, the standard of living is higher, as measured by the number of cars and television sets. But beneath the surface, behind the numerous faces on the high street, it is a different story. He was not referring primarily to levels of crime and the fear that crime brings into many people's lives – for crime is a big problem in Africa, too. Nor was he referring to the weather – infinitely preferable in Africa! His concern was what he saw of human relationships in Britain: serial monogamy, bewildered and neglected children, the loneliness of elderly parents living so far away from their children. What is the point, he asked, of so-called 'development' if it so often leads to fragmented relationships and social isolation?

Strong bonds in the relationships of an individual should not be regarded as an optional extra, only relevant for a lucky minority. For it is by our relationships that we define who we are. The wicked stepmother in the story of *Snow White and the Seven Dwarfs* had to appeal to the mirror on the wall to tell her 'who was the fairest of them all' precisely because she could not assess her own beauty, or understand her own character, outside a comparative framework made up of other people. It is through our relationships with other people that we come to know ourselves.

The relationships factor also provides the clue to whether people take care of each other in times of crisis. In the summer of 1993, a television crew filmed an elderly lady (an actress) falling down in the street, to see how long it would take for a member of the public to stop and help. In the first location, a village street, it took just two minutes before someone stopped to help; in the second, a busy shopping mall, the elderly lady had to wait 45 minutes for the first offer of help. How willing we are to help a stranger is determined in part by how well we know them, or expect to know them. Villages facilitate close interactions; huge cities generally undermine them. A sense of duty or obligation is determined in part by the individual's religious belief, parental upbringing and perhaps their genetic code, but in part it is a matter of how we order both public and private life.

Or take another example. Suppose you play golf once a month at the local golf club and frequently play with the same partner. One month when you go for the game, you find she has contracted ME and so will be unable to play again for some time, probably several years. What is an appropriate response? A bunch of flowers? A card? A phone call? Each or all of these – but it is unlikely you will feel the need to provide a 'meals on wheels' service each day for the next five years. However, if your mother living a few streets away contracted ME, simply sending a single card might seem an inadequate response over a five-year period. Again, the obligation we feel depends on the closeness of our relationship. When we grow old, how we will be treated will depend largely on the number and closeness of the relationships we have formed earlier in life.

To say that a person's well-being depends fundamentally on the quality of his or her relationships appears, at one level, to do no more than state the obvious. Even the observation that quality in relationships is essential to the success of all economic, political and social systems hardly strikes one as profound. The importance of integrity and trust, for example, is widely recognised as essential to the efficient working of markets.[1] Yet in a culture that places extraordinarily heavy emphasis on financial achievement and individual fulfilment, relationships are seldom given priority even at the personal level, let alone in public policy. It is perhaps because relationships are largely taken for granted, and consequently remain 'invisible', that the relational structure of our society has been allowed to sustain so much damage.

One reason for the lack of public concern about what is happening to our relationships in society is perhaps an awareness of the disadvantages of relational proximity in a society where relationships have already deteriorated. At certain points in the lifecycle or under certain conditions, people want privacy and independence from obligations more than they want long-standing relationships and security. Young people past childhood often find too close a proximity of relations to be oppressive. Similarly, there are phenomena such as the loveless or brutal marriage, child abuse, familial bullying, individual stereotyping and scapegoating, and so on. These phenomena cannot be passed over lightly.

For many critics, our stress on the benefits of relationships will come across as sentimentalism, to be contrasted with the actual behaviour of people which, in their view, consistently endorses choice as presented by free markets. For example, a customer may often prefer facelessness because it permits him or her to insist on a precise definition of the product or service they want, without confrontation. Also, it helps the shy or cautious to avoid being 'sold to' or persuaded through strength of personality rather than on real service need or the merit of a product. Since buyers often distrust traders, and often with reason, 'mechanical' or 'transactional' trading has benefits in placing relatively greater power with the buyer in each individual act of trading.

To some extent, the perceived advantages of relational distance are a consequence of relationship breakdown, which becomes self-reinforcing in a downward spiral of fragmentation. In addition, we must recognise that there are differences of relational need and attitude between individuals, and between the generations, so that some will need more personal space than others. However, it is generally 'the strong' who seek and benefit from such space, and the weak and disadvantaged who gain when community is emphasised. In any event, relatively few would deny that extreme liberal capitalism has taken individual choice and freedom to a point where these 'goods' have become 'not-so-goods'. It is time to redress the balance.

It is still important that we attempt to define what we mean by a 'good relationship'. Research undertaken as background to this book revealed that among agencies dealing with breakdown in family and local community relationships, there was general agreement that long-term, committed, stable relationships benefited all parties, and especially children.[2] 'Long-term', in this context, refers to at least the period of the parenting role, say 16–20 years. Commitment is not necessarily indicated by the existence of a marriage certificate or some formal arrangement, but is more an attitude of priority given to the relationship. It assumes that the relationship is indissoluble, and that every effort will be made to resolve conflicts when they arise. Such relationships are characterised by affection, attachment, self-sacrificial giving and mutuality, and have a dynamic sense of moving forward together.

Hidden pressures on close relationships

Close personal relationships are increasingly difficult to sustain as we approach the twenty-first century. It is worth pausing to ask why. There is no inherent reason to believe human beings have become less interested in relationships, or less ethically motivated, than earlier generations. The reasons appear to lie in a number of converging factors which lie largely outside the individual's span of control. However, to respond to these forces requires first that we understand them.

The role of technology, and in particular the information revolution, in moulding our relationships can be both constructive and damaging. Telephone, fax and electronic mail (e-mail) make it far easier for me to keep in touch with my mother, who lives in Nairobi. Opportunities for regular contact and conversation now extend from one end to the other of our global village. But equally, the sheer number of people I am now in touch with

6 Building a Relational Society

means that, inevitably, my relational capacity is spread more thinly as it extends over a greater surface area. Ultimately, we will know less and less about more and more people until we know nothing about everybody. As the communications facilities continue to improve, and so too does access to information, close personal relationships built on a sustained input of time and commitment will require more deliberate and difficult choices to exclude other, more superficial relationships.

The globalisation of world markets is also putting pressure indirectly on close relationships in a variety of ways. Growing numbers of the workforce are required to move, and to move more frequently over greater distances. Yet such mobility is the antithesis of what is required to build relationships in the family and in the neighbourhood. Lack of social integration as a result of mobility explains both regional and community size variations in the divorce rate in the United States.[3] Similar results have been found in Canada.[4] A study by Robertson of hospital doctors and their families has documented the kind of stress that mobility brings about for family life:

> These wives found that mobility was isolating because it both severed established ties with relatives, friends and neighbours and placed them in new and unfamiliar situations. When moves were frequent, feelings of non-belongingness were on-going ... building up new relationships was usually a lengthy process.[5]

Less than half of the British population ever have a proper conversation with their next-door neighbours.[6] In response to global competition, many companies are extracting longer hours of work from employees, and on shorter-term contracts, eroding further the basis of stable marriage and parenting relationships. The catalogue of knock-on effects is a long one.

Many actions by government, often inadvertently and indirectly, also put pressure on close personal relationships. The transfer of decision-making from local government to central government in the 1980s was carried out in the context of an ideological battle to prevent what was perceived to be an abuse of power by a small number of local authorities. One effect, however, of strangling local finance has been to remove an important incentive for local co-operative initiative and a basis for building relationships in the community through shared goals. Rapid closure of coal mines after a seven-month warning period, rather than a fifteen-year warning period as in other European countries, may have helped keep down the cost of fuel, but it has had a devastating impact on the households of the miners directly affected by the closures.

At a more subtle level, the materialism of Western culture undermines the value we put on relationships. Perhaps this is most clearly seen in the way we treat elderly people. A materialistic ethos has marginalised elderly people, so that they tend to be excluded from status-giving roles.

Participation in society has come to be defined in terms of paid employment, so that the extensive involvement of women and elderly people in the voluntary sector, and in the physical, emotional and spiritual support of the extended family, are constantly undervalued. The role of grandparents as perpetuators of the cultural legacy of the family is hard to measure in financial terms.

Above all, it is probably our attitude towards the pursuit of personal psychological satisfaction which has the greatest influence over close relationships in the household. As marriage is no longer a passport to either economic security or social status, perhaps we should not be surprised that those making the self-sacrifice involved in sustaining a marriage relationship should seek some benefit in terms of personal satisfaction. However, unrealistic expectations loaded onto the marriage partnership may now be placing extra pressures on some couples who are not emotionally equipped to cope. We now know too much about the effects of divorce on children to allow the single-minded pursuit of personal fulfilment to be sufficient justification to terminate a marriage.[7]

The ultimate end-product of attempts to create relationships founded entirely on choice, and without commitment, is the 'virtual community' of the Internet. As John Gray has argued, people join such so-called communities not as a result of the accidents of birth or history, but by personal choice. There is no gender, ethnicity or religion. You can join when you like, and leave when you like. You have no responsibilities, duties or obligations. Formed in the bodiless ether of cyberspace, virtual communities satisfy human needs for communication without any of the traditional constraints. Virtual community is community at zero cost.[8]

Mapping the relational base

'Family' and 'community' have proved increasingly difficult words to use in public discourse. Neither is easy to define. 'Family' now covers a variety of organisational arrangements, from a single parent with a child to an extended kin-group with as many as 60 or 70 members. Equally, the word 'community' is used at one moment of a small, local neighbourhood and at another of a professional association of businessmen that has a formal meeting once a year. Neither term gives any indication of the closeness of relationships involved, nor is there any basis for comparing the influence of one or the other in the life of the individual.

One way over the difficulties produced by the words 'family' and 'community' is to express both in the common language of relationships. What it means to be 'family' is, in essence, a matter of relationship, even if there has been no direct contact for years. Our relationships in the past become part of our identity. At the other end of the spectrum, the 'local community' has no significance whatsoever in our lives if we live a lifestyle which gives us no contact with our next-door neighbour. The term 'community' ceases to have content in any geographical sense. However, for most people, both family and community are important aspects of their identity, because they contribute to what we wish to call 'the relational base'.

There is a general sense in which society has a 'relational base' – a foundation of relationships whose quality and effectiveness determine social wellbeing. In this respect, a relational approach puts forward a theory of society which is both supplementary to and distinct from the conventional models. Neither the dominant liberal-individual conception of society as an aggregation of pre-social individuals nor the organic conception of it as a body politic gives adequate account of interpersonal relationships. Yet without relationships, neither individuality nor society can truly be said to exist. To use the term 'relational base', therefore, is to draw attention to one of society's most vital elements, and to plug a terminological gap that would otherwise have to be covered, inadequately, by a phrase like 'social structure' or 'social ecology'.

There is a sense in which the individual, too, has a relational base, meaning the network of his or her significant relationships, and it is in this sense that we wish to use it here. At its simplest, the individual's relational base can be represented using a set of concentric circles, the relationships entered as crosses, and the level of significance measured by distance from a central point (see Figure 1). The diagram in effect ranks a person's relationships on a single scale. There can be wide variations in both the number and distribution of entries, but in general the inner circles will contain some arrangement of close family and friends where relationships are characterised by a high level of intimacy. The outer circles will typically be filled by those where either there are high levels of intimacy but infrequent contact, or frequent contact but less intimacy. Such relationships would generally include those in the workplace, the neighbourhood, social clubs, and so on. By mapping the relational base, even in this subjective way, therefore, it is possible to gain an impression of what 'family' and 'community' mean to a given person. They constitute, in fact, a relational environment in which the individual exercises influence, and from which he or she derives support.

My relational base would also be measured not by the subjective measures of how much I 'like' each person who is in contact with me, but by how much 'relational proximity' I have with them, which has been defined in terms of five aspects, or 'dimensions' in which people get to know and understand each others' thoughts and behaviour.[9] These five dimensions of relationship are as follows:

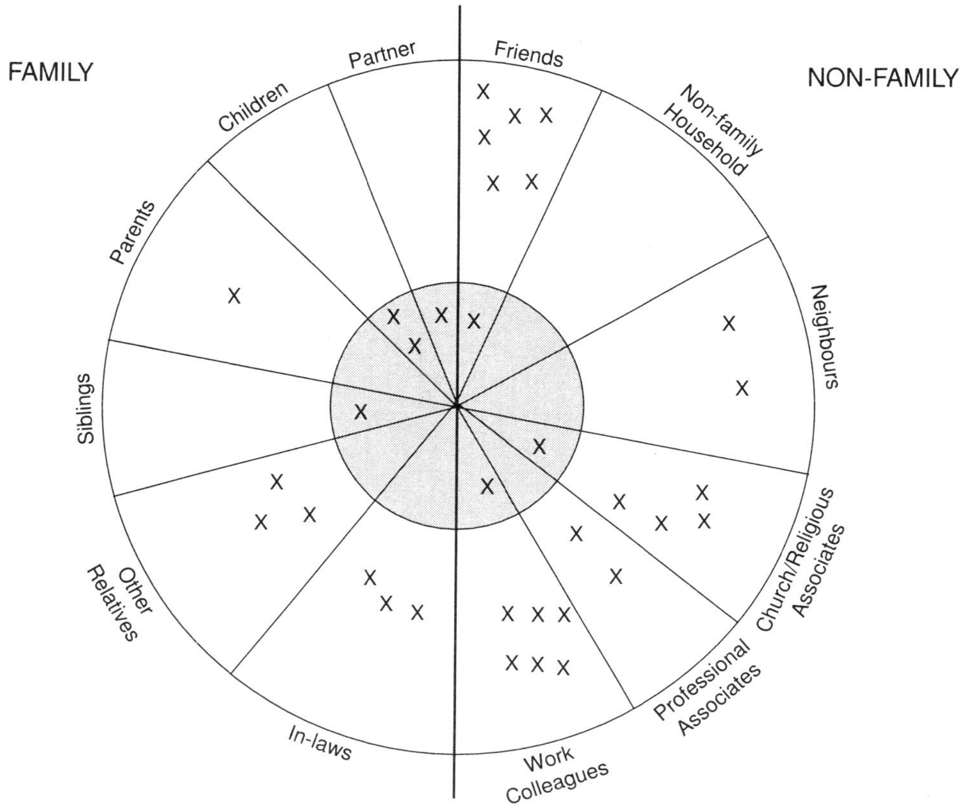

Figure 1.1 An individual's relational base

- **Directness** – the extent to which people meet *face-to-face* rather than having contact through a third party or through impersonal media;
- **Continuity** – the extent to which people meet frequently, regularly and over a sustained period of time;
- **Multiplexity** – the extent to which people have contact in more than one role or context, so that they can see how people respond in different situations and can understand other dimensions of another person's background and lifestyle;
- **Parity** – the extent to which people meet as equals, not in terms of role or status, but in terms of their sense of personal worth or value;
- **Commonality** – the extent to which people have common purpose and common experience, as these help to cement and deepen relationships.

Broadly speaking, these provide a quantifiable measure of closeness, or 'relational proximity', between two or more people.[10] They describe the 'structure' of personal relationships, and they constitute the necessary preconditions for 'empathy', an understanding of how other people feel and react, even when people do not necessarily like each other. However, they tell you little about 'intimacy', for intimacy depends on a voluntary self-giving to another and requires self-disclosure, which automatically makes the individual vulnerable. Nevertheless, the loss of a person with whom you have had long and extensive contact can occasion bereavement, even if you did not especially like them (i.e. even without intimacy).

There are particular life-stages and events at which the priority and importance of relationships should be recognised. Entries in the inner circle of the relational base confirm what could be deduced equally well from psychological evidence or a flip through the lonely hearts column in the newspaper: that people need relationships, and in particular, though individuals vary, need at least one other person to whom they are not merely known, but close. Here, of course, it becomes obvious that the relational base surrounding an individual is subject to flux in ways that cannot be captured by taking a cross-section at a single point in time. Circumstances change, friends come and go, relatives die or are born, and the pattern of the individual's relationships shifts accordingly. Often, these mark particular life-stages and events at which relational (as opposed to merely technical, financial or medical) support is required. It is at these points where the case for setting down explicitly relational public policy objectives is most compelling.

During at least two phases, for instance, the individual will be heavily dependent on others: early childhood and extreme old age. It is not enough to feed a child and keep her clean, nor is it enough merely to commit an elderly person to even the most expensive comforts of residential care. In order to grow into the full potential of her humanity, the infant needs not only nourishment, but love and human contact. Seven or eight decades later, she will need exactly the same thing – however easily these relational needs may be overlooked by the next generation, and however unpalatable the privations of old age are in a culture that can bear only youth and health. Between the dawn and the twilight of life, of course, occur many critical events in which a person's relationships are basic to survival and well-being: bereavement, long-term illness, childbirth, redundancy, parenthood, responsibility for a sick person, stress at work, criticism, disappointment. Perhaps more significant than any is the process of socialisation, since language skills develop and complex learning processes start to occur through close family relationships.

The positioning of relationships in social and geographic space influences the nature and quality of the term 'community'. Community is not the automatic result of individuals or families occupying the same residential area. It requires the establishment of long-term, cross-cutting, shared-interest relationships. Where these do not exist, either because the 'privatisation' of the middle-class home environment puts such contact at a premium, or because rapid rates of inter-regional as well as much intra-regional mobility mean that households pass through neighbourhoods rather than integrating with them,[11] the local community becomes defined less by its common consciousness than by its linkage to the same shopping centre.

Sources of common purpose as the foundation for community are now often based on interest and choice rather than on residential location. Individuals belong to overlapping communities of Scout troops, golf clubs or Round Tables, or, on a higher scale, to 'virtual communities' of subscribers to the same motoring organisation or magazine, the other members of which they seldom, if ever, meet. However, the problem with non-geographic communities of all forms, other than those where the relationships are based on kinship, is that in times of stress or difficulty, it is too easy for the strong individual to opt out or leave. In general, the weaker and more vulnerable members of society do not become members of such groups or associations, except in cases where they have a strong localised presence, such as a retail co-operative or credit union. By definition, they have little to 'give', as measured in finance or professional expertise, and because their very presence would place an obligation on others in the community, they are seldom invited in.

It is generally only in those communities defined by locality (i.e. neighbourhood) or kinship (i.e. family/extended family) that duty and obligation find expression towards the disadvantaged on a sustained basis.[12] These are what Dahrendorf describes as the 'communities of fate' versus 'communities of choice'.[13] Geographic proximity is essential to provide a whole range of personal support services, from taking an elderly person shopping to cutting their toe-nails. Certain forms of psychological comfort and support can only be given by those who have known a person over many years. Paid professional support services are limited as an alternative to family and neighbourhood support by both their cost and by the range of human need they can reasonably be expected to meet. It is, therefore, *real* community – kin and neighbourhood – rather than *virtual* community which most needs to be protected and encouraged by public policy.

Rebuilding the relational base: A goal for public policy

While politicians on all sides are now agreeing that community, and even family, are 'a good thing', there is little consensus yet on what government could or should do to sustain and develop strong local ties.

A major reason for this arises out of the reluctance to interfere in the 'private' domain of family life now expressed by both the Right and the Left in British politics. On the Right, the concern to minimise the role of the State and to promote individual liberty and choice takes precedence over 'social engineering'. On the Left, the commitment to freedom of choice in personal lifestyle and individual rights has led into a political cul-de-sac, where the competing rights of mothers, fathers and children cannot easily be accommodated without an unacceptably burdensome legal strait-jacket.

The current public debate on revitalising community and family, and more particularly, the parenting function and community, fails tragically to address the roots of the problem.

First, there has been a tendency for the debate to polarise around the so-called 'traditional' and 'modern' camps which have conducted sterile dialogues on 'What is a family?', interesting to pressure groups and think-tanks but irrelevant to most people's lives.

Second, both Left and Right, in pursuing their arguments to their logical conclusion, often appear to arrive at solutions which are primarily *economic* and not *relational*. Thus, the government talks about creating the right conditions in which families can make choices about the best childcare for their children. The Left calls for universal public provision of pre-school education.

Third, public attention focuses on the impact of policy instruments which directly impinge on family relationships, such as the Child Support Agency and the recently-renewed attempts to change the law on divorce. Little thought is given to monitoring the impact of other actions of government which can have just as much influence over relationships – but of an indirect and, presumably, unintended nature. There are several reasons for this, not least the absence of any over-arching mechanism of government to bridge the divide between different departments of State. A youth crime committee which requires co-ordination by the Home Office, the Department of Social

Security, the Department of Health and the Department for Education will find it difficult to reach a consensus on the most effective policy options.

It is the thesis of this book that a new basis for discussing family policy is long overdue, and moreover, that it is possible to discover a considerable measure of common ground between the traditionalists and the modernists, the 'ethical socialists' and the 'egoists', as the different camps have been labelled.[14] This consensus is formed around a belief that it is the quality of relationship which sustains families and localities, and that relationships characterised by *long-term commitment* and *stability* will generate the level of obligation which in turn creates citizens out of autonomous individuals.

Policies which effectively enable stable relationships to be sustained over the long term must become the goal of public policy. If a political party were to adopt as part of its motivating mission to rebuild the *relational base* in our country, it would have in its hands a plumb line to measure any and all aspects of the actions of government – a measure which goes beyond and before the ability of the economic base to foster personal well-being.

Needless to say, if that party were committed to moving towards a more relational society, it would ultimately need to devise a new economic strategy, with new financial instruments, new patterns of business organisation, new savings and investment institutions, a new ethos to govern provision of health, education and welfare, new styles of architecture and new layouts of inner-city housing.

However, the motivation for these changes will come not out of a determination to achieve economic efficiency as a means of keeping one step ahead in the global market. Rather, the underlying motivation must come from perceiving the deeper need in human beings for relationship and belonging, for connecting with other people in ways which generate trust, respect and the willingness to care.

Building a society where relationships matter

The contributors to this book are all experts in their own fields of public life. They each bring another facet into building the case for the primacy of human relations to individual well-being and the better functioning of society. Their task has been to *relate* their insights and expertise in the fields of social science, psychology, ethics, economics, business and so on to what, in their view, enhances the human dynamics within families and communities.

The chapters in Part I of this book introduce the theme of why quality relationships can and should be sustained by public policies. They represent the expertise of those who have studied trends in family relations over recent

14 *Building a Relational Society*

decades from a predominantly theoretical and empirical perspective. They bring together the arguments from social psychology, sociology and ethics for the importance of stable, committed relationships for both individual well-being and a healthy society (see Chapters 2–5).

The authors of Part II (Chapters 6–8) have all been involved in voluntary organisations operating at the grass roots, where the consequences of fractured relationships are most keenly felt. They take a more detailed look at the effect of public policies and practice on particularly vulnerable relationships: those between couples (and especially married couples), the parent–child relationship, and inter-generational relationships. Each contributor also examines some of the costs associated with the breakdown of these relationships and how these might be remedied.

The next two parts draw together evidence from public figures, practitioners and commentators on some of the major contemporary developments which are putting pressure on relationships between people, especially in their families.

Chapters 9, 10 and 11 in Part III concern the complex causal interactions between global industrial developments and the labour market and employment conditions in Britain, between employment opportunities and employees' expectations, between the daily demands of breadwinning and bringing up a family. In attempting to unravel these interconnected factors, these three chapters, one by a trade unionist, one by an industrialist and another by an academic and mother, show how the goal of strengthening the relational base can not only begin to bridge the traditional divide between employer and employee, but also provide a basis for agreeing a new balance of roles within the home.

Other specific pressures on relationships form the focus of Part IV: new technologies, fiscal and welfare policies, the financial markets and the urban built environment (Chapters 12–15). We are frequently told how important new technologies are to our future economic and commercial prosperity: who is asking how they impact our relational balance sheet (see Chapter 12)? Is there any evidence to support the case that the level of welfare payments and the structure of taxes does alter family behaviours (see Chapter 13)? How has deregulation in the banking world affected the relationship between borrower and lender (see Chapter 14)? Can the structure of our cities and the physical layout of the urban environment determine whether there exists a sense of alienation or a sense of community (see Chapter 15)?

Chapters 16–18 in the concluding part respond to the issues raised in the book by the earlier authors. They point the way forward and chart a course towards a more relational society. One key chapter demonstrates the need to make more consistent impact statements on forthcoming government legislation to more accurately predict the potential effect on relationships (see Chapter 17). The final chapter draws together the different strands from the book as a whole, sets out an agenda for redirecting the priorities of public policy in support of relational concerns and shows how a judicious use of the public policy instrument can bring about a strengthened relational base.

Together, these contributions bear witness to a remarkable consensus emerging from many avenues of our public life: the understanding that the very fabric of our social existence, our relationships, has come under sustained pressure, and how we ignore the importance of relationships to the well-being and identity of the individual at our collective peril. They paint a picture of the immense impact which public policy and corporate strategies have on the personal relationships within our neighbourhoods, families and households. They trace the connections between, on the one hand, new developments in global markets and information technology, and on the other, our experience of pressure and tension in personal relationships both at work and at home.

Above all, they argue that the priority accorded to economic concerns at the end of the twentieth century needs to be matched by an equal commitment to relational priorities in the new millennium. We are left with the overwhelming sense that if we can give attention to just one focus in our public and private lives in the future, it should be the relational dimension of our individual and collective lives. Let us make sure that we strengthen these invisible strands of loyalty, trust and obligation which cause our social fabric to cohere, and minimise the tangible and increasingly potent pressures pulling apart our closest relationships.

References

1. See, for example, Matthews, R.C.O. (1981) 'Morality, Competition and Efficiency', *The Manchester School of Economic and Social Studies*, No.4, December, p.293.
2. Baker, N. (1994) *Planning for Survival: A Family Policy for the Twenty-First Century*, Jubilee Policy Group.
3. Glenn, N.D. and Shelton, B.A. (1987) 'Regional differences in divorce within US', *Journal of Marriage and the Family*, Vol.49, No.3, August; Shelton, B.A. (1987) 'Variation in divorce rates by community size – a test of the social integration explanation', *Journal of Marriage and the Family*, Vol.49, No.4, August.
4. Trovato, F. (1986) 'The relationship between migration & the provincial divorce rate in Canada 1971–1978: a reassessment', *Journal of Marriage and the Family*, Vol.48, No.1, February.
5. Robertson, F.E. (1981) 'Mobility and the Family in Hospital Medicine', *Health Trends*, Vol.13, pp.15–16.
6. Ezard, J. (1995) 'Peering round curtains at people who live next door', *The Guardian*, 10 November.
7. See, for example, Elliot, B.J. and Richards, M.P.M. (1991) 'Children and Divorce: Educational performance and behaviour, before and after parental separation', *International Journal of Law and the Family*, Vol.21, p.481.

8 Gray, J. (1995) *The Guardian*, 10 April.
9 Schluter, M. and Lee, D. (1993) *The R Factor*, Hodder and Stoughton.
10 For an example of how relationships can be measured using these five dimensions in a prison context, see Brett, C., Schluter, M. and Wright, M. (1995) *Relational Prison Audits*, Scottish Prison Service Occasional Paper No.2.
11 See Lee, T. (1968) 'Urban Neighbourhood as a Socio-Spatial Scheme: A Study of Cambridge', *Human Relations*, No.21, p.259.
12 For example, see Wilmott, P. (1986) *Social Networks, Informal Care and Public Policy*, Policy Studies Institute.
13 Dahrendorf, R. (1979) *Life Chances*, Weidenfeld and Nicolson.
14 Dennis, N. and Erdos, G. (1992) 'Families without Fatherhood', *Choice in Welfare*, No.12, IEA Health and Welfare Unit.

2 Committed relationships: Current trends

Ceridwen Roberts

Introduction

It is difficult to produce comprehensive data on the variety of social relationships people in Britain have with one another and, in particular, to discuss the extent and nature of 'committed relationships'. We just do not collect information in this way and would have some difficulty in operationalising or measuring 'committed'. There are data from a variety of sources, however, about a range of family and friendship relationships, which are drawn on for this chapter.

Because the concept of 'commitment' has a qualitative dimension reflecting processes in, and therefore the quality of, a relationship, it is not adequately captured by the measures available through national statistics. Put simply, we cannot assume that all relationships which endure embody similar degrees of commitment and that the people in them are necessarily more caring and committed than people whose relationships break down or where contact is less frequent. Commitment cannot be simply correlated with duration or frequency of contact.

The starting point of this chapter is the key relationship between the couple. After looking at the changing nature of this relationship as marriage is increasingly supplemented by cohabitation, the chapter examines the nature of the adult–child relationship, asking if there has been a reduction in parental commitment to children. The wider inter-generational dimension of commitment is then considered by exploring the links between adult children and their elderly parents, increasingly under pressure as the policies of community care take effect.

Committed relationships may often go beyond the vertical parent–child–grandchild line to embrace wider family links of adult siblings, aunts and uncles and so on, and also friends and sometimes neighbours. Although we know much less about this aspect of people's lives, it is important not to exclude it. For some people, or at some stages of people's lives, friendships may be as important as, or even more important than contact with biologically close family members.

Couple relationships

Almost all adult men and women will make at least one couple relationship of significance during their lifetime to the extent of living with that person in a shared household. Increasing numbers will have more than one relationship, although we do not know much about the general pattern of lifetime adult relationships. For the vast majority, the couple relationship will still be formally recognised through the legal institution of marriage. Marriage is still something most people are likely to experience at least once. Currently, about 6 out of 10 adults in Britain are married, and even more have been married at some time but are now widowed, separated or divorced.[1] Some of those who are still single (21%), most of whom are under 35, will marry in due course.

Estimates suggest that the heyday of marriage was the 1950s and 1960s. In 1971, about 96% of men and 93% of women would have married by the age of 50. Estimates for more recent generations are lower, reflecting some of the important changes in the marriage and divorce rates since then. There is no doubt that the number of marriages has been falling steadily over the last 20 years. Indeed, the figures for 1993 show the lowest marriage rates for 50 years and the lowest level of first marriages this century.[2] These rates have led to estimates that 77% of men and 78% of women today could expect to have married by the age of 50, which is a substantial drop from the earlier, historically high levels.

In part, this decline in marriage can be explained by people marrying later, as well as by the rise in divorce over the last 20 years. Figure 2.1 illustrates these trends, which, if they continue, would mean that 37% of new marriages are likely to end in divorce. The UK has one of the highest divorce rates in the European Union (but it also has one of the highest proportions of married population). Increasingly, people are divorcing after shorter periods of marriage. Of marriages which took place in 1981, 10% had ended in divorce within 4.5 years, compared with 10% divorcing within 6 years in 1971 and 10% divorcing after 25 years in 1951.

However, this rise in divorce cannot be taken to mean that people are abandoning relationships, or indeed marriage. Britain also has one of the highest marriage rates in the European Union. An increasing proportion of the marriages which take place are second or subsequent marriages (up to a third of all new marriages in the 1990s, compared to a fifth in the 1970s),

```
                                 500 ┐
                                     │                               ─── Marriages
                                     │                               --- Divorces
                                 400 ┤
```

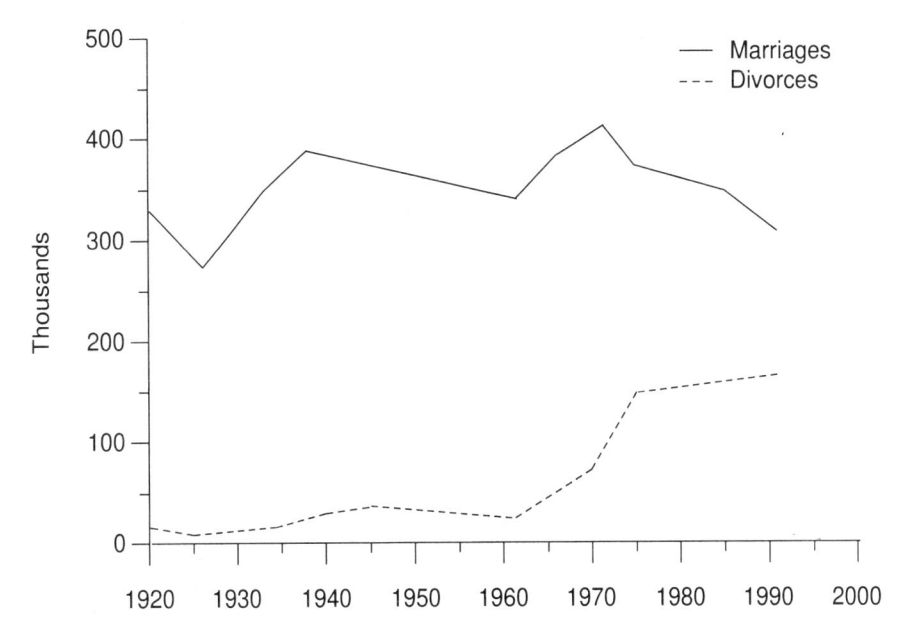

Figure: line graph of marriages and divorces, 1920–2000

Source: OPCS (1990 and 1993) *Marriage and Divorce Statistics*, OPCS Series FM2, HMSO.

Figure 2.1 Total numbers of marriages and divorces per year in England and Wales, 1921–91

which suggests that for many people the failure of a previous marriage has not led to disillusionment with the institution itself. More striking, perhaps, is that the fall in marriage rates since the early 1970s has been accompanied by a rise in cohabitation. So lower marriage rates do not mean adults are eschewing relationships, even if they are delaying marriage.

Cohabitation is not a new phenomenon. We have always had some,[3] particularly post-marital cohabitation, for example when divorces were difficult to get, or while people waited for them to come through. What is new is the growth in 'nubile cohabitation' – living together before marriage. This has become increasingly common as the average age at first wedding has moved from 22.6 for men and 24.6 for women in 1971 to 25.5 and 27.7 respectively in 1991. In the 1950s, only about 1 in 20 women lived with their future husband before the wedding; this rose to 1 in 10 in the 1960s, 3 in 10 by the late 1970s, nearly 6 in 10 in the late 1980s and 9 in 10 by the early 1990s.[4] The speed of this change has been quite dramatic and may partly explain the popular assumption that marriage has been eclipsed. But it is important to look at these figures in a broader context. Overall, about 7% of the total adult

20 Building a Relational Society

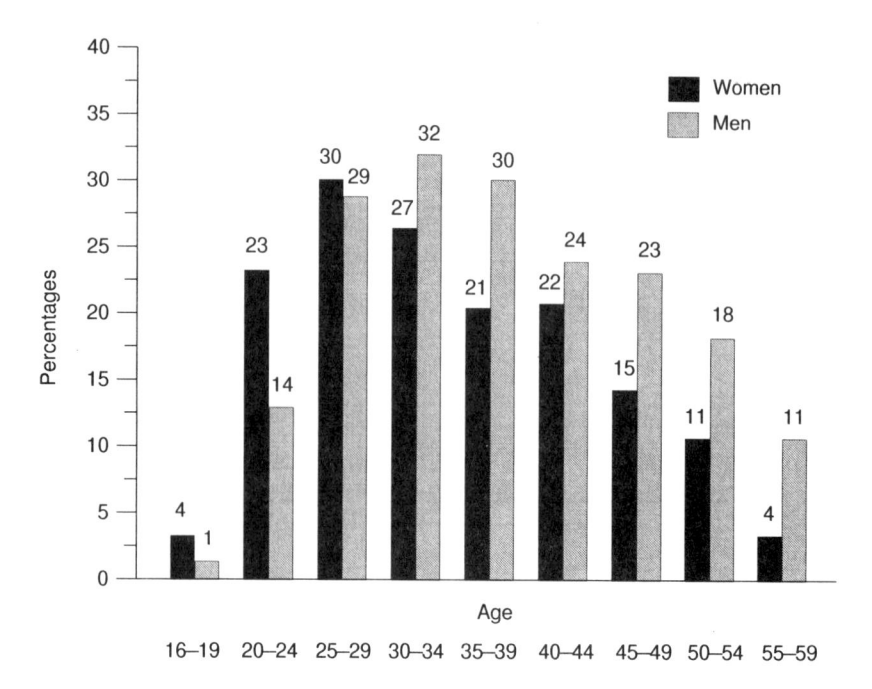

Figure 2.2 Percentages of non-married men and women cohabiting by age, 1990–93, Great Britain

Source: Derived from Haskey (1995).

population aged 16–59 are cohabiting. This rises to about 18% among those not currently married.

Cohabitation is still a transitory stage for many people. As analysis of the British Household Panel data shows, cohabitation is still a short-term activity – lasting on average about two years by the early 1990s, and, in the majority of cases, ended by transition to marriage.[5] As a consequence, cohabitation tends to be associated with younger age groups, as Figure 2.2 shows.

Facts and figures about cohabitation are only part of the story. We still do not know very much about *why* people cohabit and whether we are beginning to see, as in some Scandinavian countries, the emergence of long-term and stable relationships which are replacing legal marriages, even if, as *social institutions*, they seem little different to many marriages.

Haskey's recent analysis of the General Household Survey has both shown the rising average duration of periods of cohabitations and given us an idea of the incidence of longer-lasting cohabitations. About 17–18% of cohabiting men and women reported they had been cohabiting with their partner for seven years or more. Of course, a snapshot picture may underplay the durability of these relationships. We have no way of knowing, for example, what proportion of those cohabitants reporting durations of less than two years (41% and 39% of cohabiting men and women respectively) will go on to have long-lasting relationships.

The evidence to date shows that cohabiting relationships in Britain seem disproportionately more likely to end than marriages, and the marriages to which they have given rise seem more likely to end in divorce than marriages which were not preceded by a period of cohabitation. But there are large biases in the data because of the self-selecting factors at play. For example, the small minority of people who cohabited before marriage in the 1970s and early 1980s may have different attitudes to marriage and therefore exhibit different behaviour in marriages than those who did not. It is therefore rather early to make any definitive assessment about the duration, stability and, by implication, commitment of cohabiting relationships. It is also important to remember that periods of cohabitation at different stages of people's lives may have different meanings. Regrettably, there has been little research on this to date.

If the legal context of committed relationships has been changing, so too have the economic and social roles men and women play and the internal dynamics of the couple relationship. No discussion of commitment can ignore the fact that compared with 50 years ago, there has been a sea change in our attitudes and behaviour. The assumptions of the 1950s that women stayed at home when they married, to rear their children and look after their breadwinner husbands, have gone. In the 1990s, we are more likely to expect both partners to be economically active, even when children are very young. There is much more emphasis on individual fulfilment and economic independence, even if, for the majority of women with children, this is illusory, as they are still the primary domestic worker and secondary wage earner in the family, often working for low wages in part-time jobs.[6]

As Utting, in his review *Families and Parenthood*, reminds us, social historians have suggested that the 'differentiated' and 'complementary' model of marriage which the distinct economic roles generated has been increasingly replaced by the 'symmetrical' or 'companionate' marriage.[7] Here, the emphasis is less on the institution of marriage than on the personal liking and shared activities of the couple – a more private understanding of the relationship, and one which is likely to be invested with more expectations of personal happiness and fulfilment than in previous eras and therefore more likely to lead to disillusionment and strain. It is not difficult to see that this may be a more socially fragile institution as a consequence.

Box 2.1 illustrates the distinction David Morgan identified between these two types of marriage, although it is worth remembering that these are ideal types, and in practice, most couples experience elements of both as their relationship evolves.

> **Box 2.1 The shift from 'institutional' to 'relationship' marriage**
>
> Marriages based on a clear division of male and female roles have given way to relationships where personal liking and shared activities are more highly valued:
>
> | *Institutional* | *Relationship* |
> |---|---|
> | Less freedom of choice of marriage partners | Greater freedom of choice of marriage partners |
> | Marriage linked to wider societal/kinship obligations | Marriage relatively separate from wider obligations |
> | Emphasis on economic aspects (property/sexual division of labour) | Emphasis on emotional/interpersonal aspects |
> | Public emphasis | Private emphasis |
> | Marriage as one set of societal relationships | Marriage as *the* central adult relationship |
> | Relative 'inequality' (patriarchy) | Relative equality (companionship) |
> | Sexuality linked to procreation | Sexual dysfunction treated as 'marriage problems' |
>
> *Source:* Morgan, D.H.J. (1992) 'Marriage and Society: Understanding an era of change', in Lewis, J., Clark, D. and Morgan, D. *Whom God Hath Joined Together: The Work of Marriage Guidance*, Tavistock/Routledge, cited in Utting (1995).

The parent–child relationship

Popular concern about the apparent decline of committed relations between adults emphasises the effects on children of experiencing marital discord and dissolution. Most attention is paid to the wider social costs of this, whether manifested in the rising social security budget to support lone-parent families, the costs of rising juvenile delinquency, or the longer-term costs of increasing numbers of children under-performing at school and being unemployable. The pain of individual children and the emotional costs to them, are less likely to be considered, although the *Exeter Family Study* went some way to rectifying this bias in our perspective.[8]

However, moral panics about the death of the family or the growth of single parenthood obscure the wider picture of parent–child relationships. The vast majority of adults will be parents at some point, although an increasing minority of adults (20% of the current cohort of childbearing women) will not have children, either through choice or because they cannot have them.[9]

For most parents, having children will be a central part of their lives, even though the period of dependency and living together is relatively short, so that parent/children families are a minority (24% in 1993) of all British households.[10] Contrary to popular accounts, most children (74% in 1991) live with both their parents, who are overwhelmingly likely to be married (71% were married in 1991, and 3% were cohabiting). The remaining quarter will be living with a lone parent (19%), almost always the mother (18%), in a step-family (about 7%), or in some other arrangement (less than 1%).

This snapshot, while an important counter to the sensational, popularist accounts of social change, cannot convey the extent to which individual children will experience change in their family structure as they grow up. In practice, we do not know how much change children do experience, although there are some pointers. One of the biggest legal changes in the structure of parent–child relationships over recent years has been the dramatic rise in extramarital births. Over a third of babies are now born outside marriage, although birth registration statistics show that in 1992, three-

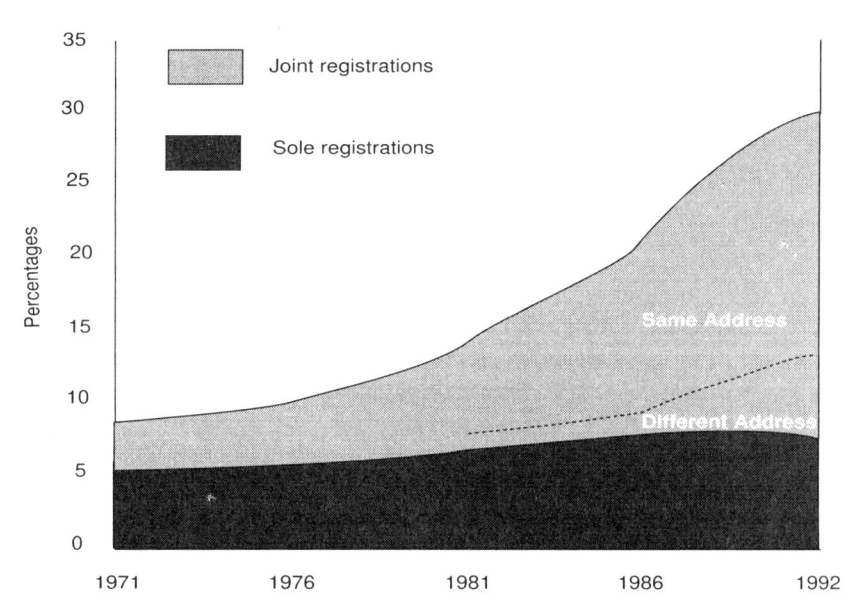

Note: The proportion of births outside marriage has trebled since 1971.
Source: CSO (1994) *Social Trends*, HMSO.

Figure 2.3   Extramarital births as a percentage of the total (by registration)

quarters were registered by both their parents, and over half (55%) were registered by parents at the same address (see Figure 2.3).

Research on long-term cohabiting mothers suggests that many marry the father of their child in time – there is a 'steady flow into marriage',[11] while some do not see the need to, and others expect or hope to marry when the situation is right.[12] But a change of legal status may not constitute a significant or meaningful change for the child – life may go on as before. This is far from the case when parents separate.

In 1992, 168,248 English and Welsh children under 16 experienced their parents' divorce, double the 1971 figure, as Table 2.1 shows. Moreover, children are experiencing the divorce of their parents at younger and younger ages. The Office of Population Censuses and Surveys (OPCS) estimates that if this trend continues, then 1 in 4 children will see their parents divorce before reaching 16, compared with 1 in 5 in the 1970s.[13]

Table 2.1 Children affected by divorce, England and Wales

Age	1971	1981	1992
0–4	20,734	40,281	54,510
5–10	40,700	67,582	70,954
11–15	20,870	51,540	42,784
Total	82,304	159,403	168,248

Note: Twice as many dependent children experienced their parents' divorce in 1992 compared with 20 years earlier.
Source: OPCS (1993) *Marriage and Divorce Statistics*, HMSO.

The consequences of this are more difficult to state with precision. A growing body of evidence from both the United States and recent British studies suggests that the effects of divorce may be more enduring than the immediate aftermath of dissolution. Children whose parents separate are at greater risk of adverse educational, health and behavioural outcomes compared with their peers from similar social backgrounds whose parents stay together. As Burghes's careful review of the evidence shows, modest but statistically significant differences in reading and arithmetic skills, general health, psychological adjustment, delinquency and personal relationships have been observed. These children are more likely to leave school earlier, fail to get educational qualifications, leave home earlier due to friction, enter cohabitation, marriage and parenthood earlier than their peers and have poorer mental health.[14] Burghes stresses that there is no inevitable post-divorce path along which *all* children will go, but *on average*, the outcomes for these children are poorer than for comparable children whose parents did not separate.

The reasons for this have been disputed, as has the incidence of difficulties. Some researchers have suggested it is still a minority of children who experience these poorer outcomes.[15] It is also not clear whether they are caused by the poorer economic circumstances these families live in post-divorce, or result from the effective loss of a parent, namely the father. About half of children have no contact with their father two years after family breakdown.[16] It is also possible that these findings are the result of experiencing parental conflict, which may have had damaging emotional or psychological effects on children. The likelihood is that a variety of factors interact. Certainly, recent evidence about the increased risks of poorer outcomes for children in stepfamilies shows that poverty alone is not the cause and suggests that the experience of multiple transitions and disruptions may make things harder for some children.[17]

Parental commitment to children cannot be simply measured by the extent to which parents stay together during young children's lives or by the frequency with which they see their children after breakdown. The quality of the parent–child relationship is also important and is not necessarily contingent on the child's family structure. Research over the last few years has examined the links between family structure, deprivation, parenting styles and juvenile delinquency and suggested no simple link. Indeed, the most recent review of the evidence argues:

> Marital discord, divorce and re-marriage, like poverty, can be seen as important stress factors that make it more difficult to be an effective parent. The parent–child relationship is, however, the *direct* mechanism through which these factors appear to exert their influence over children.[18]

These ideas underlie the increasing call for there to be more public intervention to support parents, more access to quality pre-school education (to supplement existing parental care) as well as better parent–teacher co-operation to deal with early evidence of difficulty, such as truanting, and to underpin more relationship education for children.[19]

However, while the political focus has been on the minority of children who offend and whose parents are seen as unable to control them or as uninterested in their children's well-being, there has been a wider debate about parental commitment to children which, as yet, has not attracted much attention in Britain. People like Sylvia Ann Hewlett or Amitai Etzioni in the United States have begun to ask whether parents are neglecting their children and not translating a commitment to them into time spent with them. This focus is broader than the minority of delinquent children and suggests that many more children are being deprived of the essential aspects of good-enough parenting – time and concern.[20]

In very different ways, Donald Hernandez,[21] empirically, and John O'Neill,[22] theoretically, take this theme further and suggest that the increasing emphasis on the market in our society is undermining the ability of families to care for one another, even to the extent of parents' commitment to their children being placed under increasing stress. The demands employment makes on both parents, either to make a living at all or to comply with the pressures of work, reduces the value placed on children and the time available for them.

These are alarming ideas which need to be considered seriously. They are basically asking whether the structural preconditions for commitment in all sorts of personal and family relationships are being eroded (see Chapter 1). It is ironic that these broader questions are being asked at a time when the pressure on families to care for elderly members is increasing, when the spotlight is moving to the relationships that adult children have with their elderly parents, and when interest in the extended family is re-emerging.

Adult child and elderly parents

It is a commonly held belief that the bonds of kinship and community are very much looser than they once were. The assumption is that the two-generation family of parents and children has replaced the larger three- or four-generation family. The individual is now seen as very much more socially isolated, with older people being particularly at risk.

Although it is believed that the extended family has all but disappeared for most people, at another level, a lot is still expected of it. Politicians and policy-makers see it as the right place for the care of the old and dependent. Moreover, the absence of good childcare often means that many working mothers have to rely on relatives by default to fill the gap.

Despite this expectation of family care, very little is known about the extended family in Britain. Most studies of family and community life are now over 30 years old, and many of these were partial and incomplete – focusing on working-class or middle-class families in small locations like London or South Wales. Therefore, at no time, now or in the past, have we had a complete picture of the extended family in this country and the care and support it offers to its members.

The extended family is also invisible to statisticians. Families are assumed to be equivalent to households. Our key sources of national social data emphasise the narrow nuclear family. The General Household Survey, for example, defines the family as either a married or cohabiting couple on their own, or as a married or cohabiting couple/lone parent and their never-married children, provided these children have no children of their own.

Yet there is a growing body of evidence that most people belong to some form of extended family, and that inter-generational support is alive and well. In fact, the ageing of the population means that there are now more three- and four-generation families than ever before. More children are likely to know their grandparents and even their great-grandparents, something quite unthinkable in the past.

Reviewing the support available to people from relatives, neighbours and friends, Peter Willmott concludes that most people belong to some form of extended family which they can rely on for help and support, and that there are committed relationships spanning the generations.[23] He identifies four main types of extended family in Britain.

The first type, the 'local extended family', is characterised by regular and frequent contact, with considerable mutual assistance. Willmott estimates that about 1 in 8 of the population fit into this category. It is more common among the working class than the middle class.

The second type is the 'dispersed extended family'. Because it is not local, contact is less frequent, but still weekly. Typically made up of parents and their married children, it accounts for about half the population.

The third type Willmott describes as the 'dispersed kinship network'. Many in this kinship type live quite a distance from other relatives, and contact is maintained by telephone, letter or visits. Assistance is available in an emergency, and this type of family may be transformed into the local extended family type when an elderly parent falls ill or needs assistance – the parent staying with or moving to live near a married son or daughter. About a third of the population are estimated to belong to such families.

The final type is the 'residual kinship network'. Relatives are rarely seen, and contact is maintained by letters or Christmas cards. No family care is available to people in this group, and clearly, there are low levels of commitment to the relationships. Only about 1 in 20 of the population belong to this family type.

Using Willmott's typology, it is possible to suggest that well over half the population have regular contact with their extended family, which also provides mutual aid and assistance, and that a further fifth can call upon relatives in a crisis. In fact, only a very small proportion of adults, some 5%, are isolated and do not have anyone that they can call upon for help.

Empirical support for Willmott's hypothesis comes from a study of kinship and friendship carried out on a small but nationally representative sample of British adults as part of the 1986 British Social Attitudes (BSA) Survey.[24] Contrary to popular assumptions, British adults whose parents are still alive see them quite often. About half of those whose mother is still alive either visit or have a visit from her at least once a week. Nearly a third live less than 15 minutes away from their mother, and nearly three-quarters live less than one hour away. Similar patterns were found for those whose father was still alive. These findings seriously challenge the view that children move far away from their parents when they grow up.

Visiting may be one indicator of commitment to a relationship; the ability to ask for help in difficult circumstances is another. The British Social Attitudes Survey again showed the strength of family commitment. After their spouse/partner, most people would turn to other relatives, such as parents or children, for practical help. Only when borrowing a large sum of money would they look outside the family (to a bank), but even here, a large proportion of adults would approach their parents or adult children first. These British results are borne out by similar studies in Australia.[25]

Further evidence of wider family commitment manifested through kinship support for relatives comes from surveys of informal carers of disabled and elderly people. In 1990, 10% of adults in Britain were caring for a parent or parent-in-law, 4% for other relatives, while 4% reported giving some care to friends and neighbours.[26] Overall, it is estimated that there are 6.8 million carers in the country – 2.9 million men and 3.9 million women. The most heavily-involved carers, devoting 20 or more hours per week to caring, were those caring for a parent, a parent-in-law or a spouse.

The economic consequences of this type of committed care are important. For example, the British Medical Association has recently estimated the saving to the taxpayer through this unpaid care by families, friends and neighbours at £34 billion per annum, about the same as the National Health Service annual budget.[27] The social consequences are dramatic and difficult to quantify.

Kinship support for families flows down the generations as well as up. After parents, grandparents are the most important source of childcare in Britain. This is a major way in which parents help their adult children. In surveys, the care provided by grandparents is usually masked by categorising it as informal care by close relatives. But studies in the 1980s and since show that the key role grandmothers in particular play while parents are at work is not diminishing.[28]

Despite evidence of widespread extended family support, which is indicative of certain levels or types of commitment, there appears to be no clear consensus among the population about how this should be translated into responsibility for relations. For example, a recent study showed that twice as many people thought that an elderly person should move into an old people's home as believed that they should live with a relative. Two in five adults even maintained that they had no responsibility to care for their aged parents.[29]

This suggests that people do not necessarily see the family as the front line of support in times of need, but whether this is evidence of lack of commitment is harder to say. Finch and Mason's survey showed that people agree that the wider family should be the first line of assistance only in 'deserving cases' – where the need arose through no fault of the person who needed assistance, or where the need was fairly limited. These are beliefs, however, and people's actions may be different when faced with the reality of their own family situation.

Even so, the findings suggest that government policies promoting more care by families, such as care in the community, are based on shaky assumptions that there is some set of fixed moral rules whereby families will automatically support dependent relatives. Finch and Mason argue that family care is not automatic, but must be negotiated over time. Moreover, these negotiations take place in the context of long histories of inter-personal relationships. As a result, people develop different commitments of different strengths to different people. They may be willing to support their aged parents, but not more distant relatives, such as aunts and uncles.[30]

More research remains to be carried out into the extent and meaning of wider family interaction. In particular, we still know very little about the relationships and commitments people have with their adult siblings and their children. Hopefully, this will be revealed by the research funded by the Economic and Social Research Council being undertaken by the Family Policy Studies Centre and Social and Community Planning Research. This repeats and extends the 1986 British Social Attitudes Survey of kinship and friendship. Not only will this look at changes in family contact and support between 1986 and 1995, it will also explore family members' patterns of practical help.

Relationships with neighbours and friends

As with the extended family, very little is known about the extent or quality of relationships with neighbours and friends because this has not been studied systematically. Sometimes, relatives and friends are treated as if they are the same. Yet are friends and relatives really interchangeable, and do people have different expectations about or commitments to friends compared to relations? Clearly, friends and neighbours may be very different too. Some neighbours become friends, but a distinction between the two is usually drawn and implies not only a different kind of relationship, but also different types of commitments.

The limited evidence available suggests that most people have regular contact with their neighbours and friends and are able to turn to them in an emergency. For example, a study in 1991 of people aged 65 and over found that three-quarters saw relatives or friends at least once a week. Those living alone were more likely than other elderly people to see their relatives and friends frequently. Over four-fifths talked to their neighbours at least once a week; only 12% never saw their neighbours. Social isolation does, however, increase with age, presumably because many more very old people are housebound.[31]

The 1986 BSA Survey of kinship and friendship showed that nearly 9 out of 10 people have one or more close friends, and over two-thirds see their best friend at least once a week. People are far more likely to see their best friend weekly than their sister or brother. Nevertheless, kinship plays a far more important role in people's lives than friendship. Friends are important for companionship, but it is relatives people turn to for practical help and support, except for problems with a spouse or partner.[32]

Help from neighbours can also be important. Reviewing the research in this area, Willmott argues that neighbourly help tends to be more common in rural areas than in towns. Help among neighbours is more common for things like looking after keys, looking after pets and plants, and borrowing food and shopping, but large proportions of people report that neighbours help with house maintenance and repairs, look after children and help during illness.[33]

Neighbourly help can be particularly important for older people. One of the most important roles neighbours can play is 'keeping an eye' on the elderly person, as well as shopping and generally friendly contact. But these are fairly loose types of relationships; only in the most exceptional cases do neighbours carry out the more difficult forms of intimate personal care. This is usually left for the family, especially a female relative.

Conclusions

Knowledge of the extent and types of committed relationships people have in our society is fairly limited. Most attention so far has been paid to the couple and parent–child relationship, but even here, more is known about the demographic structure or legal form of these than about the internal dynamics and processes involved in maintaining quality and committed relationships.

Not enough is known about why some relationships work well and why some people can maintain their commitment to each other and their relationship under the most apparently adverse conditions. We also need to know more about the context of relationships and examine more closely the extent to which wider societal, especially economic, values are inimical to committed relationships, or at least put them under increased pressure.

Finally, it is important to realise that there usually needs to be a healthy interplay between the types of relationships people have with their close and more extended family, as well as with their friends and neighbours. We need to know more about the quality of these wider, non-familial relationships too. Their absence may well mean that too much of an emotional and social load is carried by a few family links which may be increasingly unable to bear the burden.

Acknowledgements

I should like to thank my colleague, Francis McGlone, for his assistance and advice on the extended-family sections of this chapter.

References

1. OPCS (1993) *General Household Survey*, OPCS Series GHS No.24, HMSO.
2. Haskey, J. (1995) 'Trends in marriage and cohabitation: the decline in marriage and the changing pattern of living in partnerships', *Population Trends*, No.80, HMSO, pp.5–15.
3. McRae, S. (1993) *Cohabiting Mothers: Changing marriage and motherhood?*, Policy Studies Institute; Kiernan, K.E. and Estaugh, V. (1993) *Cohabitation, Extra-marital childbearing and social policy*, Occasional Paper 17, Family Policy Studies Centre.
4. Haskey, op. cit.
5. Buck, N. and Scott, J. (1995) 'New evidence on cohabitation spells from the British Household Panel Study', paper given at Marriage and Divorce Seminar Group, 5 July, quoted in *Family Policy Bulletin*, July.
6. Joshi, H., Dale, A., Ward, C. and Davies, H. (1995) *Dependence and independence in the finances of women aged 33*, Family Policy Studies Centre.
7. Utting, D. (1995) *Families and Parenthood: Supporting Families, Preventing Breakdown*, Joseph Rowntree Foundation.
8. Cockett, M. and Tripp, J. (1994) *The Exeter Family Study: Family breakdown and its impact on children*, University of Exeter Press.
9. Condy, A. (1995) 'Choosing not to have children', in *Family Policy Bulletin*, April.
10. OPCS, op. cit.
11. McRae, op. cit.
12. Burghes, L. with Brown, M. (1995) *Single lone mothers: Problems, prospects and policies*, Family Policy Studies Centre.
13. Haskey, J. (1990) 'The Children of Families Broken by Divorce', *Population Trends*, No.61, HMSO.
14. Burghes, L. (1994) *Lone Parenthood and Family Disruption: The outcomes for children*, Family Policy Studies Centre.
15. Utting, op. cit.
16. Bradshaw, J. and Millar, J. (1991) *Lone Parent Families in the UK*, Report No.6, Department of Social Security, HMSO.
17. Kiernan, K.E. (1992) 'The Impact of Family Disruptions in Childhood on Transitions Made in Young Adult Life', in *Population Studies*, Vol.46, pp.213–34.
18. Utting, D., Bright, J. and Henricson, C. (1993) *Crime and the Family: Improving Child-rearing and Preventing Delinquency*, Occasional Paper No.16, Family Policy Studies Centre, p.3.

19 Utting et al., op. cit.
20 Etzioni, A. (1993) *The Parenting Deficit*, Demos; Hewlett, S.A. (1991) *When the Bough Breaks: The Cost of Neglecting Our Children*, Basic Books.
21 Hernandez, D. (1993) *America's Children: Resources from Family, Government and the Economy*, Russell Sage Foundation.
22 O'Neill, J. (1994) *The Missing Child in Liberal Theory*, University of Toronto Press.
23 Willmott, P. (1986) *Social Networks, Informal Care and Public Policy*, Research Report No.655, Policy Studies Institute.
24 Finch, J. (1989) *Family Obligations and Social Change*, Polity Press.
25 Millward, C. (1992) 'Keeping in Touch – Extended Family Networks', *Family Matters*, No.32, August, Australian Institute of Family Studies.
26 OPCS (1992) *General Household Survey 1990*, Monitor SS 92/2, HMSO.
27 BMA (1995) *Taking Care of the Carers*, British Medical Association.
28 Martin, J. and Roberts, C. (1984) *Women and Employment: a lifetime perspective*, HMSO; Brannen, J. et al. (1994) *Employment and Family Life: a review of research in the UK (1980–1994)*, Research Series No.41, Employment Department.
29 Finch, J. and Mason, J. (1993) *Negotiating Family Responsibilities*, Routledge.
30 Ibid.
31 OPCS (1994) *General Household Survey 1991*, No.22, Supplement A, HMSO
32 Finch, op. cit.
33 Willmott, op. cit.

3 The effects of relationships on well-being

Michael Argyle

Introduction

In this chapter, we shall examine the effects of the main relationships – marriage, friendship, family and work – on several aspects of well-being – health, mental health and subjective well-being. Some of the research in this area takes the form of statistical relationships, for example between being married and being happy; we need to know which is the direction of causation here – perhaps only happy people get married, perhaps some feature of personality is responsible for both conditions. However, there is a certain amount of longitudinal research to settle this issue.

We shall see that relationships are extremely important for well-being, and that there are serious consequences when they go wrong or break up. These consequences are measurable in terms of unhappiness, mental and physical ill-health, even mortality, and for the children of divorced parents, a much higher rate of delinquency and other personality problems.

There may be some negative results here: it has been suggested by some that the family is stifling and bad for mental health; there is certainly a lot of conflict between spouses, even violence. However, the effects may be different for different populations, such as men and women, or different classes, though we shall confine discussion to the cultures of Europe and North America.

Marriage

Health

Many studies have found that the married are, on average, in better health and live longer. Table 3.1 shows American statistics for death rates per

Table 3.1 Marital status and mortality

Cause of death	Death rates for white men (per 100,000)			
	Married	Single	Widowed	Divorced
Coronary disease and other myocardial (heart) degeneration	176	237	275	362
Motor vehicle accidents	35	54	142	128
Cancer of respiratory system	28	32	43	65
Cancer of digestive organs	27	38	39	48
Vascular lesions (stroke)	24	42	46	58
Suicide	17	32	92	73

Cause of death	Death rates for white women (per 100,000)			
	Married	Single	Widowed	Divorced
Coronary disease and other myocardial (heart) degeneration	44	51	67	62
Cancer of breast	21	29	21	23
Cancer of digestive organs	20	24	24	23
Vascular lesions (stroke)	19	23	31	28
Motor vehicle accidents	11	11	47	35

Source: Lynch (1977).

100,000 for some of the main causes of death.[1] It can be seen that all the single conditions have higher rates than for the married, so that these results are probably due to marriage causing good health, rather than those in good health being more likely to marry (actually, they are, but this is quite a small effect). The benefits of marriage here are greater for men – probably because wives look after husbands better than vice versa – and mutual care in the family is part of the explanation of these benefits. The death rate for widowers is elevated by 40% during the first six months; the effect is much greater for the younger widowed, and when the death was unexpected. Being divorced is worse than being single or widowed, perhaps because of distress caused by the emotional conflict and feeling of failure or rejection.

The nature of the illnesses affected gives another clue, for example cirrhosis of the liver. The married do better because their 'health behaviour' tends to be better, for example less drinking and smoking, better diet, more compliance with doctor's orders. There is another reason for the benefits of marriage – positive emotional bonds strengthen the immune system.[2] So it is not surprising that the quality of marriage is also important; those who are cohabiting do nearly as well, except that they are more likely to break up, with the negative consequences we have seen in Table 3.1.

Mental health

In terms of official statistics, the married do well here. The number of married individuals who became mental hospital inmates in Britain in 1981 was 260 per 100,000, compared with 770 for the single, 980 for the widowed and 1,437 for the divorced.[3] Part of this is probably due to partners being able to look after each other, so that hospitalisations can be avoided. Again, the divorced come off worst, perhaps partly because their mental disturbance made divorce more likely. There is also a much higher rate of suicide and suicide attempts among the divorced – about four times as high as for the married.

A classical study was carried out by Brown and Harris[4] and has been replicated many times. They found that for women who had an intimate relationship with someone 'you can talk to about yourself and your problems', stressful life events made only 10% depressed, compared with 41% of those without such a relationship; care was taken to ensure that the illness came after and not before the stressful events (Table 3.2).

Table 3.2 Depression, stress and social support (% depressed)

	Support		
	High	Mid	Low
Women who had stressful life events	10	26	41
Women with no such events	1	3	4

Source: Brown and Harris (1978).

There are several ways in which marriage might contribute to mental health. Perhaps the experience of attachment or bonding, which was so important in childhood, is important here. Perhaps confiding emotional problems and receiving sympathetic support, perhaps help with dealing with the source of stress, is responsible.

Happiness

Surveys of happiness or subjective well-being show that the married are happiest. In an American sample survey, Veroff et al. found that 41.5% of married women (35% of men) said that they were 'very happy', compared with 25.5% of single women (18.5% of men) and 15.5% of divorced women (18.5% of men).[5] It is sometimes thought that it is men who benefit from marriage; the truth is that men benefit more than women, but women also gain a great deal. Could these apparent effects of marriage be due to reverse causation: do only happy people get married? No, because the great majority of people do get married (92%), which is far greater than the proportion who are initially very happy. Also, we found that marriage is by far the greatest source of reported satisfaction of the whole range of relationships. We found three satisfaction factors, and marriage scored highest on all of them: (1) instrumental and material satisfaction, (2) emotional support, and (3) companionship in shared activities (see Figure 3.1).[6] It was on the first of these factors – instrumental and material satisfaction – that marriage was most different from other relationships; friends scored nearly as high on the third – companionship in shared activities – for example.

Why is marriage so rewarding? The reason is probably that married couples do a great number of very rewarding things together, such as sex, shared leisure and shared family life.

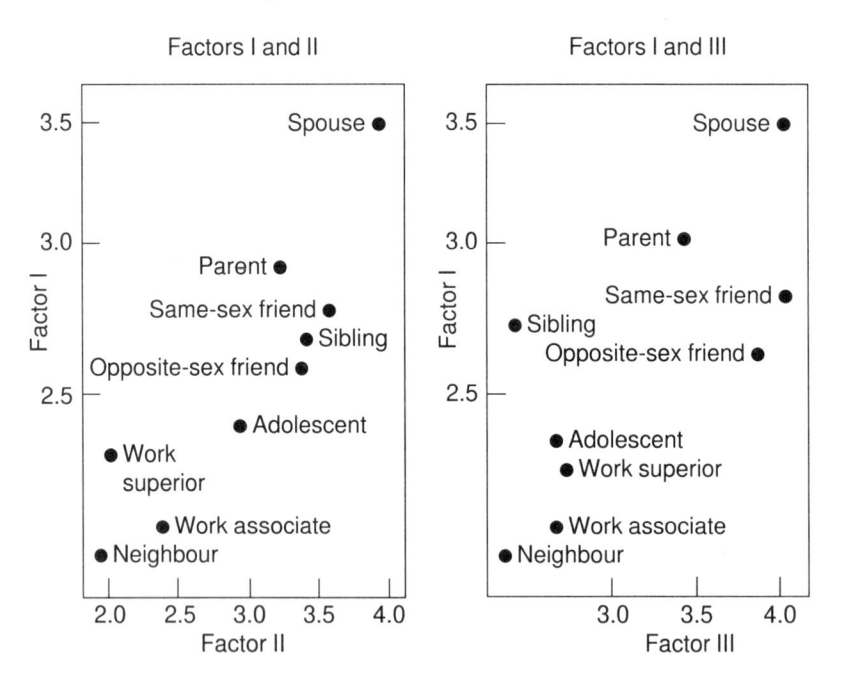

Notes: Factor I = material and instrumental help; Factor II = social and emotional support; Factor III = common interests.
Source: Argyle and Furnham (1983).

Figure 3.1 Relationships plotted on the satisfaction dimensions

Conflict in marriage

Marriage may be the most satisfying relationship, but it also creates the most conflict.[7] Britain has the highest divorce rate in Europe, about 40%, and in the USA, violence is reported by 28% of the married population. The divorce rate is a little lower in other European countries, partly because of the higher proportion of Catholics, though the effect of Catholicism on divorce has diminished; there are probably more separations. And in Southern Europe, there are still many extended (and Catholic) families, with large networks of kin to support the marital relationship. Statistics from North America and Britain show that those who are actively religious have about half the divorce rate of others, and that the divorce rate is lowest for Mormons, Jews, Hutterites and Mennonites; there was less effect for Catholics or liberal Protestants, and mixed marriages had a high rate, the Catholic/Mormon combination being the worst.[8]

Why is marriage so difficult? The main reason is probably that spouses live at close quarters and have to agree on a large number of issues – major and minor aspects of their life together where co-ordination is necessary. Since each is different, in sex, and to some extent in background and personality, they will have different ideas about these matters. They may not have the social skills or the willingness to resolve disagreements co-operatively or constructively, resorting to abuse and violence instead.

Children are a major source of low marital satisfaction, especially when they are aged under 5, and even more when they are adolescents, though at other times they are a positive source of satisfaction. The other main sources of conflict are unfaithfulness, lack of rewardingness and drink. Wives complain most about husbands neglecting them, demanding too much sex and treating them as inferior; husbands complain about wives being sexually unresponsive, bitchy and preoccupied with their appearance.[9]

In all relationships, but especially in marriage, commitment – the determination to stick to it and make it work – is very important. Students of relationships have analysed commitment in terms of the rewards and costs of staying and leaving; for example, commitment will be greater when there are 'investments' which will be lost, such as children, shared friends and jointly-owned property.[10] However, this underestimates the power of emotional attachment, which can be just as great between spouses as between parents and children. In both cases, the loss of the relationship is experienced as a devastating emotional loss. Table 3.1 showed the effect of bereavement and divorce on death rates from various causes; divorce is actually worse than bereavement, though the death rate for widowed men is 40% higher than that for married men of the same age during the first six months after the death of their wife. Similar results are obtained for mental health and happiness.

Cohabitation is increasingly practised by couples before marriage, or instead of marriage. The Church of England has recently declared that this is not a sin. A proportion of young people engage before marriage in what has been called 'serial monogamy' – they live with several people, one after another. Cohabitation usually represents a lower level of commitment than marriage and gives less security. Some regard having children as equally committing, but those who do marry say that the main reason is to make a commitment.[11] Those cohabiting are found to be nearly as happy as the married; but the rate of breaking up is much higher – three times as high in Sweden, twice as high in Britain.[12]

Friendship

We have stressed the importance of marriage, but some other relationships also have powerful effects on well-being. Friendship is the most important relationship for students and adolescents before marriage, for the bereaved after it, and for the single. Friendship is particularly important for the old and has major effects on their well-being.

Happiness

Many studies find that people are in a positive mood when with their friends, compared with being with family or alone – indeed, friends have been found to be the main source of joy. This is partly because of the enjoyable things that friends do together. We found in an Oxford sample that the most characteristic friendship activities were dancing, tennis and other joint leisure.[13] This may look frivolous, but these activities also integrate people into close-knit social networks of companionship and social support. The biological point of friends may be help and co-operation in serious matters, and it is reinforced by positive, non-verbal signals, like smiling, which are very characteristic of behaviour between friends – though friends also spend a great deal of time talking. In a later study, we found two groups of leisure activities which were associated with happiness: (1) teams, clubs and pubs, and (2) parties, dances and debates.[14]

Leisure groups, like tennis clubs, voluntary work groups, churches (which can be regarded as leisure groups) and others, are a major source of friends. These groups produce a high level of social support; some of my results shown in Table 3.3 show that people say that some of their closest friends are members of these groups.[15]

Leisure groups generate a lot of positive emotion at their meetings and are an important source of happiness. Belonging to churches has the greatest effects for old people, and it is participation in the church community which

Table 3.3 Leisure and friendship relationships

How close are your main relationships with other members?

Closer than other friendships	Religious	37%
	Voluntary work	29%
	Total	11%
Very similar	Musical	78%
	Social	54%
	Sport	41%
	Dancing	40%
	Total	40%
Different	Political	60%
	Voluntary work	43%
	Evening classes	43%
	Total	22%
Less close	Sport	40%
	Evening classes	37%
	Hobbies	33%
	Total	27%

Source: Argyle (1996).

is mainly responsible. For young people, dancing is the greatest source of joy, and all forms of sport and exercise induce positive moods.[16]

Mental health

Several large-scale studies have found an effect of networks of friends and neighbours on mental health, for example, one by Williams et al. in Seattle.[17] Sometimes, these effects have been found to be as great as those of marriage. How are these benefits of social support obtained? Emotional support, like sympathetic listening, may not always work. Nolen-Hoeksema asked subjects what they did if they felt depressed.[18] Women often shared their troubles with a sympathetic friend, which made them more depressed; men more often engaged in vigorous exercise, which enabled them to forget their troubles. Better results are obtained by helping people to solve problems, providing companionship and cheering them up. Acceptance and love may again be the most important factors.

Loneliness is a source of depression, suicide, alcoholism and poor rates of recovery from illness. It may be due to social isolation, in turn due to lack of social skills. However, some individuals who say they are lonely actually spend as much time with friends as others; the problem can be that they do not talk about sufficiently intimate topics with them: there is insufficient self-disclosure. Some do not understand what friendship is about, that it requires concern for the other's welfare, loyalty and commitment. Social skills training can do a lot for people without friends by making such individuals more rewarding, improving their non-verbal communication, correcting conversational problems, improving self-presentation and instructing on the rules and skills of particular situations or relationships. Keeping friends requires similar skills and knowledge. We studied a large sample of lost friendships and found that a major factor was breaking certain rules, especially 'third party' rules, about keeping confidences, standing up for friends in their absence, being jealous of other relationships.

Mutual-help groups, like Alcoholics Anonymous and many others, have become very popular, especially in the USA, where nearly 4% of the population belong to them now. It is likely that the companionship and support to be obtained from leisure groups could do as well. Sport is widely recommended as a treatment for depression, and the effects are probably due as much to the social as to the physical aspects of sport.[19]

Health

The effects of friendship here are modest; the ill are usually cared for by their families. However, close relationships, producing positive moods, can affect the immune system. And the bereaved can be helped by the support of friends.

Work relationships

Happiness

Job satisfaction is one of the main components of overall life satisfaction, and most people at work are happier than those who are unemployed. One of the main sources of job satisfaction is relations with others at work. Workers of all kinds are happier with their work if they belong to small, cohesive groups, where there are opportunities for interaction, and especially if they are popular. Supervisors can be a source of dissatisfaction but can also be a major source of satisfaction, if they use the right skills and look after their subordinates.

There has been disagreement over how important work relations are. However, we found that there are several kinds of work relationship – with those who become friends in the usual sense, those who are often seen at coffee or lunch but only at work, those whom workers like seeing but don't bother to have coffee or lunch with, and those they would rather not see at all. With co-workers in the closer categories, there is a lot of help and co-operation at work, but also a lot of pure sociability, such as joking and teasing and discussing personal problems.[20] This is important for productivity too, since those who establish close relations while playing games and telling jokes over coffee are also to be found helping and co-operating over the work.[21]

However, work relations are very weak under some kinds of technology. Old-fashioned production lines were like this, since it was impossible to hold any conversation; in textile mills, the noise may be too great to talk. Some kinds of automation also break up working groups by isolating workers at distant control stations. The great contribution of the Tavistock Institute of Human Relations was to show that the same equipment can be combined with a variety of social arrangements, some of which are far more humanly satisfying than others; technology does not need to be a source of low job satisfaction. The Japanese have been alert to some of these issues and try to keep working groups intact for many years, thus creating continuity and security.

Mental health

Work is often found stressful, though those not at work may be even more stressed. Stresses arise from overload, time pressure, repetitive work, role conflict and other causes; family and friends cannot help with problems at work, but workmates can. Social support from the working group has been found to buffer work stresses, partly because it causes them to be seen as less stressful.[22]

Support may consist of tangible help, information, integration into a social group, or attachment to a confidant. Again, supervisors can be a source of stress, or they can provide help and support and solve problems; they can be trained to do this better. Burke and Weir found that managers received most support at work from others who were young and of lower status, often female, and outside the immediate work setting.[23]

Health

There is a lot of stress-related illness at work, including arthritis, ulcers, high blood pressure, cholesterol and heart attacks. These are the main illnesses and conditions which cause 31.5% of men and 18.7% of women to die before the age of 65. A number of studies over a wide range of occupational groups have shown that stress has little or no effect on these aspects of health when there is strong support from co-workers and supervisors.[24] Part of this is probably due to the emotions which are generated by close social relationships strengthening the immune system.

The unemployed

The unemployed are often very unhappy, depressed, apathetic, have low self-esteem, have higher rates of physical illness, alcoholism and death, and their wives and children are also adversely affected.[25] But is unemployment really a cause of these troubles, or possibly an effect of them? Banks and Jackson found with a sample of British school-leavers that unemployment was a cause of mental ill-health rather than vice versa.[26] Social support at home can alleviate these effects. Cobb and Kasl studied men who had lost their jobs; of those who had a supportive wife, 10% became arthritic in two joints, compared with 41% of those who did not.[27] Some of the unemployed find satisfying things to do, and a few are happier than they were before as a result. There has been some success with the young unemployed from providing sports training and facilities, which of course involves a new set of co-operative relationships.

Most of the retired are quite content, often more so than those at work. However, one of the main things that they miss is the companionship of the people at work. Some replace work with voluntary work, some with further education, others with leisure groups – all of which provide relationship support.[28]

Family relationships

The effect of parents on children

Parents have a powerful effect on the present and future well-being and personalities of their children. A close relationship with mother during the first two years of life produces many benefits. Sroufe et al. found that even by 12–18 months, securely-attached infants are more co-operative, socially competent and show more positive emotion.[29] When they are older, these children continue to be happier, co-operative, popular and to have high self-esteem.

A warm relationship with parents throughout childhood has many desirable consequences, while those who are rejected are more likely to become delinquent, aggressive, neurotic, even schizophrenic. The Gluecks found that

60% of a large sample of delinquents had been rejected by their fathers, compared with 19% of a non-delinquent control group; they had also received harsh and erratic discipline.[30] However, there is a research problem here – the delinquents may have been rejected *because* they were delinquent. Nevertheless, it is becoming increasingly clear that it is poor relations with parents which are the main cause of delinquency.[31] Parents need to provide discipline which is not too strict, not too permissive, gives explanations and is consistent. The control of adolescents is particularly difficult, but it is more successful when parents use persuasive, consultative and fair methods, and set clear limits.[32] In the case of schizophrenia, there is another problem: the causal linkage is partly genetic, and the rejection may be a consequence of difficult behaviour.

When parent–child relations are disrupted by divorce or death of a parent, many undesirable consequences for children may occur. There is often immediate disturbance, such as bed-wetting and tantrums in the under-5s. Later physical health may be affected, and there is an increased probability of developing asthma, ulcers and eating disorders. Mental health is affected more: the percentage with later psychiatric illness is about five times as high for the children of divorced parents.[33] Social behaviour is adversely affected – the children of divorcees are more likely to be aggressive or withdrawn and to leave home early and form unsatisfactory sexual relations, ending in another divorce. They do worse academically at school or college and are more likely to become unemployed. The delinquency rate is much higher, 28.6% by age 21 in one study, compared with 14% of boys whose parents were still married.[34] All these results are partly direct effects of the divorce – through feeling rejected by one parent. In addition, it is more difficult for a single-parent to perform effective child-rearing. There are often financial problems for single-parent mothers.[35]

Many divorced people remarry, which is good for them, but not always so good for their children. The majority of children under the age of 5 at the time of remarriage get on well with the step-parent, but many older children find it difficult to cope with their new step-parent and his or her children. Step-families are also likely to have lower incomes and worse living conditions than intact first families.

Relations between adult kin

The most important kin relations are between parents and adult children and between siblings. For many people, there is frequent contact with kin, often daily, especially for those who are unmarried, for the elderly, and for those who are working-class. Recent American studies have found the same.[36]

People spend their leisure time with their friends, but when they need

Table 3.4 Help by friends and relations

	Middle-class	White-collar	Working-class
Advice on a personal matter:			
Friends	64%	67%	39%
Relatives	34%	33%	58%
Source of financial loan:			
Friends	26%	23%	9%
Relatives	74%	73%	86%
Main source of help in child's illness:			
Friends	39%	45%	19%
Relatives	56%	55%	77%

Source: Willmott (1987).

serious help they turn to kin, for example with money, jobs, housing, serious illness or the law. This is more the case with working-class individuals (see Table 3.4).[37]

The reason for this class difference is that working-class people are less geographically mobile; in Bethnal Green, it was found that 24% of working-class adults under 65 lived in the same house as a married child, 23% within five minutes' walk, far more than the middle-class adults in Woodford.[38] There are even greater differences between families in different cultures. In the Third World and in Southern Europe, the family is much more important, larger groups live together, there are stronger obligations to help, and a wider range of kin is recognised; the family provides the social security system. There are also considerable gender differences in all cultures – it is mostly women who keep in touch, hold the family together and provide all this help, especially maintaining the links between mothers and daughters, and pairs of sisters.

Kin relations, unlike friendships, usually last indefinitely. What is the explanation of the helpfulness and the enduringness of kin relations? The 'selfish gene' theory certainly works for animals, but it has not been proved for humans. The emotional intimacy of the early family may produce some kind of conditioning, and this is supported by the finding that cousins stay in touch more if they were childhood playmates. Also, there are social expectations, which differ and are passed on in each culture.

The parent–child link is the most enduring and produces the greatest amount of help. This relationship is often quite severely disrupted when the children are rebellious adolescents, and sometimes for longer than adolescence; however, the relationship is nearly always restored by the twenties, and then lasts for a very long time. In Britain, 15% of the over-65s live with their children, in the USA 30%, more than this for those who are single, and many more see one of their children every day. In a British survey, 69% of the over-65s had seen one of their children 'today' or 'yesterday', and another 17% in the past week. There is extensive help with shopping and housework, and for the ill and infirm, more intimate nursing care, etc., mainly by daughters, who feel a responsibility to do this but also want to do it. It has also been found that old people have a high level of contact with their siblings, if they have any, and receive a lot of social support from this source. Many more old people would have to be placed in institutions if they were not cared for by kin; they much prefer to be with their family, and the result is that they live longer.[39]

There is also help in the other direction, from parents to adult children. We found that adults gave their parents high ratings as a major source of instrumental and material help, more than friends or siblings, though less than spouses; this is partly financial, but also includes baby-sitting and other childcare, with illness and in the house. Parents can also give help and advice with jobs.

About 95% of siblings keep in close touch, especially if they live near to one another, and in later life, those who are single or widowed often live together. There is, however, less help than between parents and children, and in later life, siblings can be more like friends. On the other hand, there is often friction between siblings; in one study, 71% reported rivalrous feelings, especially on achievement, attractiveness and intelligence. There may also be friction over who should look after elderly parents and over division of property in wills.

Conclusions

We have seen in this chapter that close relationships of several kinds have major benefits for health, mental health and happiness when they are stable and long-lasting, and massive ill-effects when they break down. In some spheres, the situation is deteriorating in much of the modern world in view of the increasing levels of marital breakdown and unemployment. Could public policy do anything to improve things?

Marriage has the greatest effects, both positive when it succeeds and negative when it fails. Divorce has become easier, and more marriages are failing. This trend might be reversed if there was more pressure to receive guidance or marital therapy, or if there were economic incentives which would encourage stability.

Not all parents are very good at it, and many could be helped to be better by more widespread use of parental education, widely used in the USA. Kin play an important role in looking after each other, especially the elderly, and could perhaps be given financial incentives to do so.

Many people are lonely and socially isolated. They could be helped by making social skills training more widely available, for example through leisure centres or evening classes. Leisure groups are important here, and there should be good physical facilities for them in every community. Automation has meant the destruction of some of the traditional working groups in industry. Maintaining such groups should be an aim of industrial technology, and efforts should be made to keep working groups intact, as is done in Japan. More important, the greatest thing that could be done in the sphere of work is to make more of it available through schemes such as workfare, or to share the work out. Failing this, organised leisure activities have also been found to produce an alternative to the satisfactions of work and the relationships which go with it.[40]

References

1. Lynch, J.J. (1977) *The Broken Heart*, Basic Books.
2. Kennedy, S., Kiecolt-Glaser, J.K. and Glaser, R. (1990) 'Social support, stress, and the immune system', in Sarason, B.R., Sarason, I.G. and Pierce, G.R. (eds) *Social Support: An Interactional View*, Wiley.
3. Cochrane, R. (1988) 'Marriage, separation and divorce', in Fisher, S. and Reason, J. (eds) *Handbook of Life Stress, Cognition and Health*, Wiley.
4. Brown, G.W. and Harris, T. (1978) *Social Origins of Depression*, Tavistock.
5. Veroff, J., Douvan, E. and Kulka, R. (1981) *The Inner American*, Basic Books.
6. Argyle, M. and Furnham, A. (1983) 'Sources of satisfaction and conflict in long-term relationships', *Journal of Marriage and the Family*, No.45, pp.481–93.
7. Ibid.
8. Beit-Hallahmi, B. and Argyle, M. (in press) *The Psychology of Religious Behaviour, Beliefs and Experience*, Routledge.
9. Argyle, M. and Henderson, M. (1985) *The Anatomy of Relationships*, Penguin.
10. Kelley, et al. (1983) *Close Relationships*, Freeman.
11. McRae, S. (1993) *Cohabiting Mothers*, Policy Studies Institute.
12. Watt, E. (1994) *For Better or Worse: The case for long term commitment in family relationships*, The Relationships Foundation.
13. Argyle, M. and Furnham, A. (1982) 'The ecology of relationships: choice of situation as a function of relationship', *British Journal of Social Psychology*, Vol.21, pp.259–62.
14. Argyle, M. and Lu, L. (1990) 'The happiness of extraverts', *Personality and Individual Differences*, Vol.11, pp.1011–17.
15. Argyle, M. (1996) *The Social Psychology of Leisure*, Penguin.
16. Ibid.

17 Williams, A.W., Ware, J.E. and Donald, C.A. (1981) 'A model of mental health, life events, and social supports applicable to general populations', *Journal of Health and Social Behavior*, Vol.22, pp.324–36.
18 Nolen-Hoeksema, S. (1987) 'Sex differences in unipolar depression: evidence and theory', *Psychological Bulletin*, Vol.101, pp.259–82.
19 Argyle (1996), op. cit.
20 Argyle, M. (1989) *The Social Psychology of Work*, Penguin.
21 Ibid.
22 House, J.S. (1981) *Work Stress and Social Support*, Addison-Wesley.
23 Burke, R.J. and Weir, T. (1980) 'Coping with the stress of managerial occupations', in Cooper, C.L. and Payne, R. (eds) *Current Concerns in Occupational Stress*, Wiley.
24 Caplan, R.D. et al. (1975) *Job Demands and Worker Health*, Institute for Social Research, University of Michigan.
25 Fryer, D. (1995) 'Labour market disadvantage, deprivation and mental health', *The Psychologist*, Vol.8, pp.265–72.
26 Banks, M.H. and Jackson, P.R. (1982) 'Unemployment and risk of minor psychiatric disorder in young people: cross-sectional and longitudinal evidence', *Psychological Medicine*, Vol.12, pp.789–98.
27 Cobb, S. and Kasl, S. (1977) *Termination: The Consequences of Job Loss*, US Department of Health, Education and Welfare.
28 Argyle (1996), op. cit.
29 Sroufe, L.A., Fox, L.E. and Pancake, V.R. (1983) 'Attachment and dependency in developmental perspective', *Child Development*, Vol. 54, pp.1615–27.
30 Glueck, S. and Glueck, E.T. (1950) *Unraveling Juvenile Delinquency*, Harvard University Press.
31 Farrington, D.P. (1992) 'Explaining the beginning process and ending of anti-social behaviour from birth to adulthood', in McCord, J. (ed.) *Facts, Frameworks and Forecasts: Advances in Criminological Theory*, Vol.3, Transaction Publishers.
32 Argyle and Henderson, op. cit.
33 Wadsworth, M.E.J. (1984) 'Early stress and associations with adult health behaviour and parenting', in Butler, N.R. and Corner, B.D. (eds) *Stress and Disability in Childhood*, Jon Wright.
34 Ibid.
35 Watt, op. cit.
36 Argyle and Henderson, op. cit.
37 Willmott, P. (1987) *Friendship Networks and Social Support*, Policy Studies Institute.
38 Willmott, P. and Young, M. (1960) *Family and Class in a London Suburb*, Routledge and Kegan Paul.
39 Argyle and Henderson, op. cit.
40 Argyle (1996), op. cit.

4 Short-term relationships: Reaping the liberal whirlwind

A.H. Halsey

In Chapter 3, Michael Argyle has argued that long-term relationships are socially good. Is there a reciprocal case – that short-term relationships are socially bad? It is obvious enough that permanent bonding has net effects to be desired. But the calculus is not simple. Close and closed communities can be oppressive, and 'back-to-back' relationships may protect a person's health and welfare, threatened by face-to-face candour. Apparently learned rabbis sometimes discuss the conditions under which men might, *pro bono publico*, be encouraged to lie to their wives. So, although arguing against short-term relationships, I fully realise what a convenience it is to buy a ticket from a clerk or a newspaper from a shop assistant without demanding that the same clerk or the same shop assistant is always there to serve me.

The liberal inheritance

To put the matter much more abstractly, we can say that the secular problem of morals in Western Europe has always been to optimise the relation between the main political values of liberty, equality and community rather than to maximise any one of them. This triad of values has occupied the centre stage of political debate in Europe since the French Revolution. It is noticeable, however, that one of them – originally *'fraternité'* – has become 'community', partly because of the advance of feminism, but also because of the clarification of ideas like solidarity, cohesion and *koinonia* (the fellowship of sharing) which have been such crucial influences, especially in the twentieth century. Above all, the centrality of community, for all its vagueness, derives from its status as a precondition for seeking the other two values.

To analyse the problem of stable relationships, we can, as Michael Young and I did recently in our pamphlet *Family and Community Socialism*,[1] start from George Eliot's novel *Silas Marner*. Silas was unjustly thrown out of the narrow community of his chapel, migrated southwards to live among strangers, and set himself to work as a weaver. He was a marginal individual, connected to others only through the market for his cloth. His reaction was to hoard gold from his earnings. But, as the tale runs, he was robbed of his gold and left with a golden-haired infant child. He then had his own glimpse of socialism. As Eliot puts it:

> In old days there were angels who came and took men by the hand and led them away from the city of destruction. We see no white winged angels now. But yet men are led away from threatening destruction: a hand is put into theirs, which leads them gently towards a calm and bright land so that they look no more backward; and the hand may be a little child's.

This parable from George Eliot tells us not only that she understood community fetishism as well as her contemporary, Karl Marx; it also guides us towards priorities for the twenty-first century and warns us against a new kind of fetishism – the substitution of plastic toys for time in the relations of adults to children. Marx is mentioned deliberately – not so as to rehabilitate Marxist theories, for indeed Young and I have espoused ethical socialism all our lives – but rather to underline the shortcomings of the liberal alternative to Marxism. As John O'Neill has argued in his recent book,[2] Marxism leaves children out of account, logically and despite much rhetoric. In our pamphlet, the child is placed deliberately at the centre of social policy, by contrast with the liberal tradition which assumes mature, calculating and maximising adults who relate to others through rational bargaining in their own interests in the market. If the outcomes favour children, this is an accidental by-product of the contingency that liberals tend to be tender-hearted and especially to care about their own children. Nineteenth-century liberals were often philanthropists at the forefront of child protection and the abolition of slavery. But these altruisms flowed from social and religious commitment: they were not in any way part of the logic of individualistic and market-oriented liberalism. Thus, for example, liberals were much more likely to support private than comprehensive schooling. The latter presupposes that its proponent cares about all the nation's children, and not only his or her own. It also assumes that stable relations are most effectively sought in communities and families.

In applying liberal principles to everything, Mrs Thatcher and her successors made a fundamental mistake. They assumed that these principles would not invade the great institutions of kinship which were integral to Britain and which, paradoxically, fostered the liberal sentiment which has been so characteristic of British political and social life. But, of course, the ego-maximising principle did invade reproduction as well as production. The bargain rather than stability is the first aim. We now have marriage as a contract over the short term, with unprecedented numbers of dependent children suddenly thrown into lone-parent poverty, instead of the traditional covenant which made both parents dutiful guardians of domestic serenity for their own offspring up to at least the point of independence. We now have a society where adults are encouraged to maximise their own interests at the expense of children as well as others, who might otherwise use their citizenship to institute tax regimes capable of sustaining the collective provision for health, education and pensions which are needed for a modern rich country.

Social breakdown and crime: Tracing the connections

Recorded crime has increased in Britain on average by 5% every year over the past quarter of a century. The police recorded 1.6 million offences in 1970, 2.5 million in 1980 and 5.6 million in 1992. It may be of some comfort to some to know that 95% of these recorded offences were non-violent crimes against

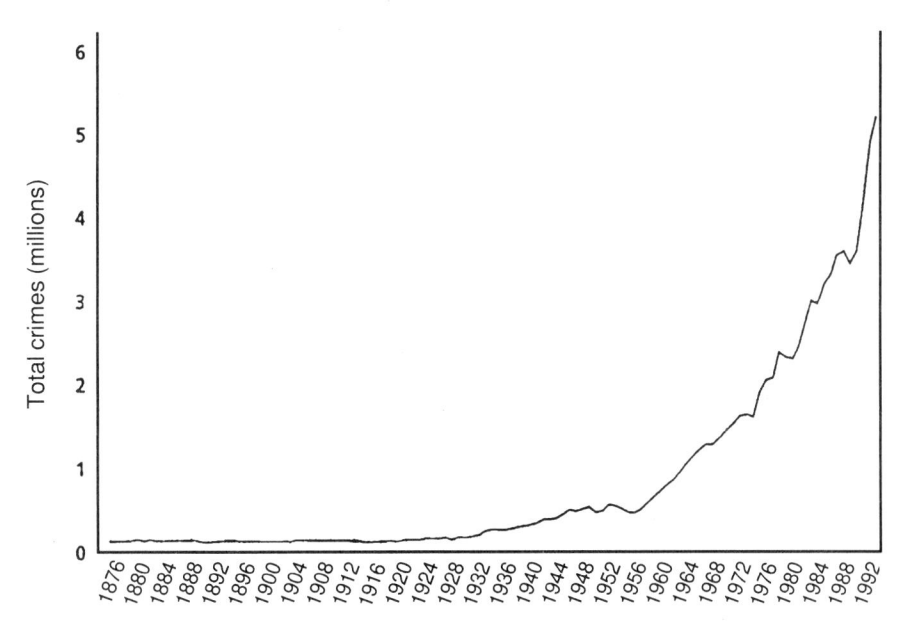

Source: Barclay et al. (1993).

Figure 4.1   Crimes recorded by the police (England and Wales)

property. But it may be of further alarm to others that crime appears on a greater scale when evidence from the 1992 British Crime Survey (based on enquiries in 10,000 English and Welsh households) indicates a total of 15 million crimes a year, many of which were no doubt trivial, and most never reported to the police.[3] One authoritative estimate is that offending rates of juveniles may have increased during the 1980s by as much as 54%. The known offending rate among young people aged 17 but under 21 has, meanwhile, risen by 13%.[4]

The records of the police and courts tell us that crime is commonly committed by young men. Over 80% of known offenders are male, and almost half are aged under 21; 1 in 5 is aged under 17. It is known from a study of people born in 1953 that 1 in 3 men, compared with only 8% of women, had been convicted of crimes on a 'standard list' of offences by the age of 35. Offending is clearly more a male than a female characteristic, and this was borne out by a Gallup survey of adults and young people in Liverpool and Guildford. Gallup was sponsored by General Accident in 1993 to survey public attitudes to young people and criminality.[5] Their findings further confirm that contemporary young people are more frequently involved in crime than were their elders or young people in the past (see Table 4.1).

Table 4.1 Estimates of teenagers involved in crime

Current age of adults	Estimate of 13–17-year-old crime in their area at the time when they were teenagers (%)
60+	3
35–59	9
25–34	17
18–24	25

	Estimate of 13–17-year-old crime now (%)
Adults	11
Juveniles	43

Source: Gallup (1993).

From their review of the relationship between family and delinquency in Britain, the authors of the Family Policy Studies Centre report, Utting et al. conclude cautiously:

it is already apparent that the tangled roots of delinquency lie, to a considerable extent, inside the family. Children whose families suffer financial and environmental poverty are clearly at greater risk than those whose parents have the income to provide them with a comfortable, uncrowded home.[6]

Yet, as the authors of the Newcastle study observed,[7] social deprivation does not appear sufficient on its own for delinquency to develop. Factors within the care-giving environment (and, possibly, in the children themselves) are seen to modify the influence of poverty and disadvantage. A similar conclusion was reached by Michael Rutter and Henri Giller in their review of the literature on juvenile delinquency.[8] Noting that any statistical relationship between social status and delinquency in the Cambridge Institute of Criminology longitudinal survey study disappeared once the influence of poor parental supervision was taken into account, they concluded:

> the indicators are that most of the modest association between class and delinquency is probably due to the parental and family problems sometimes associated with low social status, rather than low social status per se.[9]

The rise in crime over the past 20 years has been shown by David Dickinson to be closely correlated with unemployment.[10] The Cambridge survey of 400 predominantly white inner-city males born in 1953 powerfully reinforces Dickinson's findings. At age 8–10, the significant predictors are: (1) economic deprivation, including low income, poor housing, unemployment spells experienced by parents; (2) family criminality, including convicted parents and delinquent siblings; (3) unsatisfactory parenting (too authoritarian or too unbonded), and (4) school failure.[11]

A further, and in this case massive, study is *Psycho-Social Disorders in Young People*, edited by Sir Michael Rutter and Professor David Smith.[12] These editors put their interpretative emphasis less on unemployment and sexual abuse and more on post-war freedom and individualism. But these levels of causative abstraction are not necessarily incompatible.

One associated interpretation of the evidence is that the causation is genetic. *Homo homini lupus est* ('man is a wolf to man') was Freud's summary, but the question of whether wickedness and cruelty are built into the human genetic structure is not likely to be settled by a simplistic search for 'criminal genes'. Human beings are capable of everything from Belsen to the Good Samaritan. Explanations have to include both 'human nature' and the environment in complicated interaction. All we can expect here is to point to aspects of short-term relationships, especially in the family, which can be shown to have negative consequences for 'society' – meaning the welfare of all concerned.

The research findings, in summary, are that the children of parents who do not take on personal, active and long-term responsibility for the social upbringing of the children they generate are more likely to be disadvantaged in many major aspects of their chances of living a successful life. On the evidence available, such children tend to die earlier, to have more illness, to do less well at school, to exist at a lower level of nutrition, comfort and conviviality, to suffer more unemployment, to be more prone to deviance and crime, and finally, to repeat the cycle of unstable parenting from which they themselves have suffered.

Another factor noted by the Gallup survey was that those from single-parent households were less 'crime-free' than those from other household backgrounds (mainly two-parent families). 'Innocence' was also correlated with church attendance and region (Scotland low) and with the view that parents were neither too strict nor not strict enough. Some further clue to the sources of criminal involvement is also perhaps to be found in the low satisfaction recorded by the children of single-parent households and among those who are unemployed, or who have a record of being in trouble with the police, and confess to having taken soft or hard drugs. There is a matrix of correlation here which, while it does not in any way isolate the disrupted family, points to a significant increase in the probability of offending from non-traditional children.

Parental control

Much analysis of rising crime focuses on alleged decline in control over young people by their parents. The mobility, migration and age segregation of modern populations is well known, and much publicity is given to the evidence of marital breakdown through divorce and separation as well as to the rise of parenthood outside marriage. Births outside conventional wedlock have now reached 30%. The Gallup survey threw some light on relations between the generations. There is a fair consensus between young people and adults that parents today are less strict than they once were. Moreover, modern young people are overwhelmingly of the opinion (80%) that parents have it 'about right' while adults thought that 30% of *their* parents were too strict.

But it is significant that in the group discussions, some adults pointed out that although they came from large and poor families, this did not mean that they were willing to go out and rob elsewhere to satisfy their desires as adolescents. Moreover, it was equally significant to hear young people saying that at least some of their shop-lifting activity, as well as joy riding in cars, was for the sake of the 'buzz', and not necessarily related to money. Some would steal for the excitement it gave, even if they had the necessary money in their own pockets.

The Gallup survey showed that young people now live in a markedly more permissive moral climate and also do more forbidden things (except smoking). The gap between parental prohibition and actual behaviour was 9 for young people and minus 19 for adults. In other words, modern parents forbid only 11% of the list but young people nevertheless do 18% of them. The last generation forbade 47% of the list, but they nevertheless did 28% of them. Traditional obedience to parents is still there. Both generations mostly observe the rules, but young people less so. The proportion of those who always or mostly do what their parents told them has fallen in the last generation from 76% to 63%.

Concerning relations with the police, it appears from the Gallup survey that many fewer adults in their day were confident that their parents would have made excuses for them or covered for them if they had been caught committing a criminal offence. In other words, solidarity between parents and the police seems to have declined. But we should also notice that in the last generation, this absence of confidence on the part of children was much greater among those who had not been in trouble. The experience of being in trouble among young people actually increases their confidence that their parents will support them. We should also notice that parents, teachers, the police and head teachers of schools commanded heavy respect from today's adults when they were adolescents. Finally, we should note that there is fairly wide-spread cheerfulness about spontaneous recovery from youthful crime. Adults are especially confident that juvenile deviants will grow up to be respectable, law-abiding citizens.

Whatever their views about the causes of crime, it is significant that parents are accorded the responsibility for tackling youth crime. The question was put only to adults: 40% held this view, and 32% mentioned the police. Governments, courts, schools and other agencies are relatively negligible, though in the discussions it was notable that school teachers tended to see themselves as a first port of call for families in trouble.

Family fragility

Is the cure, then, to improve the lot of children by strengthening the family? The need is urgent. Some of the best evidence comes from the longitudinal studies which have followed the samples of children born in 1946 (the Douglas study), the 17,000 children born in 1958 (the National Child Development Study) and the later study of children born in 1970. The children featured in all these studies have now grown up and are themselves having children, so some of the long-term effects of disruption in one generation can be looked at. When this was done for the 1946 sample, the children who experienced their parents' divorce before they reached 15 had lower levels of attainment at school as well as more emotional disturbance and more delinquency, and were themselves more prone to divorce or separation than those whose parents had remained married.

The 1958 sample has been examined in the same way, and the outcome is, if anything, more dire. The people whose parents' marriages broke down are more likely to finish school at the minimum age and to leave home before they are 18, are much more likely to suffer from psychological problems, and the men are much more likely to be regular smokers. For children with a divorced parent and a stepfather or stepmother, the differences in comparison to families with two natural parents are even more striking. Girls in stepfamilies run twice the risk of pregnancy outside marriage while teenagers, and we know from other evidence that they run more risk of sexual abuse too, not infrequently from stepfathers. Girls and boys in stepfamilies are twice as likely to leave school at age 16. David Willets summed up the evidence by saying 'better death than divorce, better single parent than step-parent'.[13]

But in all three birth cohorts, the children of divorced parents were in a minority, and most children came from families where there was no such breakdown. This continues to be so. In 1985, 80% of children under 16 were living with both their natural parents. This is a key figure from the point of view of child protection and nurturing. But the statistic has been moving the wrong way. The 80% has, on a later reading, become 70%. Increasing proportions of children are being born and brought up without a committed father.

Children without their own two parents are also different in other vital respects. Their families are often inharmonious before there is any open break. Moreover, in our chronicle of child neglect, a prominent place had to be given to poverty, and the children from broken homes and of lone parents who never had a two-parent home to 'break' were, on the whole, also poorer. If the children were disturbed, was it because they were poorer, or because their parents had split up? The answer has to be that it was often both, and beyond these two influences were many others which, for really firm conclusions to be justified, would have to be taken into account and their relative importance assessed. We have to recognise that we are dealing with a complex interaction, for instance between parental breakdown and poverty. Poverty can cause the breakdown; the breakdown can, and usually does, cause poverty. The two factors can work together to produce the kind of downward spiral from which it is difficult for either adults or children to escape.

Even in saying that, we are, of course, generalising. For particular individuals, it is not necessarily like this at all. Whatever the situation of the parents, what matters most is the quality of the care the children receive; this can be excellent in any family circumstances. Hewitt and Leach put forward a proposition which is incontestable:

> Individual children thrive in any kind of family where they are well cared for by loving parents or parent-figures.[14]

As long as there are loving parents or parent substitutes, the kind of family they are in may be of little consequence. Yet it cannot be denied that many children are in distress and that the numbers are apparently on the increase.

Conclusions and cures

It is clear that rising crime is a national problem of high magnitude. It is also clear that having divorced parents and being born outside marriage are becoming commonplace for children. Whereas once 80% of children grew up under the care of two married parents, it now appears that the twenty-first-century child will have a less than even chance of doing so.

How can we reverse these trends and encourage those which could create and sustain stable, long-term relationships in family, school, neighbourhood and work?

I believe that redistribution of income, redistribution of time and redistribution of concern is even more of a necessity than it has been in the past. My concern with future stability requires that redistribution should have a primary new purpose – a massive redistribution in favour of children.

Richard Wilkinson, in a report published by Barnardo's,[15] traced the decline of children's quality of life to the wrong-way-round redistribution there has been under recent governments, from the poor to the rich, from children to adults, and generally to the increasing gap between richer and poorer. I would add that the origin of disorder and anomie is to be found in the declining standards of familial commitment. If the trends are not checked, Britain and many other countries are going to become moral wildernesses filled with wild children roaming the streets in search of revenge against older generations who seem to have turned their backs on them. This is a new challenge for our entire civilisation, and one that has to be grasped if society is not going to rot from the bottom up.

Child poverty of the familiar kind has to be tackled, and radically. But there is also time poverty, which can bite into all social classes. Children can get too little of the time of their parents. Inside even the affluent home, the individual can be paramount – individual parents who go out to work before their children go to nursery or school, and the individual's own friends and own interests take a precedence. The result can be a loss of collective cohesion in the family. This has sometimes gone so far that the members of the family rarely even eat together. The commensality – the eating together – which Max Weber regarded as so necessary to solidarity will hardly survive the microwave.

If they do not get enough of the time, attention and love of one or both of their parents, the children may not build up enough trust, enough of a sense of security about their attachments, to be able to strike out when the moment comes into independence and self-reliance, and to reach maturity with enough of the capacity to love which is generated by the love and affection that they once received. If their childhood is serene as well as stimulating, later on, they will be able to combine self-reliance and the self-interest which will give brio to life with that ability to transcend self-interest and regard the interests of others as in some way their own which is the sinew of any society. If that does not happen, they may become determined to make society suffer in reprisal for what they have suffered and without necessarily being aware of the origins of their destructiveness. Lack of self-respect can redound on others. It can only be destructive to love thy neighbour as thyself if you do not love yourself at least a little.

Family covenant

The family is at the heart of enduring relationships. It goes beyond contract. It teaches people the most precious ability of all, the ability to transcend self-interest and regard the interests of others as in some way their own: the kind of altruism which is at the heart of the collective conscience and which holds all societies together. When it is working well, the family is the seed-bed of the virtue from which all the civic virtues stem, just as, when things go wrong, it can be the fount of all the vices. And the family works well when it is complete, where there is an intact marriage, a steady income and relatives in proximity or easy communication.

How then can we best support families in living up to these ideals? It would help if there were in existence a proper family conciliation service covering the whole country; if the law were reformed to remove, or much reduce, the legal disabilities from which cohabiting parents suffer at present, and if the government were to give some support to the moves being made to establish a 'family covenant' which seeks to bond parents more closely together when a child is born, so that their chances of staying together are improved. For those who do not want a formal church baptism, the birth can be recognised by a family covenant ceremony which is more than just for naming the child: it is the occasion for the solemnisation of a moral commitment by the parents to cherish, nurture and shelter their child; for the appointment of godparents, and for the grandparents not just to meet (which they may never have done beforehand if there has been no marriage), but to undertake to support the parents and their grandchildren. It would, among other things, be welcome to the family covenant movement if the government would allow civil naming and commitment ceremonies to be conducted in registry offices, and so put them on a par with civil marriages.

This applies also to parental responsibility agreements. At present, unmarried mothers are considered in law to have exclusive responsibility for their children. Unmarried fathers have none unless they opt in for joint parental responsibility by means of a special agreement. The law should be changed so that the presumption is that, where fathers and mothers have both signed the birth certificate, they intend to share responsibility unless they want to opt out of it. Opt-out would take the place of opt-in.

Basic income

I cannot see that a stable society can in future base income distribution solely on employment. Transfer the claim upon income from work to citizenship (or contribution to society), and the whole scene would change. The best version of the basic income is that put forward by Professor Atkinson.[16] He believes that a main reason why a basic income has not been introduced, despite it having been advocated for so long, has been the unconditionality of it. It was to be paid to everyone, irrespective of deserts, and although this is politically acceptable for children, it is not for adults. Although I prefer the term 'basic income', he suggested 'participation income', and his term certainly brings out the essence of his scheme: the income would not be for everyone, including people who made no contribution to the welfare of the community, but would be conditional on their 'participation'. People could be considered as participating on grounds of:

- work as an employee or being self-employed;
- absence from work on grounds of sickness or injury;
- inability to work on grounds of disability;
- being unemployed but available for work, engaging in approved forms of education or training;
- caring for young, elderly or disabled dependants, undertaking approved forms of voluntary work.

The whole issue of the basic income would matter less if we could expect an early return to the full employment of the first decades after the Second World War. But the economy has been showing no signs of yielding that. Rather the opposite. The secular trend has been towards greater unemployment, higher in the trough of each successive depression and at the peak of each successive boom. There are over a million long-term unemployed, and after being out of work that long, many are unemployable. Many other young people have never been in work, especially men and especially the low-skilled. The problem could be due in part to the decline of manufacturing and in part to the greater difficulty of bringing up children who will turn out to be employable. If the measures for family support I am proposing were effective, there could be fewer unemployable people. But, for the moment, employable or not, the level of unemployment is wretchedly high in boom times, and higher still in slump.

Those for whom the economy cannot find jobs are, through no fault of their own, often plunged into consequential poverty, and their children with them. Until means are found of restoring full employment, the unemployed, and especially the long-term unemployed, could remain in a kind of moral limbo, stigmatised and deprived of respect in the eyes of their children and other members of the family. A basic income for everyone, employed or unemployed, would at least help to soften a new division into two nations – the employed, to whom more is given, and the unemployed, from whom so much is taken away.

Education and extended-kin surrogates

The plight of children is also an outcome of how much resource goes into education and the other public services which have been developed in the twentieth century to support, augment or substitute for the family. Teachers, health visitors, social workers and the police are all part of the State apparatus of child support; they are the extended-kin surrogates which are so characteristic of modern social development.

It is high time that the percentage of Gross Domestic Product recorded as being spent on education at the end of the 1970s should be restored and exceeded. But we also want to make the function of the schools in support of parents and, beyond that, the parental role of the schools more specific. The ideal is that schools should consider themselves *in loco parentis* and even '*in loco grandparentis*', but with the aid of actual parents and grandparents.

The immediate and justified response of many teachers to any notion of a 'parental role' for them, without more resources being assigned for the purpose, is rejection; it is incompatible with limited professional time and responsibility. The job of a teacher is already harassing enough.

True. At the same time, the problems of parents (especially if they have ordinary, paid work) are aggravated by the practice of schools in closing down in mid-afternoon and for holidays which last weeks or months. These practices are a strange Victorian hangover from the period when State schools were influenced so much by the public schools which had long holidays and played games in the afternoons. The closure times also made more sense in State schools when most mothers were housewives, at home in the afternoons when their children got out of school, and likewise in school holidays. Their children did not have to have latchkeys; it was enough for the mothers to have them. But all that has changed and is continuing to change as more and more mothers go out to work, and, as that happens, it becomes more and more indefensible for schools to close their gates when increasing numbers of their pupils have nowhere to go except to an empty house.

The next step in aligning school and family should be to regain lost ground and lay a duty upon local education authorities and on schools to look after their pupils up to six o'clock on weekday evenings and during holidays. This would be in the interests of children as well as parents. Schools would be open for any pupils who wanted to stay on in the afternoon to do their homework or, better, to play games and do other things – drawing, painting, photography, model-making, drama, dancing, pop music, computing – which there is not enough time for in school hours.

But for any such extension of the pastoral and educational functions of the school, new staff will be needed: auxiliaries on a large scale to supplement the ordinary teaching staff. Some of these would need second contracts to cover the extra time they would be putting in, especially if they were going to be involved in organising a new educational auxiliary service.

Where would the new auxiliaries come from? The conjunction of two figures – in 1991 there were some 12 million children under the age of 16 living in the United Kingdom, of whom 9.3 million were in school, and there were 12 million people of 65–79 years of age – suggests a plausible answer. Many retired people are as fit as ever they were, possessing valuable skills and with many years of healthy life ahead, and their own experience of bringing up children to draw on. They have the indispensable asset of not being as busy as their adult children. In all societies, grandparents, with their experience of child-rearing, have had a role as reserve parents. In Britain, grandparents are often close at hand. In a national sample of adults in Britain (according to a recent survey), of those whose mothers were still alive, 53% had their mother living within five miles, and of those whose grandmothers were still alive, 47% had their grandmother living within the same five-mile radius.[17] Although there has not been any recent research on what grandparents – grandfathers as well as grandmothers – do for their grandchildren, common observation suggests that they do a great deal.

I want particularly to reassert my belief in comprehensive schooling. If community is the aim, an essential precondition is to be brought up with a full range of other children. Apart from schooling, I also applaud the expansion of post-secondary education along the path to mass, recurrent and universal provision. And I want to see opportunities for all parents to choose part-time pre-schooling combined with parental childcare. In short, I hope for public services of the highest quality for childcare, education and training which will worthily complement the upbringing of children by their own parents.

Continuity makes community

Children are the foundation of community, or at any rate they were so before the car and molesters invaded their territories and drove them off the common land and the common street. If allowed to follow their own inclinations, children are drawn to others of their own age who are having the same unique experience of being 3 or 5, 8 or 13, and they form their own little groups accordingly. They can be accompanied through their childhood by the same people whom they got to know early on. The vital ingredient for friendship is continuity. 'Old friends' is not a meaningless concept, even for children of 10.

This continuity depends upon remaining in the same place. Many older people know how important this is, or at any rate was, when they were children, especially if they were brought up in villages or small towns, or in cities too, if their parents lived in settled communities. They learned about the place when they were at their most impressionable, and many people remain deeply attached to it and to the people they first discovered beyond their own parents and family. They learn about their society not so much by being taught as by following the example of others and by absorbing the values that the others take for granted. The main part of education consists of an apprenticeship to a number of different adults and learning by absorbing and sensing what they do.

When people are born and bred and stay in the same place, the community does not have to be built up by deliberate decision: you only need community development officers when there is no stability of residence. Given time, people who live together become attached to each other. I am not saying for all, but for many, repeated interaction produces a morality which, despite those who fall by the wayside, is generally observed. The children get to know each other. They bring their parents together. They grow into adults who know each other because they knew each other.

If the adults stay together even beyond that, they marry each other and have children. The next generation of children then has an ever more dense web of relationships to join. Parents become grandparents and great uncles and aunts to supplement the parents below them and the ordinary uncles and aunts. The kinship system that develops is also a friendship system. The friends of your relatives can be, at one remove, your own friends, and the relatives of your friends can become almost as though they are your own relatives. Time may not heal, but it certainly generates collective social relationships if allowed to develop in a limited space.

Fellow feeling, which is at the heart of morality, comes from children and other people living together, and the longer they live together, the better the chance it has of developing. Society can regenerate itself in this way by children and adults learning the old lessons of loyalty, kindness and tolerance which are the underpinning of any society. But we have to acknowledge that, as it works out in practice, there is a constant tussle between the experiences which add to human solidarity and those which threaten it, and which are set in motion whenever people move from one district to another. There is not much doubt which tendency has in recent years been winning out.

Acknowledgements

This chapter has drawn heavily on two sources: M. Young and A.H. Halsey, *Family and Community Socialism*, (Institute for Public Policy Research, 1995), and A. H. Halsey, 'Teenage Trouble', in *Youth Crime in 90s Britain*, (Gallup, 1993).

References

1. Young, M. and Halsey, A.H. (1995) *Family and Community Socialism*, Institute for Public Policy Research.
2. O'Neill, J. (1994) *The Missing Child in Liberal Theory*, University of Toronto Press.
3. Barclay, G.C. et al. (1993) *Digest 2: Information on the Criminal Justice System in England and Wales*, Home Office Research and Statistics Department.
4. Utting, D., Bright, J. and Henricson, C. (1993) *Crime and the Family: Improving Child-rearing and Preventing Delinquency*, Occasional Paper No.16, p.7, Family Policy Studies Centre.
5. Gallup (1993) *Youth Crime in 90s Britain*, Gallup.
6. Utting et al., op. cit.
7. Kolvin, I. et al. (1990) *Continuities of Deprivation?*, ESRC/DHSS Studies in Deprivation and Disadvantage, No.15, Avebury.
8. Rutter, M. and Giller, H. (1983) *Juvenile Delinquency – Trends and Perspectives*, Penguin.
9. Farrington, D.P. and West, D.J. (1990) 'The Cambridge Study in Delinquent Development: A long-term follow up of 411 London males', in Kaiser, G. and Kerner, H.-J. (eds), *Criminality: Personality, Behaviour, Life History*, Springer-Verlag.
10. Dickinson, D. (1995) *New Economy*, Summer.
11. Farrington, D.P. et al. (1988) *Cambridge Study in Delinquent Development: long term follow-up*, mimeograph, Cambridge Institute of Criminology.
12. Rutter, M. and Smith, D. (1995) *Psycho-Social Disorders in Young People: Crime trends and their causes*, John Wiley.
13. Willets, D. (1993) *The Family*, Contemporary Papers No.14, W.H. Smith.
14. Hewitt, P. and Leach, P. (1993) *Social Justice, Children and Families*, Institute for Public Policy Research, p.14.
15. Wilkinson, R.G. (1994) *Unfair Shares – The effects of widening income differences on the welfare of the young: A report for Barnardo's*, Barnardo's.

16 Atkinson, A.B. (1995) *Incomes and the Welfare State*, Cambridge University Press.
17 Young, M. and Halsey, A.H. (1995) *Family and Community Socialism*, Institute for Public Policy Research.

5 Postmodernism: Mutual society in crisis

Graham Cray

> Western civilisation suffers from a strong sense of moral and spiritual exhaustion. Having constructed a society of unprecedented sophistication, convenience and prosperity, nobody can remember what it was supposed to be for.[1]

> The truth is that we are in a time of transition, an in-between period when the old is dying and the new has yet to be born. The values, assumptions and structures that have governed us for so long have come to their logical end, and we now find ourselves at a dead end. But new values, patterns and institutions have not yet emerged. We are caught in the middle, stranded between paradigms.[2]

> There is a widely shared sense that Western ways of seeing, knowing, and representing have irreversibly altered in recent times: but there is little consensus over what this might mean or what direction Western culture is now taking. Has modernity really come to a close, or has it simply undergone a change of appearance?[3]

Western culture is going through a major upheaval at the close of the twentieth century. The quotations given above are but a random selection from many which could be taken from a wide variety of religious, political, sociological and philosophical perspectives. The overall debate about the nature and future of modernity and the significance of postmodernity[4] is beyond the scale and scope of this chapter; but the questions about the possibility of a coherent and genuinely communal society which are raised by that debate are central to the concerns of this book.

Modern certainties

Western culture as we know it took its intellectual shape in the seventeenth century. It has proved to be an extraordinary world view, transforming the West and influencing much of the rest of the world. It took its original shape in response to the breakdown of unity and authority in Europe which was a social and political consequence of the Reformation. Both civil and religious authorities were split between Catholic and Protestant loyalties, and Europe experienced a century of religious wars – believed by some to be the historical root of secularism.[5] Europe needed a new basis for authority and a framework of unity which allowed adequate diversity and religious tolerance.

In his search for absolute certainty, the French philosopher René Descartes identified the human capacity for reason ('I think therefore I am') as the foundation for all reliable knowledge. In England, John Locke distinguished between the public and private spheres of life. The public sphere was to be controlled by reason alone – only what could be rationally and 'scientifically' proved was to be believed and acted upon. Tradition lost its primacy and was restricted to the private sphere, where anything could be believed. Society's unity was to be preserved by keeping religious authority, together with other traditional sources of knowledge, apart from the public square, where objective scientific reason was to reign supreme.

The concept of progress, adapted from the theological idea of providence and a secularisation of the Christian view of history, developed in the same period to express an ideological confidence in the capacity of reason to forge a better world. The contemporary understanding of 'history' was also formulated in the same era.

These developments, of course, had a profound effect on how persons in society were viewed, the repercussions of which are still with us today.

The search for a modern ethic

The Enlightenment world view has been spectacularly successful, and nothing should be allowed to detract from its achievements. None of us would wish to return to a pre-scientific world. But the scientific and technological brilliance of the modern era has not been matched by an equivalent ethical achievement. By comparison with the visible scientific achievements of recent centuries, the attempt to derive universal moral standards from autonomous reason has proved futile.

The philosophers and ethicists of the early modern era were in many ways blinded by the light of their scientific colleagues' success. The sense of liberation was intoxicating. Immanuel Kant, the father of modern ethical theory, spoke of:

> The emergence of human beings from a tutelage to which they had voluntarily acceded ... Tutelage is the inability to make use of one's own understanding without being guided by another. Dare to know, have the courage to make use of your own understanding! That is the slogan of the Enlightenment.

Kant assumed and trusted the autonomy of rational human self-consciousness. For him, individual human reason possessed the power to discover the truth about the human race, the world and God *and* assumed that rational, autonomous human beings had the capacity to live in accordance with that truth. Released from tutelage to authoritarian dogma, human beings could all discover for themselves what *the* truth was, *and* they could live it morally. Kant's 'categorical imperative' insisted that morality derived from reason must be universal. Once, through reason, we have discovered rational, universal moral values, it is our duty to live them, and the will to perform that duty is the essence of morality. Kant emphasised the significance of knowledge, together with the will to live in its light. As a Christian, he took little notice of that aspect of Christian teaching which focuses on the human tendency to know what is right and choose *not* to do it, or to know what is right and to lack the moral character or strength to do it.

Despite his Christian faith, Kant rejected the idea that ethical judgements should be derived directly from Christian revelation, although he had no doubt that autonomous reason would lead to the affirmation of traditional, Christian moral values. He wrote of the necessity for human beings to treat one another as ends and not merely as means. He held out a vision of a 'kingdom of ends' in which each member treated the others in this way. In practice, Kant *assumed* the rational validity of Christian ethics and was not himself in any doubt as to what constituted the moral law; he never doubted for a moment that the maxims he had learned from his own virtuous (Lutheran) parents were those which could be vindicated by a rational test.[6]

However, Kant's presuppositions about autonomous reason, a rationally demonstrable universal morality and the will and capacity of human beings to know and to do what is right, together with his belief that reason, morality and (human) nature were in harmony, have proved unsustainable on the basis of Enlightenment assumptions. Modern ethical theory has failed to establish a rational basis for universal morality. The search for an objective moral standard derived from reason alone has resulted instead in an almost total subjectivism or emotivism, where all evaluative judgements, and more specifically all moral judgements, become nothing more than expressions of preference, expressions of attitude or feeling, in so far as they are moral or evaluative in character.[7]

In practice, the Enlightenment world view's incapacity to deal with issues of purpose (these having been exiled to the private sphere) rendered it incapable of answering questions about universal moral values, because, as Alasdair Macintyre explains, 'Once the notion of essential human purposes or functions disappears from morality, it begins to appear impossible to treat moral judgements as factual statements.'[8]

Postmodern origins

The link between the era of Immanuel Kant and our postmodern day is found in the work of Friedrich Nietzsche. Kant had claimed that ethics could not be grounded in revelation, but only in the free human will. But Nietzsche denied the existence of the universal rationality which Descartes had assumed and which Kant had used as the basis of a universally recognisable rational ethic. For Nietzsche, 'Truths are illusions which we have forgotten are illusions.' There is no Truth, only a range of perspectives from different social contexts. What each individual sees depends entirely upon their particular vantage point. Underlying *all* truth claims is human self-assertion, the 'will-to-power'. Universal ethical claims are partly self-delusion and loss of memory ('a mobile army of metaphors which ... come to be thought of, after long usage by a people, as fixed, binding and canonical') and partly cowardice. It is the weak who submit to them and project upon them a fictitious universal force which alienates them from their true selves. For Nietzsche, Christianity was the ideology which reinforced this alienation. Authentic human autonomy lay in 'the death of God'.

In the face of Europe's wars of religion and intellectual scepticism, Descartes had sought a new certainty and social unity through individual, autonomous reason; Kant proposed a universal, rationally accessible ethic. Nietzsche began the demolition of any understanding of autonomous, universal reason, reduced moral truth claims to competing perspectives and autonomous, individual reason to self-assertion and the 'will-to-power'. The ethical dimension of the Enlightenment dream had deconstructed itself.

In the twentieth century, the perspective that so-called rational truth claims are often as not disguised power plays has been developed by Nietzsche's postmodern intellectual successors, for example Jacques Derrida, Michel Foucault and Jean-François Lyotard. In Derrida's words, 'The white man takes his own mythology ... for the universal form of that which he must still wish to call Reason.'[9]

The history of this century, with two world wars, the Holocaust, the nuclear threat and the environmental crisis, has also made us challenge previous assumptions about the automatic goodness of scientific knowledge and new discovery in human hands, that perhaps, after all, there is no inherent connection between knowledge and its beneficial use.[10]

In his study of the holocaust, sociologist Zygmunt Bauman has made it clear that *both* its horrifying technical efficiency and its total lack of ethical compassion were characteristic of the modern era, and that: 'In a system where rationality and ethics point in opposite directions, humanity is the main loser.'[11]

The twentieth century has seen a significant and near-total breakdown between the technological and ethical arms of the Enlightenment project.

While progress in scientific research was achieved in all areas, the contemporaneous moral progress which would have prevented the misuse of science was lacking. Despite the development of a highly efficient macro-technology which has spanned the world, the spiritual energy which could have brought under control the risks of technology which were felt everywhere did not develop to the same degree. Although it generated an economy which expanded and operated worldwide, it has not produced the resources of ecology for combating the destruction of nature by industrialisation, which is equally worldwide. Over the centuries, a system of political democracy has been established across Europe and in many countries beyond. However, what has not been established is a morality which can work against the massive power interests of the different men of power and power groups. Thus, 'The Enlightenment itself shattered some of its own basic assumptions'.[12]

Mutual society in crisis

As the effective basis for a mutual society (Kant's 'kingdom of ends'), the Western world view is now in crisis. Three elements in particular have contributed to the undermining of community and social cohesion at various levels.

Individualism

Enlightenment theory was essentially individualistic. Personal autonomy was of the essence of the human. Human fulfilment was to be found in freedom *from* the restraints imposed by others. This also has proved double-edged. At its best, this has led to an invaluable emphasis on human rights. At its worst, it has undermined any personal or shared sense of mutual responsibility. To 'do our own thing' is to be human, not to find our being in reciprocal relatedness with our neighbour.[13]

The breakdown of bonds of commitment and mutuality at family, local and national levels is the harvest reaped from a partial understanding of what it means to be human, mistaking the individual for the personal and ignoring the relational altogether.

Reason and power

Unity in the public square was to be maintained by the *neutrality* of reason. Great emphasis was laid on the objectivity of 'scientific' knowledge. This has been undermined by two developments: first, the recognition that there is no such thing as a purely neutral, presuppositionless knowledge – what we see depends, in part, on what we expect to see and the perspective from which we look, for *all* knowledge is perspectival. Second, there has been a re-examination of the relationship between truth and power. It has become increasingly clear that the so-called neutrality of truth in the public square was in fact the particular truth of those in power. In Michel Foucault's words, 'We are subjected to the production of truth through power and we cannot exercise power except through the production of truth.'[14]

As a consequence, the public square is now full of formerly excluded groups competing for the right to be heard:

> Both society and polity in developed countries are now full of power centres which are outside and separate from government ... The new pluralism of the polity focuses on power. It is a pluralism of single cause, single issue groups – the 'mass movements' of small but highly disciplined minorities. Each of them tries to obtain through power what it could not obtain through numbers or through persuasion.[15]

This has had as powerful an impact on national communities as on regional or local ones. There is a tendency to break down into smaller and smaller political or ethnic units to *secure* community identity, just when such security seems impossible apart from intercommunal partnership. This explains why governments are weak, 'not because the voters have deliberately elected weak governments or because politicians are weak individuals but because that is the nature of the world at the close of this century'.[16]

Progress undone

Despite many extraordinary scientific and technological advances, the twentieth century has seen the collapse of the myth of progress. Two world wars, the Holocaust, the nuclear threat and the environmental crisis have undermined the ideology of an ever-improving civilisation. It is not merely that some global problems seem beyond our capacity to solve, but that the major crises we face have been caused or aggravated by our modern presuppositions. Contrary to the univocal optimism of classical Enlightenment thought, Ulrich Beck has shown how 'In advanced modernity the social production of wealth is systematically accompanied by the social production of risks.'[17]

Progress has turned out to be just another ideology with a limited shelf life. But its demise has undermined much of Western culture's social coherence, because 'Modernity was not merely the Western Man's thrust for power; it was also his *mission*, proof of moral righteousness and cause for pride.'[18]

The initial impact of Enlightenment thinking was to create a society with a sense of liberation from the past and a shared vision of modern history as a movement with a direction. The collapse of the ideological assumption of progress has resulted in a loss of confidence in a significant future. Social coherence depends strongly on a sense of shared history and shared hope for the future. We only know who we are if we have a notion of how we have become and of where we are going.[19]

But many moderns are left as participators in a 'perpetual present',[20] which is equally lacking in coherence, but which provides an extremely comfortable consumer culture in which most people are able to live, for the moment, without shared answers to the question 'Why?', an essential component of a corporate ethical vision.

There is a substantial intellectual debate as to whether or not the Enlightenment era is over, whether we are in 'late modernity' or 'post-modernity', but theorists on both sides agree that the integrating point of late modern or postmodern society is consumerism. Belonging to Western society is focused in the freedom of consumer choice:

> In present day society, consumer conduct (consumer freedom geared to the consumer market) moves steadily into the position of, simultaneously, the cognitive and moral focus of life, the integrative bond of the society, and the focus of systemic management ... In our time individuals are engaged (morally by society, functionally by the social system) as consumers rather than as producers.[21]

But even if life is no more than a market, the market still needs at least minimal ethical principles, and it is in no way clear where they are to be found.

The postmodern difference

Postmodernity, the social form of Western life at the end of the twentieth century, has been described as 'modernity's surprising outcome'. The philosophers and ethicists of the Enlightenment, whether Christian, deist or atheist, all believed in an objectively rational world discoverable by objectively rational people which would lead to a harmonious and objectively rational and thus unified society. In practice, the line of thinking that leads from Descartes's principle of radical doubt to the deconstructionism of Jacques Derrida has left us with nothing to be sure of apart from what we individually feel. If rational objectivity lay at the heart of the Enlightenment's ethical dream, inevitable and unbridgeable *difference* lies at the heart of the postmodern ethical experience. Where does this leave our perception of humans in relationship?

Fragmentation and pluralism

From a philosophical perspective, truth claims are seen as relative and are under suspicion as power plays. From an everyday perspective, global electronic technology makes pluralism and relativism seem self-evidently true. Which of the many fragmented electronic messages from different cultures and eras should we believe? Life is also fragmented. Academic disciplines tend to develop in isolation from one another. We are a society of the expert, yet lacking a shared sense of the meaning and coherence of the whole. Our identity seems to depend on a variety of roles which we are expected to play in different contexts. We are to be one person at work, another at home, another at leisure, with little sense of any stable personal centre or of any set of integrating relationships.

On the other hand, Western society is increasingly a global society; a ubiquitous commodity culture which emphasises consumer choice while simultaneously restricting it by offering the same choices everywhere:

> On the surface there is diversity and variety in modern life, but beneath the surface there is a pressure for homogeneity which in effect nullifies them.[22]

> Modernity once deemed itself as *universal*. It now thinks of itself as *global* ... Universal was to be the rule of reason – the order of things that would replace slavery to passions with the autonomy of rational beings, superstition and ignorance with truth ... Globality, in contrast, means merely that everyone everywhere may feed on McDonald's burgers and watch the latest made for TV docudrama.[23]

Paradoxically, we are a global society with no shared ethic beyond the right to consume (if you have the means) and to compete in the market place.

The self made self

The change of aspiration from a universal to a global society is paralleled in a change in the perception of the self. From the perspective of the Enlightenment, personal identity was found in a 'centred' self, rational, in control and shaping the world and its future. The postmodern self, on the other hand, is 'decentred', inundated by a multiplicity of clamouring voices proffering alternative identities, for the moment or for each context. For some, this offers at least the illusion of liberation. We can make ourselves whatever we choose to be within the (illusory) range of options, because 'If identities are essentially forms of social construction, then one can be anything at any time as long as the roles, costumes and settings have been commodiously arranged.'[24]

For others, the combination of an (apparently) unlimited range of choices and identities, in the absence of any shared ethical value system, results in a defensive withdrawal from society. The self 'contracts to a defensive core ... emotional equilibrium demands a minimal self', resulting in 'selective apathy, emotional disengagement from others ... a determination to live one day at a time'.[25]

Neither a perpetually self-creating self nor a withdrawn, minimal self is capable of the moral and social re-envisioning of society, since 'If life lacks any meaning beyond the meaning we pour into it, it is perhaps not surprising that care is quickly collapsed into self interest.'[26]

The postmodern dilemma

The postmodern dilemma is that we have lost our belief in a shared moral vision, or even the possibility of one; but we know from personal experience that moral questions do not go away. Zygmunt Bauman claims that postmodernity's demolition of modernity's belief in universal reason allows us to see the nature of the moral dimension with fresh, if daunting clarity:

> The breaking up of certain modern hopes and ambitions and the fading of illusions in which they wrapped social processes and the conduct of individuals alike, allow us to see the true nature of moral phenomena more clearly than ever. What they enable us to see is, above all, the 'primal' status of morality. Well before we are taught and learn socially constructed and socially promoted rules of proper behaviour ... we are already in the situation of moral choice.[27]

In facing moral dilemmas, questions of how I relate to the 'Other' are primal. They are inherent in our human condition. According to Jonathan Sacks:

> A private morality is no more possible than a private language.[28]

> Society is a moral exercise ... We cannot live alone. But we cannot live together without conflicts. How we resolve those conflicts determines the quality of our lives as members of families and as citizens.[29]

The loss of the Enlightenment belief in a rationally demonstrable ethic has, in one sense, cleared the way for a more adequate ethical framework, but at the price of an inherent suspicion towards any attempts to develop one. Postmodernism has demolished too much. If 'difference' is, in effect, the new absolute, where can ethical coherence be found?

A growing number of theorists are coming to the conclusion that postmodern nihilism, descended from Nietzsche, has indeed demolished too much. If morality is 'primal' to our humanity, then it requires some form of mutual framework between human beings. Questions of value and mutuality continue to demand a response irrespective of contemporary philosophical preferences for 'difference' and 'local narratives'. Postmodernity has a task ahead, to 'call for the creation of a common framework of assent, which alone can guarantee the continuation of a global diversity of voices'.[30]

The meeting table

The American Christian writer and political activist Jim Wallis has written recently of the contemporary opportunity for a 'meeting table'. Wallis recognises that Western society is undergoing a profound transition (see his quotation at the beginning of this chapter). He also recognises that people of many different faiths, ideologies and value systems are coming to the same conclusion. He uses the image of a table where they can all meet, openly acknowledging their particular and different perspectives, but united in a common concern: the discovery of a new moral framework for Western societies. A similar view has been expressed by the Chief Rabbi:

> We will search, as we have already begun to do, for an ethical vocabulary of duties as well as rights; for a new language of environmental restraint; for communities of shared responsibility and support; for relationships more enduring than those of temporary compatibility; and for that sense, that lies at the heart of the religious experience, that human life has meaning beyond the self.[31]

A Christian theological perspective

The remainder of my contribution will be written from the perspective of a convinced Christian, drawing also on Jewish sources. This is not an invasion of the public sphere by the private – that distinction is no longer tenable in its original form. Rather, it is a specific contribution from the conviction that *all* knowledge is perspectival. Nothing is seen, known, learned or discovered from a position of detached neutrality. There is no place outside of human society from which to observe human society. All knowing takes place on the basis of a world view accepted by faith (and revised on the basis of experience).

This does not mean that all truths are inevitably relative. Relativism is not the logical consequence. One particular perspective may give a more satisfactory account of reality than another. So I make no attempt to hide my conviction that Christian truth is public truth and that the claims of Christ are made upon every human person. I recognise that Christianity is in this way a 'metanarrative' of just the sort distrusted by postmodern theory, but I deny that it is inevitably oppressive. However, I do not ask my readers to accept these claims. Rather I place upon the table a Christian contribution to the search for a renewed ethical framework, to be assessed on the basis of its merits rather than its origins.

Much that has proved of value in our society but which now seems under threat is the direct, long-term consequence of the impact of the Christian faith upon British culture. Many people with no practical contact with the Church have eaten the fruit of a Christian perspective without necessarily being aware which tree it grew on. As our society undergoes a major shift, it is appropriate to bring to the table dimensions of a Christian world view which addresses our need for ethical coherence.

A vision of society based on a vision of God

Any Christian social vision must begin with the Christian understanding of God. When Christians speak of God, they mean the Holy Trinity, one God yet three persons. This is not a doctrinal dissertation, so I will not attempt to make the lengthy, nuanced statement that would be needed to define this further. However, this belief is not the complex creation of theologians with nothing better to do. It is the inevitable outcome of the central Christian claim that God has revealed himself to humankind and come to our rescue in the particular person of Jesus Christ.

Christ, whom we believe to be truly God, related to the one he called Father. This same experience of personal relationship to God the Father through his Son becomes real and actual for Christians by the help of another, whom they know as the Holy Spirit. Christians believe in the Trinity because there is no more adequate way to explain the experience of their faith and worship.

This belief has direct and substantial consequences for a Christian world view. Through this lens, reality is seen to be essentially personal and social. The sense of personal existence and the necessity of relationships come from an understanding that the creator of the universe is personal and relational and seeks relationship with humanity. Theories that see reality as essentially impersonal (whether materialist or those of Eastern faiths), or that see persons as *essentially* individuals, are rejected.

In the light of the environmental crisis, some of those who link the solution to the spiritual dimension of human beings have taken a monist or pantheist perspective, collapsing the world and persons into God. The Christian world view denies this on the basis that Jesus the Son came to reveal *both* the Creator's commitment *to* the world and his radical distinctiveness *from* it. This frees humans to see their purpose (a vital category for social ethics) as that of stewards of the impersonal creation in relation to the personal God.

At a time when philosophy is highly sensitive to the fact of oppression and the abuse of power, the Christian world view affirms that sacrificial love, not inevitable violence, is the ultimate building block of reality because the character of the triune God is revealed in the life, character and death of Christ. This frees Christians to sustain hope for change at a time of collapsing community and sustains the belief that love is stronger than violence.

The vision of God as Trinity also addresses the tension between unity (which tends to collapse into homogeneity or dictatorship) and diversity (which can result in social disintegration). The Christian view of society allows for both mutuality and particularity.[32]

The nature of personhood

The Judeo-Christian understanding, taken from the early chapters of the Bible, is that humans are created 'in the image' of this God. This is developed and illustrated in the partnership of male and female. At the heart of the concept of image is that of relationship. Humans are sufficiently like God to be able to relate to God personally. They are also created to be interdependent with one another and to share the stewardship of the earth. This fundamentally challenges the shared perspective of modernity and postmodernity that the essence of the person is an autonomous individual. Humans are *essentially* relational. It is only in relationship with our fellows that we grow into our true personhood and individuality. This is an essential insight to bring to the meeting table if the communal dimension of Western societies is to be restored.

Although this insight, that 'personal identity and individuality are neither asocial nor presocial, but arise out of one's relations and community with others',[33] arises from Christian doctrine, it is, I believe, sustainable on the basis of the basic evidence of human society. The very use of terms like 'I' or 'my' only makes sense (like morality) in a corporate context. 'I' is not referring to a thing (e.g. my 'self'), but 'to my position as a point location relative to others, and referring to that point as the location from whence communication may originate and with which communication may be conducted'.[34]

The contemporary attempt to identify the self by looking within and over against others is at the cost of ignoring the other, equally formative, dimension of human reality:

> A common picture of the self as drawing its purposes, goals and life plans out of itself, seeking 'relationships' only insofar as they are 'fulfilling', is largely based on ignoring our embedding in webs of interlocution.[35]

Covenant relationships

Not only is the relational nature of human reality central to a Christian world view; so also is the understanding that human persons are made for lasting, stable relationships and were created with the capacity to sustain them, at least when in such a relationship with God. The relationship between God and his people is described as a covenant, and God's character as one of faithfulness or 'steadfast love'. A life made up of short-term or broken relationships is deeply damaging and falls short of our purpose and potential capacities as humans. No wonder our social ethical life is in such disorder.

Community, purpose and time

From a Christian perspective, humans find their identity in relationship and their shared sense of purpose from a sense of vocation and hope for the future, which encompasses the dynamic development of the physical world and of human society, not just a caretaking function.

Identity is found in the narrative, the story we tell ourselves about ourselves:

> A person's identity is not to be found in behaviour, nor – important though this is – in the reactions of others, but in the capacity to keep a particular narrative going. The individual's biography ... must continually integrate events which occur in the external world, and sort them into the ongoing 'story' about the self.[36]

But the narrative has to be both social (if it is to integrate with the external world) and temporal, that is moving towards a perceived future. Our current tendency to live in a 'perpetual present' is an illusion which cannot be sustained forever. Visions of the future are learned in communities of belief; they are hard to sustain in isolation.

My life has a unique purpose as a chapter in a larger narrative, and thus 'I become connected to the community's past and future.'[37] This renewed sense that our stories are part of a larger, meaningful story has been affirmed by the discoveries of cosmology:

> The universe has a biography, a story of life. This is a story which moves forward, which accumulates, which points ahead. The stories which are visible in the lives of individuals are not some kind of aberration in a universe which basically goes round in circles.[38]

True humanity

But it makes a great difference to the nature of hope whether or not we believe we live in a personal or an impersonal universe, whether or not the universe's story is part of God's story. Christians base their belief in a personal universe in the promises of Jesus Christ about the destiny of the universe and of human persons within it. In the person of Jesus, Christians see not only a model of true humanity, but also the one through whom it becomes possible for all humanity to live a life marked by justice and self-sacrifice.

This requires an approach to ethics that is concerned with character as much as justice. Charles Handy makes the same connection:

> The new freedoms and the new choices will only survive if those who exercise them take time to look over their shoulders, if they genuinely have a care for others as well as for themselves, others beyond their families and their own institutions. ... We need a new religion to save us, or at least a new fashion. Fraternity, the care for others as much for oneself, must be our guiding ethic.[39]

Handy identifies the need for 'a new religion' (or an old one reappropriated) because he recognises the link between morality and spirituality. It is the religious communities of this land that have nurtured the values of mutuality that we most urgently need:

> Religious communities are not communities manufacturing and then maintaining values. Values for them are grounded in an attempt to understand external reality at its most profound level. In short they are grounded in metaphysics.[40]

The Christian doctrine of God found its first form in worship expressed in response to Christ. Such worship now carries the values which can help restore a relational society:

> The absolute dignity of otherness is a spiritual proposition. Religious commitment may yet prove to be its best defence.[41]

In writing this, I am deeply aware of the capacity of all religions for intolerance, oppression and bloodshed. I do not offer an instant solution. But I remain convinced that if the Judeo-Christian faith does not bring its insights to the meeting table, our society will face a critical moment without its most significant resource.

> There is a large element of hope that I see in Judeo-Christian theism, (however terrible the record of its adherents in history), and in its central dimension of a divine affirmation of the human, more total than humans can ever attain unaided.[42]

References

1. Longley, C. (1995) 'Foreword', in Sacks, J. *Faith in the Future*, Darton, Longman & Todd, p.x.
2. Wallis, J. (1994) *The Soul of Politics*, Orbis (US edition), p.5.

3 Snyder, J.R. (1988) 'Translator's Introduction', in Vattimo, G., *The End of Modernity*, Polity, p.vi.
4 See Lyon, D. (1994) *Postmodernity*, Open University Press.
5 Pannenberg, W. (1988) *Christianity in a Secularised World*, Student Christian Movement (SCM), Ch. 1.
6 Macintyre, A. (1990) *After Virtue*, Duckworth, pp.43–4.
7 Ibid, pp.11ff.
8 Ibid, p.59.
9 Derrida, J. (1981) *Writing and Difference*, Routledge, p.213.
10 Allen, D. (1989) *Christian Belief in a Postmodern World*, Westminster/John Knox Press, p.5.
11 Bauman, Z. (1989) *Modernity and the Holocaust*, Polity, p.206.
12 Kung, H. (1994) *Christianity*, Student Christian Movement (SCM), p.766.
13 Gunton, C. (1993) *The One the Three and the Many*, Cambridge University Press, p.65.
14 Foucault, M. cited in McHoul, A. and Grace, W. (1993) *The Foucault Primer*, University College London Press, p.59.
15 Drucker, P. (1989) *The New Realities*, Butterworth/Heinemann, p.71.
16 McRae, H. (1994) *The World in 2020*, HarperCollins, p.205.
17 Beck, U. (1992) *Risk Society*, Sage, p.19.
18 Bauman, Z. (1992) *Intimations of Postmodernity*, Routledge, p.xiv.
19 Taylor, C. (1989) *Sources of the Self*, Cambridge University Press.
20 Jameson, F. (1983) 'Postmodernism and Consumer Society', in Foster, H. (ed.) *Postmodern Culture*, Pluto Press, p.125.
21 Bauman (1992), op. cit., p.49.
22 Gunton, op. cit .
23 Bauman, Z. (1995) *Life In Fragments*, Blackwell, p.24.
24 Gergen, K. (1991) *The Saturated Self*, Basic Books, p.184.
25 Lasch, C. (1984) *The Minimal Self*, W.W. Norton, pp.15 and 57.
26 Gill, R. (1992) *Moral Communities*, University of Exeter Press.
27 Bauman (1995), op. cit., p.1.
28 Sacks, J. (1991) *The Persistence of Faith*, Weidenfeld, p.44.
29 Sacks, J. (1995) *Faith In The Future*, Darton, Longman & Todd, p.12.
30 Connor, S. (1989) *Postmodern Culture*, Blackwell, p.244.
31 Sacks (1991), op. cit.
32 Gunton, op. cit.
33 McFadyen, A. (1990) *The Call to Personhood*, Cambridge University Press, p.29.
34 Ibid.
35 Taylor, op. cit.
36 Giddens, A. (1991) *Modernity and Self-Identity*, Polity, p.54.
37 Sacks (1991), op. cit., p.45.
38 Williams, R., quoted in Tilbey, A. (1992) *Science and the Soul*, SPCK, p.97.
39 Handy, C. (1995) *The Age Of Unreason*, Arrow, pp.208–9.
40 Gill, op. cit.
41 Sacks (1995), op. cit., p.124.
42 Taylor, op. cit., pp.520–21.

Part II

Vulnerable relationships

6 Till death do us part?

David French

The Roman Catechism of 1566 said of marriage:

> The primary reason for marriage is the community of man and woman for the purpose of mutual help so that together they will more easily be able to bear the difficulties of life and especially those of old age.

One of the more frequent observations about marriage in our time is that it has become 'companionate', an arrangement for the 'mutual help' of man and woman, arguably not very different from that view of the Roman Catholic Church in the sixteenth century.

Plainly, however, a great deal has changed, and these changes are now reflected in statistics about marriage, cohabitation and divorce rates which, at the least, should give us pause for concern by the speed of the trends they reflect. So what has changed? Should we be concerned? And what of the future?

This chapter takes a look at some of these questions, mainly based on the experience of RELATE as the leading couple counselling agency in Britain today.

Modern marriage

For at least 50 years, research studies have tended to show that the capacity to form strong affectional bonds is central to our survival and development from the first days of life onwards. The capacity to make satisfying relationships forms the basis from which we explore and manage our experience of the world: we make a decent central relationship, we manage to be good enough parents, and we hold down our jobs. Down the centuries, marriage has reflected these deep personal needs while it has also provided a clear and accepted framework for the upbringing of children, as well as a strong economic unit; and in predominantly religious societies, the teaching of the Christian Churches, as well as Judaism and other faiths, that marriage is a life-long commitment has served to provide a strong affirmation of the virtue and value of marriage.

The statistics today show us that marriage remains popular in Britain – in Europe, only Portugal has a higher marriage rate. Although this is now falling quite fast in Britain, in 1990, 69% of women and 75% of men still expected to marry at some time in their lives (compared with 85% and 90% respectively in 1980). Nearly two-thirds of all marriages survive until the death of one partner, and over one-third of all marriages are now remarriages – representing the triumph of hope over experience?[1]

One of the most notable changes of the last generation has been the pathways which people choose into marriage: one study found that, in the late 1950s, 65% of women who married were virgins on their wedding day, while nearly 60% of women who married in the late 1980s had lived with their partner first.[2] Cohabitation is most commonly a transition into marriage rather than a permanent arrangement, the decision to have children most commonly being the trigger for marriage.

The majority of those who choose to cohabit, then, may be seen as exploring or testing their commitment to each other before entering marriage – though the statistics tell us that many of these cohabitations end in separation rather than marriage. Research also shows that couples who had cohabited before marriage were more likely to divorce than those who had not.[3]

So, while most people still choose marriage, fewer are doing so; and the alternatives they choose are, on the evidence of statistics, less likely to achieve a life-long relationship.

Great expectations

What, then, are some of the pressures on a contemporary marriage? One among the most visible comes from the communications revolution. We are constantly bombarded with images of apparently ideal relationships, for example through the medium of television advertising. Everyone is beautiful, everyone is clean, everyone has enough money, babies don't seem to scream or smell or dribble. These images are, of course, unrealistic; but they raise expectations of marriage which are frequently at odds with everyday experience.

It is in the field of expectations that some of the most striking changes in marriage have taken place: expectations of love and companionship have come to be seen as the most important factors in marriage, ahead of the expectation of fulfilling the roles of breadwinner or homemaker.

A loosening of the traditional stereotypes of male and female roles has accompanied this trend. Many more women take up their own careers, or at least take on jobs outside the home; and Britain now has the highest proportion of two-income families in Europe: 60% in 1982, compared with 43% in 1973.[4]

What is frequently described as a shift in the respective roles of men and women in marriage is in practice, then, both powered by and a consequence of the changing work patterns of women. Women today have the opportunity to establish a lifestyle and identity other than homemaker and mother, and indeed, this work-related identity is now commonly accorded a higher status.

It also brings a higher level of economic freedom to today's married women than even their mothers, certainly their grandmothers, knew. Consequently, women who feel trapped in marriages which no longer fulfil those expectations of love and companionship have more realistic prospects of leaving the marriage. However, the evidence that around two-thirds of single mothers receive Income Support suggests strongly that economic independence is a more realistic prospect for single women on their own than those with dependent children.

If, then, the expansion in women's opportunities, economic freedom and consequent attitudes to marriage has been the principal influence over the last generation, what about men?

Studies tend to show that in two-income marriages, 'new man' is still an elusive and unusual species. Men's attitudes to housekeeping and domestic jobs and to childcare responsibilities have shifted much less than women's work patterns outside the home. Working women tend to retain responsibility for these roles in addition to managing a part-time or full-time job, frequently without their employer offering flexibility to adapt to family responsibilities.

It would be facile to suppose that if 'new man' has yet to develop in large numbers, 'superwoman' can cope with heavy domestic responsibilities on top of a job outside the home without a good deal of stress and a range of potential effects which impact on the whole family.

If, in addition, redundancy or unemployment hit the family, with all they commonly entail in loss of status and self-respect, it is not hard to see that disaster can easily strike a marriage in which the partners have not developed the resources or resilience to cope with setbacks together. Even those who have and who treasure the few hours they spend together at the weekend or evenings may quickly reach the stage where, keeping each other's company for 24 hours a day, they yearn for a change.

In addition to changing living patterns, the loss of a job also entails a drop in income, and anxiety about how a couple will meet their future commitments: keeping up the payments on the mortgage or paying the rent are, for many, only the largest in a string of financial commitments which are likely to be greater than a generation ago as a result of the material explosion of our age and the willingness of banks and other lenders to encourage us to stretch our spending capacity to its limits.

Along with the financial pressures, the loss of a job often means the loss of a central factor in a person's identity. Being in employment is central to our view of ourselves, to our self-esteem. How often do you meet someone socially for the first time and find that the first (or at least second or third) thing they want to know about you is where you work? That is a way by which we can frame an understanding of each other, or at least think we can: it represents standing, being someone with a role and a contribution, a location in society. It may also reflect interests and aptitudes and, indeed, may enable – often wrongly – short cuts to be taken in calculating the views and assumptions the other will hold. As Janet Mattinson put it in her book *Work, Love and Marriage:*

> People are at their happiest, strongest and most creative when the external world confirms their best and most hopeful images or they are able to transform the external reality through their own symbolism to fit these images; and ... they are at their most miserable, disturbed and weakest when the world confirms their worst fears about themselves.[5]

The external world is often the most strongly represented by work or the absence of it.

In these patterns, there are conflicting influences. Couples seek love and companionship in their private relationships in a world whose public face is characterised by increasing pressure, complexity and time constraints. Technology opens up new possibilities for communication, yet parents and in-laws are more likely to live further away and friends and neighbours are reluctant to intrude.

The challenge of commitment

The most common characteristic of all RELATE's counselling work is that couples have lost the ability to communicate with each other or have developed destructive and negative habits in doing so, in a world where the ability to communicate, to stay in touch, to exchange information, is the most powerful cement in any relationship. A commitment to the future of family life must surely be based on a commitment to nurturing communication skills and patterns of living which enable them to be practised.

For, when a marriage can be ended without financial disaster to either partner, and when society accepts divorce with sorrow but without stigma, couples have nothing better than their own resources to fall back on. When many of the signals they receive through advertising or the media serve only to raise expectations about endlessly fulfilling relationships, there was never a time when the ability to spot oncoming danger signals was more vital, when the unglamorous message of working to maintain a commitment, of openness and trust, of rediscovering the joy of a relationship once deeply cherished was more centrally important than it is now.

Indeed, a commitment to commitment itself lies at the heart of our present need in relation to marriage and family health. When besieged by the pressure of work, or lack of it, or debt, or the demands of teenage children for the latest brand of trainers, when all the conventional attitudes of our society encourage quick-fix solutions and short-term gratifications, it can require serious determination to maintain a commitment to a close relationship, however strong the bond once was.

One of the other most significant changes affecting contemporary marriage is the simple fact that people live longer. A century ago, a couple who married could expect between 15 and 20 years together. Today, the majority of men and women live until they are well into their seventies or considerably older, so that a young couple marrying in their twenties are committing themselves to upwards of 50 years living in partnership. As individuals, we grow and change throughout our lives, and pyschologists identify some eight stages in a human lifespan, with considerable periods of change between each of them. Each of us as individuals grows and develops over time; and if we look back on the person we were 20 years ago it may be hard to recognise the one we are today. Two individuals are likely to grow and change in different ways over time, even where those two are married and influence each other's development closely. In that sense, every marriage is a struggle between you, me and us; and we must surely all, if we are honest, admit to periods of discomfort, anxiety, dissatisfaction or sheer boredom in any 'normal' marriage.

If, then, these are some of the changing characteristics and pressures on marriage and families today, it is hardly surprising that in the last generation we have lived through an extraordinary period of re-evaluation and experiment in the realm of relationships. If the pill provoked the sexual revolution of the 1960s and 1970s, and economic necessity the advent of the two-income family, the widespread phenomenon of relationship breakdown has itself provoked a reassessment of marriage as the public endorsement of a private commitment. Children who grow up with the experience of their parents' divorce – and today, that is 1 in 4 children under 16 – are inevitably more likely to question the value of marriage and be more cautious about choosing it for themselves. So what of the future?

The future of marriage in a changing world

Most of all, we who are concerned with family relationships and their long-term future must start from a real world view of life as it is, rather than an idealised notion of what we would like it to be. At least, we must not succumb to cornflake-packet stereotypes if we mean to have any impact on a changing world. To do this is not to capitulate to what may be seen as unwelcome trends; and it is not to pretend – though too many commentators do – that families can function equally well whatever their characteristics. Rather, it is to face up to the reality that variety of family structures is a fact of life today.

Today, less than a quarter of households comprise couples with dependent children; in 1961, 38% of households were so composed. Today, more than 1 in 4 households consist of one person living alone; in 1961, just 11% of households were so composed.[6] Today, the divorce rate in England and Wales is six times higher than 30 years ago.

These trends are by no means all unwelcome. 'Traditional' families, at their best – two parents with a good relationship providing a strong setting for rearing their children, perhaps with a third generation in support – can be the best possible setting for all concerned; but at their worst, the same traditionally-structured families can provide a private and sometimes impenetrable setting for oppressive and demeaning behaviour, with life-long consequences. Public policy has been unwilling for too long to break through the assumption that the private world of families is no public business. It is only in the last five years, for example, that the Home Office has required police forces to recognise and act on the all too common problem of domestic violence.

What is now abundantly clear from a succession of research studies over the last 15 years is that when family relationships break down, children as well as their parents suffer. There has been some notable work which charts the effects of divorce on the mental and physical health of adults. This is hardly surprising given the extent to which divorce is now widely recognised as a highly painful and stressful experience. For example, the risk of premature death and the incidence of morbidity are higher among the divorced than the married. Divorced and separated men are more likely to be heavy smokers than any other marital status groups. Divorced women are more likely to smoke than married women; and divorced and separated men drink more heavily than married men, with all the consequent risks of other illnesses developing. Notable links between marital status and health conditions such as heart disease and cancer have also been identified.[7]

As Janet Walker, Director of the RELATE Centre for Family Studies, has said of the research on children and divorce:

Conflict-ridden families, whatever their composition or marital status, create the most difficult environment for the well-being of children as well as of adults. Research findings consistently show that children in conflict-free, lone-parent households function more adequately than those in two-parent conflict-ridden homes. The mere status of the parental relationship and the number of parents present in the home, do not ensure the optimum conditions for raising happy, healthy children. It is in high conflict families where communication is poorest that prolonged disturbance may develop and it is for those children that the prognosis is poorest.[8]

So it seems more useful to focus on the changing relationships in families than the institutions themselves as a guide to how policy and practice for families might best develop. Indeed, there is now a strong case for arguing that the future of marriage itself will be best secured by rediscovering its original purpose (remember that sixteenth-century Catholic view) and focusing policy on equipping couples to maintain the reality of 'mutual help', rather than through some misguided attempt to shore up the institution without regard to the reality of those who live in it.

Building quality relationships

The remainder of this chapter is devoted to a personal view, developed over my nine years as Director of RELATE, of the actions which government and society need to take if we are seriously to address the issue of family life through supporting family relationships.

Relationship education

First, I believe that relationship education needs to be developed systematically and widely in schools and elsewhere. By 'relationship education', I mean the development of appropriate skills, self-confidence and awareness to build and maintain good inter-personal relationships, combined with the capacity to accommodate and adapt to change.

Our approach is based on the recognition that teachers are often reluctant to take up relationship issues formally in the classroom or informally in the corridor – either because they lack the confidence to do so, often not having had any training in this field, or because they are entering a moral minefield in which the norms have become anything but clear and the risks of exposure are all too evident.

Clearly, there are a number of obstacles in the way of developing relationship education in schools at present: first of all, the legal framework here is much less well developed than it now is for sex education. Equally, the pressure imposed by the National Curriculum tends to restrict time available for other 'softer' topics such as this. More fundamental is the central concern which emerges from our recent enquiries among teachers that there appears to be very little attention given to the relationship aspect of the teacher's role during training, either at a qualifying or at an in-service stage; and, of course, the search for funding for in-service training is highly competitive. But perhaps the root of this ambivalence is the still widespread view that personal relationship matters are the sole responsibility of parents. At a time when there is now so general an understanding of the value of parents and schools working together, this view cannot be sustained.

In response to this, RELATE has focused its recommendations on the extension of training for teachers in relationship education: in initial teacher training, for newly-qualified teachers and as a component of in-service training for more experienced teachers.

Teachers are, of course, in the most prominent position in the development of relationship education with children and young people; but other key influencers include GPs, health visitors, lawyers, clergy and religious leaders, the media, public figures and, most of all, family members themselves.

For relationship education is not simply about what can be taught in schools; it is also about public awareness more broadly. It is about raising the level of consciousness of what enhances or undermines our close relationships, of better communication and deeper understanding, about finding ways to use and take advantage of the technology of the communications revolution and also about supporting family and community networks at a very personal and immediate level.

Work and the family

My second field of policy development would be to strengthen the connections between work and the family. Clearly, the central issue here goes far beyond the provision of childcare facilities, important though that is. It is about reforming the benefit system, sensible work patterns, recruitment policies, leave practices and career breaks, and so on; it involves creating a labour market so that men and women who want to work can earn the self-respect and income which come from doing so. A balance between work and family would mean that mothers could earn as much self-respect and have sufficient income from being mothers; that fathers could see and know their children; and it means recognising that family-friendly work patterns do not mean very much if you do not have any work.

Support for families

It is obviously right that support services to families should be strengthened when, for example, it still costs under £300 for RELATE to help a couple to save their marriage or minimise the damage if it ends (RELATE works with about 70,000 people a year). This work attracts only £1.6 million a year in government funding; it is high time government placed a higher priority on this field. After all, it spent £332 million in matrimonial legal aid alone in 1993-4, and the financial costs to the taxpayer if Income Support, housing, childcare or health costs were taken into account would be many times this figure.

Divorce reform

My final interest is in the field of divorce reform, in which the government signalled its most welcome intentions in the Family Law Bill in November 1995. Divorce law is, of course, itself about marriage. It is one of the strongest means we have available to model appropriate or inappropriate behaviour in the way conflicts in marriage are resolved. As the present Lord Chancellor has said, the manner in which a marriage is ended can do much to 'buttress' the institution of marriage, whether or not a couple decide in the end to go through with their divorce.

The central facts are well known. It takes two or five years to obtain a divorce on separation or desertion grounds; a median of six months if the fault-based grounds of adultery or unreasonable behaviour are used; some take as little as three months. Three-quarters of all divorces under present legislation use fault as the grounds, most commonly to avoid the wait.

The minimum period in the Family Law Bill, which would be variable in virtually no circumstances, would be one year. During this time, there would be much encouragement given to couples to reflect on the possibility of saving their marriage, to consider the options open to them, and their consequences, before proceeding with a divorce, and to examine the reality of life after divorce, for example in arrangements for co-parenting of children or in the sharing of property.[9]

To use a railway metaphor, there would be a variety of signals to direct couples into sidings where they could reflect and consider the consequences of continuing down the track. Located in the sidings would be: counsellors to help couples sort out whether they want to be on this track in the first place and, if so, to manage their way through the emotional thunderstorm which is so common an experience in divorce; mediators to help resolve disputes in as non-confrontational a setting as possible, and lawyers to seal the arrangements which had been made.

I believe that the opportunity to do these things in a siding, taking as long as necessary, would be a vast improvement on the present system. All too often at present, couples are encouraged to stay on the main track, negotiating at high speed if at all, and frequently reaching the terminus before they have settled the arrangements for property, finance or children.

Many other countries in Europe and elsewhere have reformed their divorce laws by abolishing the fault grounds and encouraging the use of mediation. In Britain, we approach the prospect of divorce reform with a more comprehensive understanding from research of its value and limitations than any other country has had available. The prospect of a framework for divorce – as outlined in the government's White Paper of April 1995,[9] preparatory to the Family Law Bill – though not being without its challenges and difficulties, will, I believe, represent a huge step forward in recognising the real experience and feelings of couples approaching the breakdown of their marriage.

Conclusion

I believe that any political party which committed itself to these four areas would command widespread public support, and I can see no more effective way of securing the future of family life than by focusing on strengthening and supporting the relationships on which families are built.

References

1. 'Marriage Today' (1994), *The One Plus One Information Pack*, One Plus One.
2. Gorer, G. (1970), *Sex and Marriage in England Today: A study of the views and experiences of the under-45s*, Nelson.
3. Haskey, J. (1992) 'Pre-marital cohabitation and the probability of subsequent divorce: analyses using new data from the GHS', *Population Trends*, No.68, HMSO.
4. Utting, D. (1995), *Family and Parenthood: Supporting Families, Preventing Breakdown*, Joseph Rowntree Foundation.
5. Mattinson, J. (1988) *Love, Work and Marriage*, Duckworth.
6. OPCS (1995) *Social Trends*, No.25, HMSO, p.31.
7. McAllister, F. (ed.) (1995) *Marital Breakdown and the Health of the Nation*, One Plus One, 2nd edn.
8. Walker, J. (1995), *The Cost of Communication Breakdown*, BT Forum, p.15.
9. Lord Chancellor's Department (1995) *Looking to the Future: Mediation and the Ground for Divorce*, Cm 2799, HMSO.
10. Ibid.

7 Children in need
Helen Roberts

All of us were children once, and this gives every adult, whether a parent or not, one kind of expert knowledge of what children need. Even so, adult memory can lead too easily to adult over-confidence. How many of us have heard: 'What the child needs is ...', frequently completed with the phrase 'a good talking to', or (even now) 'a good smack'? The Children's Society poster, 'What that child needs is a good listening to' is powerful precisely because it challenges such conventions. For while there is no shortage of suggestions on what children need, the evidential basis for a great deal of what is said is thin and subject to change over time and place. The basic requirements of children – for adequate food in their bellies, warmth in winter, a roof over their heads and the love of a good-enough parent or substitute parent – is clear. We do not need studies to show us the evidence that these 'work' as prerequisites for a good childhood. But identifying a need does not ensure that it is met. Even in a relatively wealthy society such as our own, these very basic requirements remain far from an entitlement for all our children.

The discussion of childhood and 'what children need' can frequently be clouded by the fact that a good deal of the argument is ideologically-driven, with each of the main political parties in the UK recognising the attraction of occupying the moral high ground which might enable it to be identified as 'the party of the family'. A failure of consensus in ideologically-driven areas is hardly surprising. More worrying is a lack of professional consensus on what children need. What is confidently thought to be 'right' by professionals at one time will be confidently believed to be wrong at another. Do I pick up my baby when she cries at night, or leave her? Do I feed him on demand, or at regular intervals? Do I place my baby on her back or her front in the cot, or should she perhaps not be in a cot at all, but in my bed? If, on issues as relatively clear-cut as these, there has been so little expert agreement, how much more contentious are the questions of what works in children's relationships and in bringing up children successfully within different family structures and family formations. It is important that we know what kinds of support we can give children and families to help ensure that the difficult task of parenting is carried out as well as it can be. Yet the knowledge on which such support must be based is elusive.

One term often used in such discussions about children's needs is 'good-enough parenting'. While there is no precise definition of what it is to be 'good enough', it is clear that it incorporates much more than basic material requirements, and includes both emotional and relational needs as well. It is this assumption which underpins the content of this chapter.

This chapter explores some of what we know about the significance of stable relationships in a child's life. It describes a number of issues arising both when the family (traditional and otherwise) acts as parent, and when the State acts as parent. It looks at the importance of 'family ethos' as well as 'family structure', and at the reservoirs of knowledge among ordinary parents and children about what is needed for successful family life. This 'lay' expertise remains largely untapped by professionals.

Work by anthropologists, sociologists and historians reminds us that notions of 'childhood' and our sense of what it means to be a child are not 'givens', but are themselves socially constructed.[1] Our understanding of childhood is shaped by other understandings – of the way in which society is organised, of family life, of notions of community or individualism. Hockey and James, for instance, describe an account of child-rearing practices in Matabeleland, where children were often cared for by their aunt or another female relative. Known as the 'big mother', the eldest sister offers equal care to her own children and those of her younger sisters.[2] The ways in which children are cared for are not fixed laws of nature, and there is no monopoly of virtue. This should give us cause for caution when variations of family type, family formation and family structure are used to 'explain' a range of major issues from moral degeneracy to rising crime rates. A more modest and fruitful question for those wanting to improve the lot of children is how, given the variety of ways in which children and families operate, can we best support them? What kinds of relationships between individuals, or between individuals and the State, are sustaining?

Changes in family structure and family life

Changes in family structure are described in some detail elsewhere in this volume. It is worth reminding ourselves here, however, that there have been very rapid changes in family life in the United Kingdom over the last 20–30 years. Utting describes some of these as follows:

- There are fewer children and families have become smaller; there were 11.8 million children under 16 in the UK in 1991, compared with 14.3 million in 1971.
- The proportion of babies born outside marriage has surged from 6% in 1961 to 32%.
- The annual divorce rate is six times higher than 30 years ago.
- One in five dependent children lives with a lone parent, compared with 1 in 13 in the early 1970s.
- Two out of three mothers with dependent children either have a job or are looking for work, compared with fewer than half 20 years ago.
- Between 1979 and 1992, the proportion of dependent children living in households with less than half average net income rose from 1 in 10 to 1 in 3.[3]

Adult views on family life

In 1995, Barnardo's commissioned MORI to carry out a survey to explore whether a gap exists between people's expectations of what a 'decent childhood' *should* include, and what they feel that childhood today *does* include.[4] We also looked at whether people felt that today's children have a better or worse childhood than they themselves did when they were children. The MORI survey showed that over 3 in 5 (62%) adults think that childhood today is worse than when they were children. Older people were significantly more likely to cite 'the breakdown in family structures/increase in one-parent families/the divorce rate' as something which could make the world a worse place for children (71% of those aged 55–64, compared to 46% of those aged 15–24).

While we do not claim that the results are an objective account of social change, what we were told presents a worrying picture. Table 7.1 describes just two aspects of this survey – adult views on whether a stable family life, or a loving home, was more or less likely than when they were children, or had stayed about the same: 7 in 10 adults feel a stable family life is now less likely, and over half said this of a loving home; 26% of adults expect today's children to have a worse life than theirs. In looking at these data, we need to bear in mind that notions of childhood and attitudes towards the family are socially constructed, and that adults tend to look back on their childhood with feelings of nostalgia. Nevertheless, what was very clear from the survey, as David Utting has pointed out, is the way in which 1 in 4 adults, who do not necessarily share the disadvantages of those families with whom Barnardo's works, nevertheless share some of their concerns.

Table 7.1 The changing face of childhood

Compared to when you were a child do you think that children these days are more likely or less likely to get the following things, or do you think the likelihood has stayed the same?

and

Now I would like you to think about your own childhood and compare it with the life of the average child in Britain today.
Do you think that children today are more or less likely to have the following things, or is the likelihood about the same?

	More likely (%)	Less likely (%)	Stayed the same/about the same (%)	Don't know (%)
A stable family life	11	70	17	2
A loving home	7	53	38	2

Note: In total, 1,069 interviews were conducted face-to-face, in-home, among a representative quota sample of adults aged 15+ in Great Britain. Fieldwork was carried out and between 23 and 29 April 1995 over 105 sampling points. All data has been weighted to the known profile of the British population.
Source: Barnardo's (1995).

Children's views on family life

In social research in general – including, ironically enough, research on what family life is like for children and their own hopes and fears – we are rather more likely to seek adult views than those of children themselves. There are some admirable exceptions to this,[5] and with Social and Community Planning Research, Barnardo's has recently supplemented the British Social Attitudes study by a survey of the attitudes of a sample of children and young people aged 12–19.[6]

The survey includes a number of questions about marriage and parenting. Interestingly, both boys and girls were more inclined to say that they think that family life suffers because men focus on work too much than they were to agree that family life suffers if women work full-time. We asked children and young people if they agreed or disagreed with a number of statements on marriage and parenthood. Table 7.2 shows that about half of those inter-

Table 7.2 Attitudes to marriage by gender

	Agree Females (%)	Agree Males (%)	Neither agree nor disagree Females (%)	Neither agree nor disagree Males (%)	Disagree Females (%)	Disagree Males (%)
It's better to have a bad marriage than no marriage at all	3	11	9	9	88	81
When there are children in the family, parents should stay together even if they don't get along	14	22	18	27	68	37
One parent can bring up a child as well as two parents	66	45	17	18	17	37

Note: The British Social Attitudes Survey is a nationwide annual survey carried out by Social and Community Planning Research (SCPR). In 1994, 3,469 people aged 18 or over were interviewed. In 1994, for the first time, the survey was supplemented by the Young People's Social Attitudes Survey. All young people aged 12–19 who lived in the same household as a British Social Attitudes Survey respondent were eligible for interview. Of the 735 young people eligible for interview, interviews were achieved with 580 (79%).
Source: Oakley (1996).

viewed consider that a single-parent family can do as well as a two-parent one, and most disagree with the notion that having children is a good reason for parents to stay together. Ann Oakley, considering these data, notes:

> most striking of all is the difference between the 66% of young women and 45% of young men who consider that one parent can be as good as two. Are the young women perhaps sensing here their own possible trajectories in this direction? Some may also be reflecting their own positive experiences of being raised by single mothers.[7]

As part of the same survey, we gave the young people interviewed a checklist of ambitions and asked them to pick their main one in life, followed by the next ambition in their order of priorities. Young people placed happiness at the top of their lists. If we are to bear in mind an apparently pervasive climate of greed and individualism in both public and private life over recent years, it is perhaps reassuring that being well-off is not rated as highly as happiness. 'Having a family' tied with 'Having good health' as the next most important ambition, but as a 'main ambition', fell below having a good job and being successful at work. Young people may, however, be more attached to family life than stereotypical images of conflictual youth may suggest. Almost 1 in 5 young women in the *Young People, Health and Family Life* study,[8] for instance, said that a happy family was the most important thing in life for them.[9]

Are some family structures better than others?

In an area as important as family life, not all of our beliefs are grounded in evidence. Some are grounded in our own experience as children or parents, some in religious beliefs or political ideologies. Some are probably grounded in the need to find a reason for some of the less desirable changes experienced in the last couple of decades. Some are likely to be grounded in the understandable desire of politicians of all persuasions to look to factors other than their own policies as a source of malaise.

Mothers and fathers as parents

Even when we try to move beyond the limits of our individual experience, measuring the effect of different kinds of family structure on children's wellbeing is made difficult by other factors in the lives of the children under consideration. Following Bowlby's classic study,[10] for instance, the notion of 'maternal deprivation' gained popular currency with those whose work involved caring for children. The children in Bowlby's study, however, were deprived of a great many other things in addition to their mothers, including their fathers.[11]

The studies which are perhaps best able to throw light on the effects of family structure on outcomes for children are the cohort studies, such as the National Child Development Study (NCDS) and the National Survey of Health and Development. These studies follow up subjects at more than one point in time, so that data are collected from (or about) the same person over a period of months or years. Of particular relevance in looking at the influence of relationships are the birth cohort studies, in which those included are selected into the study at birth and followed up at intervals well into adulthood. The evidence from these has been reviewed by Burghes.[12] As Holterman points out, the emotional and social impacts on children of marriage breakdown can be severe, and the practical effects – notably the reduction in financial circumstances that often accompanies the transition to lone parenthood – can be drastic.[13]

A crucial question in the interpretation of the research results and the consideration of appropriate policy responses is how far the adverse outcomes for children of one-parent families are due to lone parenthood, and how far they are caused by the poverty in which many lone parents live. We know that lone parenthood following separation is commonly accompanied by a reduction in income for the lone parent and children, and poverty is associated with poor outcomes for children. It is important to attempt to disentangle, as far as possible, the contributions made to both good and poor outcomes by family structure and by material and other factors. Without this knowledge, the evidence basis for the practice and policy interventions which can best support children and families remains thin, and our interventions and expectations of what is likely to be protective are more likely to be based on conjecture than on soundly-based understanding.

Other chapters in this volume explore some of this evidence in more detail, but it is worth reporting here a raft of research recently funded by the Joseph Rowntree Foundation under the Transitions to Adulthood initiative, which suggests some pointers on the role of family 'process' as well as family type. Work done by Sweeting and West,[14] based on the youngest cohort of the West of Scotland Twenty-07 Study,[15] looked at the ways in which different aspects of the family lives of young people related to a range of outcomes chosen as broadly representative of lifestyle (opinions, worries and aspirations; health-related behaviours; delinquency and contact with the police; education; post-school labour market position, and family formation). The authors consider both family structure (categorised as intact, reconstituted or single-parent households) and reasons for family breakdown, distinguishing between parental separation and death, as well as two aspects of the process of family life: 'family-centredness' – a measure of time spent in joint family activities, and 'conflict' – frequency of arguments between the young person and their parents. Data on family life were obtained at age 15, the dependent variables at 15, 18 and 21; thus, both cross-sectional and prospective analyses were conducted. Of the four aspects of family life, family-centredness showed the strongest and most consistent relationships with outcomes, in both males and females. While the authors are cautious about the meaning of their findings and warn that family-centredness and arguments do not, contrary to the suggestions of some authors,[16] wholly 'explain' the variations in outcome which occur in different family structures, their work does offer a different way of looking at what might be supportive for families.

We need to remember, in looking at biological parents in all kinds of family structures, that most of them, whether lone parents or dual parents, whether conventional or not so conventional, do a *good enough* job in bringing up their children. The question for policy-makers, and for service providers, is how we can better support both those families who are doing well (in many cases, with sub-optimal support) and those where there is reason for concern.

The State as parent

While there has been much discussion in recent years of the deficiencies of parents – and in particular mothers or single mothers – in bringing up their children successfully, there can be little doubt that the State as parent falls well short of the aspirations which most parents have for their children. We need to recall that those charged with the care of children separated from their families undertake *parental responsibilities* for them and are therefore accountable for the manner in which they discharge their *parental duties*.

Research by Ward[17] has shown that 'looked-after' children are often poorly educated, socially isolated and at risk of developing criminal or pathological behaviour patterns.[18] Perhaps most worrying of all is the finding that such children tend to leave the protection of the agency several years before young adults in the community leave their families and are often ill-equipped to cope with their independence.[19] The experience of being 'looked after' is thus a negative one for many children. Their educational and health needs tend to be neglected, they tend to have numerous moves, which are hardly conducive to the formation of stable relationships, and children who may have been removed from their families because of abuse are by no means guaranteed freedom from abuse while in care. If the process and experience of being in care are frequently negative, what are some of the *outcomes* for those children for whom their parent is the State?

- More than 75% of young people leave care with no academic qualifications, compared to 11% of their peers.[20]
- The national rate of unemployment for 16–24 year-olds is 17%, but for care-leavers, it is estimated to be between 50% and 80%.[21]

- Young people who have been in care are disproportionately likely to become homeless. Less than 1% of young people have been in care, and yet they form one-third of the population of homeless young people.[22]
- At least 1 in 7 young women leaving care are pregnant or are already mothers.[23]
- Twenty-five per cent of adult prisoners and 38% of young prisoners have been in care.[24]

Government policies on social security and housing are based on the assumption that young people are able to remain at home with their families. Young people aged 16 and 17 do not receive Income Support at all, but have to rely on 'severe hardship' payments. The Income Support level for 18–24 year-olds is lower than that for people aged 25 and over, and this is reflected in a lower rate of Housing Benefit for 18–24 year-olds. Yet most young people who have been in care have no choice but to live independently, and the cost of living is no different whether you are alone and unsupported at 18 or 19 or you are 25 or 26.

In England and Wales, the Children Act (1989) placed a duty on local authorities to 'advise and befriend' young people leaving care, and gives local authorities the power to provide financial assistance. However, these provisions depend upon interpretation, and the provision of services for young people leaving care is still a low priority in many local authorities.

What can be done?

Over 20 years ago, Michael Rutter wrote:

> That 'bad' care of children in early life can have 'bad' effects, both short term and long term, can be accepted as proven. What is ... needed is a more precise delineation of their separate effects and of the reasons why children differ in their responses.[25]

While much good work, some of it described here, has been done, we are still some way from being in full command of the knowledge Rutter was recommending we seek. For those researchers struggling to disentangle the various strands of the relationships between childhood experiences and later outcomes, the questions are intriguing methodological and intellectual puzzles. For those of us who have the duty and the responsibility to provide services for children and young people, we need to use the best of what we already know to suggest ways in which weak relationships – be they with biological parents or with the State as parent – can best be strengthened.

In the last few years, there has been a growing emphasis on evidence-based medicine. Many people have been shocked to discover that there is any basis other than evidence for the interventions which doctors make in our lives, and presumably the public would be just as shocked at the lack of evidence underpinning many policy or practice attempts to 'fix' parenting or make it work better. Some proposals, such as those to reduce benefits to single mothers, are alarmingly naive in their linking of cause and effect, and would have as a consequence direct damage to the most vulnerable children. We do, however, have good evidence on some aspects of strengthening relationships, both within families and between the great institutions of the State (such as health and education) and children. There are a number of things which we know we can do and where the long-term outcomes are good.[26] Irrespective of whether there is one parent or two (and we know that in many two-parent families, the parenting functions are effectively carried out by only one of them), parenting is a time-intensive and exhausting task, as well as having the potential to be, and being, for many, rewarding and fulfilling. Drawing from knowledge accrued from the cohort studies, which enables us to understand protective factors, we find that:

- Children fortunate enough to have parental enthusiasm for and interest in their education tend to do better in terms of educational attainment.[27]
- In due course, such children, as adults, are more likely than are others to be enthusiastic about their own children's education.[28]
- Parental enthusiasm also helps to fend off the risk to educational attainment presented by parental divorce and separation.[29]

Services which have been shown to make a positive difference include a number of early-childhood education interventions. At age 27, for instance, graduates of the High/Scope pre-school programme were found, in comparison with a group randomised not to receive this service, to have:

- a significantly higher level of schooling completed;
- significantly higher monthly earnings;
- a significantly lower percentage receiving social services at some time in the past ten years;
- significantly fewer arrests, including significantly fewer arrests for crimes of drug-taking or dealing.[30]

In the health arena, there have been a number of social support schemes, which have been robustly evaluated through randomised, controlled trials. One of the most radical of these is one in which mature mothers were recruited to provide support to younger mothers. At the end of this study, mothers and children in the intervention group had a better diet than the controls (who had had the normal service provided to first-time mothers), more children in the intervention group had received all their primary immunisations, they were more likely to be read to, and they were less likely to begin consuming cow's milk before 26 weeks. Mothers were less likely to be tired, feel miserable or want to stay indoors; they were less likely to display negative feelings.[31] The programme has now expanded to incorporate breast feeding support, mother and toddler groups and attention to the special needs of Travellers. In one Dublin suburb, a peer-led nutrition programme is being developed which draws on the Community Mothers Programme in terms of involving volunteers.[32] In terms of child protection, there are promising interventions in parent training[33] and in anger control.[34]

Turning to what might be done to improve the quality of parenting by the State, it is fair to point out that the children who are brought up in the care of the State are not a representative group. They are children and young people who have had difficult experiences, which have led to their being 'looked after'. However, the parenting which they receive from the State is delivered at high cost, and by 'experts'. They have the right to expect high-quality relationships and services from those to whose care they are entrusted. A crucial issue here is that (as in biological parenting) those people who have the greatest direct contact with children and carry out the day-to-day parenting tasks for children in care tend to be the least well rewarded.

While the outcomes for children parented by the State are dismal, there are measures which can be taken. The Looking After Children Project,[35] funded by the Department of Health, provides material and records to ensure that children do not get 'lost in care'. There is every reason why the State should be encouraged to lend at least the same level of financial support to those children who have been in State care as the majority of other young people can expect from their families of origin, however hard pressed they may be. Local authorities should maintain the role of an 'interested parent' in encouraging the education of young people while in State care. Greater emphasis and resources are needed to assist care-leavers in obtaining employment and training on leaving school. Arrangements for youth training under Training and Enterprise Councils should be flexible enough to enable care-leavers to complete their training programmes, and local authorities should ensure that care-leavers who are pursuing further and higher education should be adequately funded, including arrangements for vacations.

Commitments to these provide some of the ways in which the State, which itself has failed so singularly as a parent, can provide support to children and families in maintaining the kinds of relationships which, in the long term, will be supportive to us all.

Acknowledgements

In preparing this chapter, I have benefited from advice and information from my colleagues Steve Harwood, Di McNeish and Roger Singleton, but the views expressed are mine and do not necessarily reflect those of Barnardo's. I am also grateful to Helen Sweeting at the MRC Medical Sociology Unit and Suzy Aronstrom and Michele Corrado at MORI for comments.

References

1. Aries, P. (1979), *Centuries of Childhood*, Penguin; Hockey, J. and James, A. (1993) *Growing Up and Growing Old: Ageing and dependency in the life course*, Sage; James, A. and Prout, A. (1990) *Constructing and Reconstructing Childhood*, Falmer Press; Pinchbeck, I. and Hewitt, M. (1969: Vol I and 1973: Vol II) *Children in English Society*, Routledge and Kegan Paul.
2. Moyo, E. (1973) *Big Mother and Little Mother in Matabeleland*, History Workshop Pamphlet No.3, cited in Hockey, J. and James, A. (1993) *Growing Up and Growing Old: Ageing and dependency in the life course*, Sage.
3. Utting, D. (1995) *The Facts of Life: The changing face of childhood*, Barnardo's.
4. Ibid.
5. Alderson, P. (1993) *Children's consent to surgery*, Open University Press; Alderson, P. et al. (1995) *What works? Effective social interventions in child welfare*, Barnardo's/SSRU; Alderson, P. (1995) *Listening to children: Children, ethics and social research*, Barnardo's; Little, M. with Kelly, S. (1995) *A Life without Problems? The Achievements of a Therapeutic Community*, Arena.
6. Roberts, H. and Sachdev, D. (eds) (1996) *Young People's Social Attitudes*, Barnardo's.
7. Oakley, A. (1996) 'Man the Hunter', in Roberts, H. and Sachdev, D. (eds) *Young People's Social Attitudes*, Barnardo's.
8. Oakley, ibid.
9. Brannen, J. et al. (1994) *Young People, Health and Family Life*, Open University Press.
10. Bowlby, J. (1953) *Child Care and the Growth of Love*, Pelican.
11. Comer, L. (1974) *Wedlocked Women*, Feminist Books.
12. Burghes, L. (1994) *Lone Parenthood and Family Disruption: The outcomes for children*, Family Policy Studies Centre.
13. Holtermann, S. (1995) *All Our Futures: The impact of public expenditure and fiscal policies on Britain's children and young people*, Barnardo's.
14. Sweeting, H. and West, P. (1995) *Young People and their Families: Analyses of data from the Twenty-07 study youth cohort*, Working Paper No.49, MRC Medical Sociology Unit.
15. Macintyre, S. et al. (1989) 'The West of Scotland Twenty-07 Study: Health in the Community', in Martin, C. and MacQueen, D. (eds), *Readings for a new Public Health*, Edinburgh University Press.
16. For example, Edwards, J.N. (1987) 'Changing Family Structure and Youthful Wellbeing', *Journal of Family Issues*, Vol.8, No.4, pp. 355–72.

17 Ward, H. (1995) 'The looking after children project, asking practitioners to assess outcomes in child care', in Alderson, P. et al. (1995) *What Works? Effective social interventions in child welfare*, Barnardo's/SSRU.
18 Lambert, L., Essen, J. and Head, J. (1977) 'Variations in behaviour ratings of children who have been in care', *Journal of Child Psychology and Psychiatry*, Vol.18, pp.335–46; Jackson, S. (1987) *The education of children in care*, Bristol Papers No.1, School of Applied Social Studies, University of Bristol; Millham, S. et al. (1986) *Lost in Care: The problem of maintaining links between children in care and their families*, Gower.
19 Stein, M. and Carey, K. (1986) *Leaving Care*, Blackwell.
20 Garnett, L. (1992) *Leaving care and after*, National Children's Bureau.
21 Stein and Carey, op. cit.
22 Anderson, I., Kemp, P. and Quilgars, D. (1993) *Single Homeless People*, HMSO.
23 Stein and Carey, op. cit.
24 Prison Reform Trust (1991) *The Identikit Prisoner: Characteristics of the Prison Population*, Prison Reform Trust.
25 Rutter, M. (1972) *Maternal Deprivation Reassessed*, Penguin, p.128.
26 Macdonald, G. and Roberts, H. (1995) *What works in the early years? Effective interventions for children and their families in health, social welfare education and child protection*, Barnardo's.
27 Douglas, J.W.B. (1963) 'Waste of talent', *Advancement of Science*, Vol.19, p.564.
28 Wadsworth, M.E.J. (1986) 'Effects of parenting style and pre-school experience on children's verbal attainment: a British longitudinal study', *Early Childhood Research Quarterly*, Vol.1, pp.237–48; Wadsworth, M.E.J. (1991) *The Imprint of Time: Childhood history and adult life*, Oxford University Press.
29 Wadsworth, M.E.J. and Maclean, M. (1986), 'Parents' divorce and children's life chances', *Children and Youth Services Review*, Vol.8, pp.145–59.
30 Schweinhart, L. and Weikart, D. (1993), *A summary of significant benefits: the High/Scope Perry pre-school study through age 27*, High/Scope Press.
31 Johnson, Z., Howell, F. and Molloy, B. (1993) 'Community mothers' programme: a randomised controlled trial of non-professional intervention in parenting', *British Medical Journal*, No.306, pp.1449–52.
32 Johnson, Z. and Molloy, B. (1995) 'The community mothers' programme – empowerment of parents by parents', *Children and Society*, Vol.9, No.2, pp.73–83.
33 Dumas, J.E., (1989) 'Treating anti-social behaviour in children: Child and family approaches', *Clinical Psychology Review*, Vol.9, pp.197–222.
34 Barth, R.P. et al. (1983) 'Self control training with maltreating children', *Child Welfare*, Vol.62, No.4, pp.313–24.
35 Ward, op. cit.

8 From generation to generation
Wally Harbert

Revolutions such as those that have occurred in Eastern Europe and in some developing countries are accompanied by abrupt and major social and economic changes. In the United Kingdom, where, despite the Thatcher years, we have largely been shielded from major political convulsions, we tend not to notice change as it unfolds. It is only by comparing the present with what existed, say, 50 years ago that we become aware of the tremendous social changes that have been taking place and the impact of those changes on lifestyles, public attitudes and on the delivery of public services. Only with the benefit of hindsight can we see how these changes affect relationships which are normally taken for granted.

The demographic revolution

Between 1901 and 2001, the number of people in Great Britain over the age of 85 will have increased by a factor of 21 – from 57,000 to 1.2 million. Such a dramatic change is unique in the history of the world. Trends in all industrialised countries are broadly similar and will be repeated by developing countries early in the next century. Table 8.1 shows how the percentage of older people in the population has been rising, particularly those over the age of 80.

A key factor that has immense implications for the care of older people is the growing number who live alone. In 1973, 40% of people over the age of 75 lived alone. By 1993, this had risen to 50%. Sixty-one per cent of women over the age of 75 now live by themselves.[1] Forty-six per cent of people over pensionable age in Great Britain live with their partners. Eight per cent live with relatives such as children or siblings.[2]

Table 8.1 Percentage of population aged 65–79 and 80+

	1961	1981	1991	2001	2021
65–79	9.8%	12.2%	12.0%	11.4%	14.3%
80+	1.9%	2.8%	3.7%	4.3%	5.1%
All aged 65+	11.7%	15.0%	15.7%	15.7%	19.4%

Source: OPCS (1995) Social Trends, No.25, HMSO, Table 1.4.

Changing social circumstances

Living alone now has a vastly different quality about it than was experienced by older people two generations ago. People living by themselves are more isolated than in former years. Urban life is no longer punctuated by regular calls at the door, and a walk down the street no longer promises a succession of encounters with familiar faces. Largely emptied of the hustle and bustle of the workaday world, pavements are not as safe as they once were for older and vulnerable people. There are fewer pedestrians to spot and deter mischievous children, over-exuberant teenagers and criminals. Good role models on foot are hard to find in residential streets.

An army of people whose jobs once required them to knock on doors have melted away during the past 50 years. Rent collectors and caretakers with personal knowledge of people who live alone have largely disappeared. Window cleaners are hard to find. The once-ubiquitous insurance collector is becoming a rare species. Christmas club collectors are also being replaced by cheaper and more reliable arrangements. The demise of bread, milk and coal deliveries still further reduces the number of callers on the homes of isolated people; they will soon go the way of the knife grinder, the chimney sweep and the Kleeneze man. Gas and electricity meter readers are less in evidence than previously; meters can now often be read without entry to the premises, and estimated bills are more common; few households have coin boxes that require regular emptying.

In former years, pavements in residential areas swarmed with public servants and tradesmen of all descriptions. The midwife, district nurse, health visitor, the school board man, the welfare officer, the public health inspector, the policeman and the probation officer travelled by bicycle or on foot, encountering their current and previous clientele in the process; they were more likely to live in the area and be part of the local community. Who can remember bookies' runners, lamp lighters and knockers up? A walk to the corner shop has largely been replaced by a weekly car journey to a supermarket on the edge of town, so even neighbours are seen less often.

As a result, the environment appears less friendly and welcoming; more of life is lived behind the locked and bolted front door; even neighbours become strangers, and local communities are less likely to be seen by vulnerable people as positive and supportive. Although reliable figures are difficult to obtain, it seems likely that more elderly people are dying alone. Because of their isolation, they may not be found for weeks or months. In London, a body lay in a council flat for three-and-a-half years before being found.[3]

Not all people who live alone regard themselves as lonely. MORI has devised a loneliness scale. It reports that 10% of the population over 65 could be regarded as lonely in 1989, and that this proportion increased to 14% by 1995. The highest incidence of loneliness – 25% – was among people living alone. They were more likely than other older people to pass a full day without speaking to anyone, to spend Christmas alone and to receive no presents on their birthday.[4]

Changing family circumstances

In former years, older people often had an important role within the family, which was an economic, social, employment, recreational, caring and educational unit spanning several generations. Older people provided a sense of continuity and offered childcare and other skills that helped the family to function. In return, the older person received care and support. Relationships were reciprocal, and dependency was mutual. Now, many functions essential to daily living have been transferred elsewhere. The economic and social imperatives that bound the generations together have been weakened, and geographical mobility has led to physical separation. The incidence of early retirement may afford more time for older people to relate to their grandchildren, but they are now less likely to live in close proximity. With no clear role in life, and often an income that is too low to take advantage of the formal social, recreational and education services that are available, many older people no longer feel needed by their families, and feel marginalised by society.

Discussion about older people is sometimes accompanied by explicit or implicit assumptions that families provide less care than in former years. It is difficult to discover hard evidence for this, although the majority of older people believe this to be the case.[5] A study conducted in 1992 found that 22% of elderly people in the UK had daily contact with their families,[6] while 30% had contact of less than once a week. A more recent poll of 1,071 people over the age of 65 showed that 2% had spoken to no one in the previous week.[7]

A smaller percentage of elderly people are now in institutional care (less than 5%) than at the beginning of the century. Changes in society and in the nature of the care required have made it more possible for families to care 'at a distance'. Regular, face-to-face contact has been partly replaced by telephone communication; the preparation of meals has been superseded by a weekly shopping expedition and a supply of meals in the deep freezer ready for microwaving.

Although much of the unfit housing stock in the UK is occupied by older people their living conditions have generally improved. Each year, more dwellings have hot water systems, central heating, washing machines, vacuum cleaners, telephones, deep freezers, refrigerators and microwave ovens. Self-care has never been easier, and the sheer physical drudgery of providing care has been eased for older people and their families. Family life may be less cohesive and less all-embracing than in former years, but overwhelmingly, the care received by vulnerable elderly people comes from their family and friends. There is nothing to suggest that today's older people have been abandoned by their families.

It should not be assumed that the ideal model of care for older people is necessarily one in which they live in the bosom of their families. We are being made more aware of the incidence of elder abuse and of the family stresses and strains that can be caused by three generations living day-by-day in the same household. It should be noted that in Italy, Greece, Spain and Portugal, where older people are much more likely to live with their families and where daily contact between the generations is common, older people express a greater dissatisfaction with their living arrangements than any other group of older people in Europe. They complain more of loneliness, of boredom and of a lack of activity.[8] Family care can reduce opportunities for independence and self-determination and impose an unwanted lifestyle. In consequence, there has been an increasing desire for older people to be assisted to remain in their own homes and to move to forms of assisted living to maintain their independence as they become more frail.

Poverty in old age is overwhelmingly a problem affecting women. Breaks in employment to care for family members, low pay and greater longevity all conspire to ensure that many women experience poverty as they become older. The higher incidence of divorce and family break-up is also likely to increase the incidence of female poverty.

Accommodation needs

Much existing housing is unsuited to the needs of older people. Martin complained that architects tended to design buildings for fit males between the ages of 18 and 45.[9] The remaining five-sixths of the population who were tall, short, fat, left-handed, women, children, older people, and those with disabilities, were expected to cope as best they could. The impact of a disability depends significantly on the environment in which it is experienced; poorly-designed housing can imprison vulnerable people and create a disability which would otherwise not exist.

Overwhelmingly, people wish to remain living in their own homes for as long as possible. A poll in 1995 of people living in their own homes found that 90% wished to remain where they were, although some of them wanted adaptations to make the accommodation more suitable. Four per cent said they would prefer sheltered housing and 2% wanted to live with relatives. Less than 1% expressed a wish to enter residential or nursing home care.[10] Elderly people prefer to remain in contact with familiar places and to live among people who are known to them.

Yet housing has become the neglected ingredient in the provision of community care services. An examination of the government's record in encouraging the development and maintenance of a housing stock suitable for the needs of frail people is not encouraging. The number of new sheltered housing schemes and other specialised dwellings for elderly people has been dramatically reduced. Public expenditure on home improvements has dropped, and some sheltered housing is of such a low standard that it has become difficult to let.[11] Unless the government places more emphasis on specialist housing, the cost of domiciliary care and of residential care will increase dramatically.

Although less than 5% of people over pensionable age live in institutions – hospitals, residential homes and nursing homes – the question still needs to be asked: 'Why do we need traditional residential care?' I have yet to meet anyone who wishes to share a bedroom with one or more strangers or who looks forward to using a commode in a shared room (with or without privacy curtains). I know of no one who prefers to share a toilet 'down the corridor' rather than have their own close at hand. You and I can barely envisage what it is like to have no privacy when entertaining friends and to have no facility to offer them a cup of tea. We would not relish the thought of putting the possessions we have accumulated over a lifetime into a wardrobe and two drawers. Nor do we want to be placed in the position of looking forward to the death of a fellow resident in order to move into a single room. Long-term care does not have to be like that. Too often, the decision to enter a residential home is not about choice, but about the lack of adequate alternatives.

To retain their faculties, older people need to be stimulated, to make decisions and to be usefully occupied. Retirement, even with infirmity, is not a period in which to sit quietly anticipating death, leaving decisions about daily routine to others. It is a time to do new things, to find new ways of becoming self-fulfilled, to contribute something positive to the lives of others and to learn new techniques for self-care. It is difficult to see how such a view of old age can be reconciled with the traditional design of elderly persons' homes or the regimes that the layout of homes impose on both staff and residents. The residential model tends to provide a uniform service to people with varying needs and disabilities. It is therefore unnecessarily elaborate and costly for some residents, and it creates dependence. Those who enter residential care to escape social isolation can find that the loneliness becomes greater when surrounded by others.

Studies of institutions have repeatedly found that large numbers of residents do not need to be in them. In general, the proportion of questionable admissions has steadily decreased over a period of years from as many as 74% in the 1950s[12] to about 23% at the time of the community care reforms in 1993.[13] This problem has not been confined to the UK. A report in 1984 suggested that 28% of residents in French long-stay institutions could have lived at home 'with the aid of a home help or occasional nursing assistance'.[14] A study of a geriatric hospital in Barbados in 1987 identified that 40% of patients did not require hospital care.[15] It appears that service providers habitually find it easier to offer residential options than domiciliary care.

Responding to change

Changed living arrangements and family relationships are leading to a different kind of society, a society in which the family remains at the core but in which other relationships play an increasing part. Social institutions other than the family are required to extend opportunities for social interaction, for providing recreation and self-fulfilment; new ways must be found to enhance contact within and between generations. The remainder of this chapter attempts to demonstrate some of the issues that must be considered.

Large numbers of people retire early. About 25% of men aged 50–59 are now not in employment (compared with only 7% some twenty years ago), and only about half are employed until they are 65.[16] Newly-retired people can often look forward to 25–30 years of active life after collecting their gold watch – a period to take on new commitments and develop new interests.

Retirement is a time to do something different, not to do nothing. In its widest sense, the concept of 'community care' must embrace opportunities for self-fulfilment, for community service, for a purpose in life, for developing relationships and activities. Although more care services are required, we do a disservice to older people and to society when we equate retirement with the end of productive capacity and growing dependency. Overwhelmingly, retired people do not need care, and studies have shown that large numbers of them, even in their eighties and nineties, lead satisfying lives while receiving little assistance from statutory services.

Forward-looking local authorities are stimulating schemes in which older volunteers provide services to others. Such work includes voluntary visiting, after-school childcare, assistance in the classroom, advocacy, the provision of special transport, advice on home security and many other tasks that assist the local community. The sense of purpose, the new challenge and the opportunities to make new relationships which such schemes provide offer friendship, companionship and self-fulfilment to volunteers who might otherwise be isolated and lonely. They become part of the solution rather than the problem.

Opportunities for older people to lead rewarding lives have never been greater, but if they are to make sensible choices, they must be aware of what is available and be helped to plan their retirement. The educational system prepares young people for 40 years of employment. Very little is done to prepare older people for 30 years of active retirement. There is considerable scope for both the government and employers to widen opportunities for pre-retirement education.

Reductions in local authority budgets have raised the cost and restricted the number of educational courses suitable for pensioners at a time when the number of potential students is rising sharply. Similarly, pressure on local authority community leisure budgets has led to facilities like swimming baths, libraries and open spaces being under-used by older people. This is false economy. The cost to health and social services for people who are isolated and lack stimulation in their lives is likely to outweigh savings in public expenditure.

Poverty remains a serious problem for many older people; it narrows choice and makes retired people more dependent on the decisions of others, reducing opportunities for them to pursue educational and recreational pastimes. Ironically, many of today's elderly people have reduced incomes because they gave up work to care for an elderly relative and therefore were unable to build up a State or personal pension. This problem requires urgent consideration, and employment conditions should, wherever possible, be flexible enough to enable the workforce to provide care to family members when required and allow older people who wish to supplement their income by part-time paid employment to do so. More equitable arrangements for the provision of pensions to women following divorce and on the death of the main breadwinner would ease some of the financial problems faced by older women.

New administrative and managerial systems in the UK following community care reforms in 1993 were intended to improve selection arrangements for residential care. But change has taken place at a time when the health service is narrowing its focus by reducing long-stay beds, developing day surgery and encouraging early hospital discharge. Shorter hospital stays are switching rehabilitative programmes from in-patient to domiciliary services. Patients are being discharged quicker and sicker, and relatives are facing increased pressure to fill the care gap. Community services, including health provision, will need to become more flexible, more sensitive and more comprehensive. Traditional methods of managing home care are inadequate, leaving vulnerable people at risk, particularly those living alone or whose relatives are at work.

New technology offers one means of solving the problem. A community alarm enables a central control to be contacted for help even when the old person is too incapacitated to reach a telephone. A specially-designed telephone alarm unit is installed which can be activated by a button on the telephone or by pressing a small, body-worn radio transmitter with sufficient range to contact the alarm unit from anywhere within the house or immediate surroundings. Following a call, control centre staff can send whatever help is needed – a doctor, ambulance, home help, police, neighbour or relative. The benefits of such a system for elderly and disabled people are clear. Not only can they be provided with immediate help in emergencies, but they and their relatives feel a greater sense of security knowing that an accident, a sudden illness or the presence of an intruder can lead to instant action by specialist staff, volunteers or family.

The latest technology goes much further. By inserting a 'pin number' on the key pad in the home of the user, information is instantly conveyed to the control centre, which can monitor who has called, what tasks have been performed and when the contact was made. Furthermore, if a task that forms part of the care plan has not been performed, control centre staff can be alerted automatically.

Hitherto, computerised health and social services systems have been primarily tools for enabling professional carers to carry out their traditional tasks more efficiently. The new generation of technology is interactive, enabling the user to participate: it therefore changes the relationship between user and carer and between different groups of carers. New technology can provide opportunities for severely disabled people to live in ordinary domestic surroundings. It cannot be a substitute for informal contact with callers, and it can only be as good and as effective as the human response it evokes.

Long-term problems about the housing stock must be tackled. Disability and social isolation are as much a product of physical factors in the environment as of individual pathology. Increased expenditure on home improvements could lead to savings on expensive domiciliary and residential care.

The segregation of frail, elderly people from the mainstream of society into residential homes can lead to artificiality. One attempt to combat this and improve the quality of relationships within residential homes is currently being developed by the Relationships Foundation. Following successful auditing of relationships within prisons, the foundation is piloting a relational audit of an elderly persons' home in Nottingham. It aims to provide an active measure for assessing the non-material elements of care, such as the opportunities for social interaction.[17] Instead of only gathering information about the achievement of specified targets or 'soft' data about the values, attitudes or feelings within an institution, the relational audit focuses on the influence of policy and practice upon relationships.

Organised visits by school children to elderly persons' homes with planned inter-generational activities not only help children to learn about the community in which they live and the events which have shaped it, but children can be helped to develop an appreciation and respect for the knowledge and wisdom that often accompanies old age. For their part, elderly people can be helped to feel wanted and valued, as well as making new friends across the generations. After a particularly successful visit by school children to an elderly persons' home, one old lady was heard to remark: 'When I came here I thought I would never again hear the sound of a child's laughter'.

Several countries are achieving dramatic changes in the provision of long-term care. Denmark is no longer building traditional elderly persons' homes, and the construction of new nursing homes is forbidden by the government; 100% financing is available for converting nursing homes into residential apartments, accompanied by the provision of intensive care services. Wagner describes how a nursing home in Skaeville was converted and the staff redeployed in the community.[18] All accommodation for elderly people in Denmark must have its own bath and kitchen facilities.[19] In effect, the Danish government has legislated to implement the key recommendation of the Wagner Committee in the UK, that 'No-one should be required to change their present accommodation in order to receive services which could be made available to them in their own homes'.[20]

No new elderly persons' homes are being constructed in the Netherlands, and the development of special housing is being encouraged;[21] Sweden intends to replace elderly persons' homes by sheltered housing and improved domiciliary care. Meanwhile, in the UK, new residential and nursing homes are still being constructed without *en suite* facilities. While the Home Office plans to end slopping out in prisons, the social care agenda does not envisage an end to the practice in elderly persons' homes.

Self-contained accommodation that provides a satisfactory quality of life before the onset of dependency but for which increasing levels of staffing can be supplied as needs increase is likely to represent the best way forward. An elderly person denied the dignity of a front door is denied the sense of freedom, power and independence that the rest of us enjoy. It is a historical anachronism that instead of care services revolving around people, people are required to move as their physical and social needs change, producing disorientation and often considerable trauma. When accommodation is built in such a way that we do not know whether to regard the staff as part of domiciliary or residential provision, we shall know that we have finally erased the legacy of the Poor Law and the workhouse.

Older people in need of care are in danger of having solutions imposed upon them by their families or by organisations that fund care services. They need opportunities to control their own lives and to exercise choice. Increased numbers of retired people now have pensions at a level that enable them to retain that control, but many are more fearful of the kind of care that may be imposed upon them than they are of their disabilities and infirmities. A more appropriate range of services is required, based on the wishes of older people themselves rather than on the perceptions of those who have traditionally made decisions about the pattern of care services.

Much discussion about the needs of older people is centred on the provision of care services. When someone living alone dies and is not found for several months, criticism is usually directed towards statutory services. Yet the cohesion and responsiveness of society to its older members cannot rest on the provision of State care. Inter-generational family life and community activity are vital to all the generations. Where the family and local community are unable to meet the social needs of older people, other means must be made available to fill the void. Opportunities for full participation can be provided by business, voluntary organisations and government bodies.

We must seek a wider understanding of the importance of personal relationships and the part they play in sustaining better physical and mental well-being. A start may be made by ensuring that all new public policies are scrutinised to consider their impact on human relationships. Some local authorities require that reports brought before committees indicate the impact of the recommendations on disabled people, ethnic minorities and women. But this is too limiting – we need to consider relationships between people.

A greater awareness of the needs of older people and the changed social circumstances in which they live may help to change public attitudes and create a more positive climate of opinion. This will serve the best interests of us all, for although elderly people are a minority of the population, it is a minority we all hope one day to join.

References

1. OPCS (1993) *General Household Survey*, OPCS, Tables 2.10 and 2.11. OPCS Series GHS No.24, HMSO.
2. OPCS (1994) *General Household Survey*, 'Supplement A: People Aged 65 and over', OPCS.
3. Harbert, W. (1994) *A Lonely Death*, London Borough of Brent/Help the Aged.
4. MORI/Help the Aged (1995) *Independent Living*, MORI, p.15.
5. Walker, A. (1993) *Age and Attitudes: Main Results from a Eurobarometer Survey*, Commission of the European Communities, p.29.
6. Ibid., p.11.

7   MORI/Help the Aged, op. cit., p.11.
8   Walker, op. cit., p.9.
9   Martin, F. (1992) *Every Home You'll Ever Need*, Edinvar Housing Association.
10 MORI/Help the Aged, op. cit., p.31.
11 Harbert, W. (1993) *Residential Care and Housing*, Help the Aged, pp.13–16.
12 Townsend, P. (1962) *The Last Refuge*, Routledge.
13 House of Commons (1988) *26th Report of the Committee of Public Accounts: Community Care Development*, HMSO.
14 European Health Committee (1984) *The Provision of Medical and Nursing Care for Old People at Home*, Council of Europe.
15 Barbados Ministry of Health and Pan American Health Organisation (1987) *Health Care Services for the Elderly in Barbados*, Barbados Ministry of Health.
16 OPCS (1995) *Social Trends*, No.29, HMSO, Table 4.4, p.66.
17 Burton-Jones, J. (1995) *The Case for a Relational Audit of Homes for Older People*, The Relationships Foundation.
18 Wagner, L. (1989) 'A Proposed Model for Care of the Elderly', *International Nursing Review*. Vol.36, No.2.
19 Jamieson, A. (1991) 'Community Care for Older People', in Room, G. (ed.) *Towards a European Welfare State*, School for Advanced Urban Studies.
20 Wagner Committee (1988) *A Positive Choice*, HMSO, p.114.
21 Nusberg, C. (1981) 'Programmes and Services for the Elderly in Industrialised Countries', in Hobman, D. (ed.) *The Impact of Ageing*, Croom Helm.

Part III

Sources of pressure on relationships: Work versus family dilemmas

9 Stakeholders in the workplace

John Monks

Introduction

Is it still possible to build long-term relationships between workers and employers? The question may seem a little naive in a world where we are told that jobs for life have disappeared and that in future we will all have to be 'portfolio workers' undertaking a range of jobs on short-term contracts. Many of the so-called management gurus suggest that there is a need for a cultural revolution in the workplace. They argue that employees should relish their insecurity and see it as an increase in individual choice. This may be all very well for highly qualified and well-paid people who can, as John Kay of London Economics has put it, 'move from boardroom to senior common room, from radio to journalism, from Norfolk to Tuscany',[1] but such an appealing lifestyle is never going to be available to more than a small minority.

What most people want is a regular income which enables them to plan their lives with a degree of certainty and achieve a balance between work, family and leisure. When asked what they expect from work, most people talk about more than money. They want real career opportunities that enable them to develop their skills and talents in jobs that are genuinely rewarding. Perhaps most importantly, a job is about more than simply a formal contract between a worker and an employer. The quality of their relationship, or the 'psychological contract', as it has been called, really does matter. It is on the quality of this relationship that the success of a business depends. Unfortunately, the deregulated labour market of which the government is apparently so proud runs contrary to the notion of such relationships based on trust.

Far too many employees feel that they are treated by their employers as disposable commodities and as the most flexible item on the balance sheet. Indeed, the evidence of the Third Workplace Industrial Relations Survey

(WIRS3) suggests that far from there being a move towards the more enlightened treatment of people at work, bad employment practice is on the increase.[2]

One explanation for this is that the coverage of collective bargaining has declined over the last decade. In certain sectors, printing and publishing being one prominent example, trade unions have been derecognised and workers deprived of any representational rights. Many workers therefore have no channel through which they can influence their working conditions and shape management decisions that affect them. WIRS3 is explicit that there has been an aggressive reassertion of managerial prerogatives in recent times. Macho management rules, and it is not OK.

This conclusion is reinforced by the evidence of WIRS3 that trade unions have not been replaced by other workplace representational machinery. Nor have employers taken any steps to empower workers as individuals. In the vast majority of cases, an 'individualisation' of the employment relationship has simply been a smokescreen for the exercise of the so-called 'right to manage'.

At the same time, of course, unemployment has remained high. Job insecurity has increased, and people no longer have the confidence that enables them to plan for the future over the long term. The apparent decline of secure full-time employment, the growth of part-time working, the increasing use of sub-contracting and out-sourcing all conspire to create a 'feel-bad' factor. Companies have embarked upon a process of almost unprecedented change. Organisations have been 'downsized', 'rightsized' and 're-engineered'. White-collar workers are now experiencing the same degree of employment insecurity as unskilled and semi-skilled manual workers. It is hardly surprising that middle England finds the feel-good factor so elusive.

Of course, none of this is inevitable, and sensible public policy intervention can do a good deal to mitigate the worst effects of unregulated free markets. Insecurity in the workplace breeds insecurity in society, and if Britain is to maintain a high level of prosperity in the next century, then urgent action is needed to rebuild the social cohesion that is seriously threatened by the current trends. Obviously, I cannot address these wider questions in this short chapter, but what I would like to do is set out a different approach to relationships at work.

Before exploring these issues in more detail, let me emphasise that there is clear evidence that trade unions improve workplace relationships. As WIRS3 shows, unionised workplaces have lower rates of labour turnover (always a good measure of workers' job satisfaction), fewer unfair dismissals and fewer compulsory redundancies than non-union workplaces. Good employers know that it makes good business sense to negotiate with trade unions. Workers know that trade unions are the only effective, independent voice in the workplace that can defend their interests against high-handed management behaviour. To argue that collective bargaining has an essential role to play in improving the quality of relationships at work is not special pleading by trade unions – it is a matter of fact.

Of course, some employers take the view that they can develop good relationships with their workers without needing to recognise trade unions. Unfortunately, this approach has a fundamental and fatal weakness. Good practice here depends upon the goodwill of the employer. The relationship is paternalistic and, by definition, unequal. Consequently, workers can find their good terms and conditions swiftly undermined if the employer so chooses. It is the independent, collective and representative nature of trade unions which is important in this context. By enabling otherwise atomised workers to act in concert, the presence of a union ensures a fairer balance of power in the workplace. Without this balance of power, it will be difficult, if not impossible, to rebuild the relational base in the workplace.

However, simply leaving it to employers and unions to develop such relationships on a voluntary basis is unlikely to succeed. In the absence of legal backing, the worst employers will continue to adopt a hire-and-fire mentality and seek only the most shallow, purely contractual relationships with their workers. That is why there needs to be explicit public policy support for the development of best practice and long-term relationships. Employment law has an important role to play in establishing some minimum standards to guarantee fair treatment for workers. Anything less will make a programme to rebuild the relational base at work into nothing more than pious aspiration.

Insecurity at work and the culture of commitment

Let me be clear. I am not suggesting that all employees feel like the exploited workers in Dickens's *Hard Times*. Not all employers are Mr Gradgrinds, or have any wish to be. Indeed, Britain's world-class companies are providing their workers with excellent terms and conditions, investing in training and recognising that developing the commitment of people to the organisation requires more than warm words and a new mission statement. The difficulty is that public policy does little or nothing to encourage such excellence. Britain is promoted by the government as the bargain-basement economy of Europe with low labour costs and very little labour market regulation. Inevitably, workplace relationships suffer as a result, and people at work find it more difficult to balance the competing demands of work and family.

The logic of current government policy is that competitiveness can only be improved by reducing labour costs. It is not clear, however, just how far this logic is to be pursued. For example, it surely cannot mean that the UK should compete on labour costs alone with the newly-industrialised countries of South-East Asia. Total wage costs in these economies are only 30% of the UK level, which is bound to give them a competitive advantage. It is difficult to see how the British people would be willing to tolerate a reduction in living standards of this order.

Accepting labour costs as the only indicator of international competitiveness could exacerbate problems in developing countries. For example, there is a powerful case for the application of minimum labour standards within the framework of the International Labour Organisation (the United Nations agency responsible for labour standards). There is also an overwhelming case for taking effective action to tackle child labour. Initiatives of this kind could be undermined if developed countries take the view that they should reduce their own labour standards rather than seek to raise labour standards in the developing world and prevent the abuse of human and trade union rights.

Robert Bischof, chairman of the leading German company Jungheinreich, recently noted that on the government's argument, the German economy should be massively uncompetitive. Labour costs per hour are some 80% higher than in Britain and Spain, about 40% higher than Italy and France and four times the labour costs of Portugal. In reality, Germany has a very healthy trade surplus with the rest of the world, while the UK has a large (and apparently widening) trade deficit. Indeed, Germany has a trade surplus with Britain which, in recent times, has been rising.

Essentially, then, the focus of government policy is wrong. Labour costs are important, but it is unit labour costs, taking account of productivity differences, that are really crucial to competitiveness. Even though the UK has lower wage costs than many of our major competitors, our poor productivity record worsens our position.

Britain has a quality problem as well as a productivity problem. A recent survey of 500 UK companies found that:

- 50% of UK products are late to market;
- development costs overrun by 17%;
- up to 20% of engineering changes in manufacturing occur after products have gone into production.[3]

When compared with company performance in Germany, the USA, France, Sweden, Japan and Italy, 40% of the organisations surveyed exceeded the best overall UK score, judged against the above criteria.

Why should this be so? Despite government rhetoric to the contrary, the real factors influencing competitiveness are skills, infrastructure and innovation. A recent survey of economic strength by the World Economic Forum, based on the views of managers covering a range of factors affecting performance, concluded that Britain had slipped to nineteenth place in the league of the 22 wealthiest nations by 1993.[4]

- The UK's rating was particularly poor in skills and innovation. The UK was bottom of the table in the availability of skilled labour, the number of qualified engineers and industrial investment.
- The report also questioned the UK's 'hire-and-fire' culture: 'In the long run competitiveness cannot be attained if people are treated as disposable assets.'

It is clear then that many of Britain's most intractable economic problems are at least partially caused by the poor quality of workplace relationships.

In the TUC's view, the deregulation of the labour market has not delivered the improvements in performance that the government suggests. The costs of deregulation clearly outweigh the benefits. There is little evidence to suggest that deregulation has improved Britain's record on job creation. Despite the rhetoric to the contrary, Britain's performance has been below the European average in both the 1980s and 1990s. Equally, despite our deregulated labour market, unemployment in Britain remains proportionately higher than in the deregulated USA, or the more heavily regulated Netherlands or Germany.

Indeed, as the TUC made clear in our evidence to the International Labour Organisation's Committee of Experts inquiry into UK labour market policy, there is little evidence to suggest that there has been a wholesale move to flexible working. What appears to be happening is that fear of unemployment and the loss of employment rights are fuelling job insecurity. Deregulation has delivered no increase in employment and has had only a marginal effect on the so-called flexibility of the labour market. Those who argue that red tape is strangling employment growth have failed to produce the murder weapon.

On the other hand, the costs of deregulation have been felt in particular by new entrants to the labour market and re-entrants to the labour market. These groups are likely to be offered disproportionately lower-paid, poorer-quality and temporary jobs and will have fewer training opportunities to improve their skills. This is hardly a recipe for success, and these people at the lower end of the labour market rightly feel exploited and undervalued. At the same time as individual employment rights have been eroded, the government has adopted increasingly coercive measures to deal with the unemployed, culminating in the Jobseeker's Allowance.

It is not too fanciful to suggest that workers are being trapped in a pincer movement between deregulation on the one hand and increasing demands from some employers on the other. A good example of this phenomenon is the relative increase in average working time in the UK over the last decade. A Eurostat survey published early in 1995 shows that the British now work the longest hours in Europe.[5] Over the last decade, the average working week has risen in the UK while in all other EU member states it has fallen. This has been confirmed by a recent survey by the Institute of Management which suggests that around 20% of managers are working more than 15 hours' unpaid overtime per week.

TUC analysis of the government's Labour Force Survey (LFS) has identified a disturbing trend towards what can only be described as excessive working hours.[6] Despite a drop in the number of full-time employees, the number working 45 hours or more has increased from 4.7 million to 5.7 million in the last decade. Thus, while in 1984, 29% of full-timers worked at least 45 hours a week, ten years later this had risen to 36%. Much of the increase is at the upper end of the scale: the proportion of employees working 45–49 hours went up 1%; but the proportion working 48 hours or more increased from 20% to 25%, while the largest increase of all was in employees working 50 hours or more, which went up from 15% to 21%.[7]

The vast majority of those working very long hours are men. By 1994, 2.2 million men were working at least 50 hours a week. Thirty-three per cent of full-time male employees, or 2.8 million men, now work at least 48 hours a week, up from 26% in 1984. These increases correspond to the decline in the proportion of men working a 35–44 hour week, which has shrunk from 62% of full-time male employees in 1984 to 53% in 1994. Therefore, it would appear that a considerable number of men who were working a 35–44 hour week back in 1984 have significantly increased their working time over the last ten years and are now working very long hours on a regular basis.

The important point about the Labour Force Survey is that it is based on a representative sample of employees. Employers appear to assess the trend in working time rather differently, and the *New Earnings Survey* (NES – based upon a questionnaire completed by a representative sample of employers) tells a very different story.[8] In the NES sample, 7.7% of full-time employees worked 50 hours or more per week in 1994, while 10% worked at least 48 hours. This is substantially lower than the 1994 LFS figures of 21% and 25% respectively. The NES data puts a much higher proportion of employees in the 35–39 hours per week bracket and a much lower proportion working above 35 hours a week. In other words, the NES data suggests that a far greater proportion of employees work a 'normal' full-time week than the LFS data suggests. The reason for the discrepancy is clear. Employers are reporting the hours that employees are *contracted* to work, whereas employees are reporting the hours that they *actually* work. There must be real doubt whether relationships based on such different perceptions display the degree of trust and mutual respect that is required both for good industrial relations and business success.

What seems to be happening is that employees are being asked to subscribe to a culture of 'commitment' that requires them to work excessive hours. If they fail to do so, they may be seen by their employers as showing less than the required degree of enthusiasm. They may fail to win high appraisal or performance markings and may be deprived of career development opportunities as a result.

Some policy-makers have responded to the growth of excessive working hours, and the EU has sought to tackle the problem through the directive on working time.[9] The directive will introduce a ceiling of 48 hours on the average working week, measured over a three-month reference period. The UK government's unwillingness to implement the directive and the negotiation of a seven-year opt-out from the working week provisions simply compounds the problem.

Trade unions understand that economic success demands improvements in competitiveness, but we believe that competitiveness can best be achieved by valuing people. It is possible to reconcile the demands of a dynamic and competitive economy with workplace relationships based on trust which recognise that employees have social relationships beyond the workplace. However, we still have some distance to travel before we reach this desirable state of affairs in Britain.

A particular cause for concern is the re-emergence of social divisions at work which are wholly inconsistent with the notion of high-trust relationships. In the past 'them and us' was the common description of too many workplace cultures. Progressive managements and unions responded by developing single-status arrangements as a means to reduce workplace tensions. The danger now is that a new divide is opening up between those with executive pay packages and the majority of workers. In our recent evidence to Sir Richard Greenbury's committee, the TUC pointed out that pay differentials have grown considerably over the last 10 years.[10] Looking at over 1,000 companies, the average ratio between highest-paid director (HPD) salary and average-employee salary has grown from 7.8 in 1984 to 12.57 in 1994 – an increase of 61%.

The salary and bonus of HPDs rose from an average of £98,261 in 1984 to £211,629 in 1994. This is an increase of 115% in real terms over the whole period, or around 10.5% per annum. Average-employee pay in the same companies has grown from £12,601 in 1984 to £16,831 in 1994, an increase of just 34% over the whole period, or 3.1% per annum. Top pay has far outstripped pay increases for ordinary employees.

To complain about this is not to indulge in the politics of envy, as some would claim – it is the natural reaction of people with a genuine and justifiable grievance. The central point here is that differentials within a company must be felt to be fair. They should reflect the understanding that the company is a co-operative enterprise that depends upon the efforts of all stakeholders. A failure to respect this fundamental principle can only undermine the psychological contract. Indeed, by accepting excessive pay increases, British managers have abandoned their leadership role. Good relationships depend on a sense of fair dealing underpinned by an understanding that the same rules apply to all parties. Why should workers give any credibility to the strictures of top managers when there is an apparent unwillingness to accept this principle of fair dealing? How can employers develop the commitment of workers to the business unless there are some elementary guarantees of fair treatment? Surely, the correct response for the more thoughtful employers is to develop pay structures based upon shared understandings of felt fairness. That is how relationships at work can be improved.

Reaping the consequences of deregulation

This evidence shows that in Britain, we have failed to strike a proper balance between work, family life and leisure. Working excessive hours can cause stress-related and other illnesses. It is inefficient because it can cause more days lost through sickness. There is also clear evidence that excessive working hours lead to more workplace accidents. Employers should remember that a tired worker is a less effective worker. Productivity is not increased simply by requiring people to work longer hours.

That excessive hours can produce adverse social consequences should be a concern for all policy-makers. Working women with young children may be particularly prejudiced by the culture of commitment, finding it difficult to combine the demands of work and family life. Equally, men working long hours will find it difficult to share domestic responsibilities with their partners – a situation which is hardly consistent with a commitment to equal opportunities. It is not absurd to suggest that the present imbalance between work and leisure can accelerate family breakdown. Employers may not have to deal directly with the social consequences of excessive hours, but these results will inevitably have an effect on business performance.

If there is a simple way of characterising the problem, it is that government policy treats the labour market as an economic rather than a social institution. Individuals are seen as having purely contractual relationships in a marketplace that should be as unfettered as possible and regulated by nothing more than the laws of supply and demand. This vision simply ignores the human dimension and leaves no place for values like trust, respect and co-operation. If we are to meet the challenge of a new century, then I would suggest that something very different is needed. The TUC believes that an alternative approach has three essential ingredients: first, the establishment of some minimum labour standards; second, a determined effort to build real social partnership at work, and finally, the introduction of a stakeholder model of corporate governance.

Minimum labour standards

The TUC set out the basic rights that should be enjoyed by all workers in our 1993 *Employment Charter for a World Class Britain* (see Box 9.1). A basic floor of rights would have the effect of requiring the worst employers to treat their employees as people rather than disposable assets. Statutory rights would fix a base upon which unions could build through collective bargaining. Far from being a 'burden' on business, as the government suggests, minimum labour standards are both an essential element in any policy to move British employers towards longer-term investment plans and a necessary base for any reconstruction of the psychological contract.

Box 9.1   TUC Employment Charter

All people at work should be entitled to:

- A safe and healthy working environment;
- Equal treatment at work regardless of sex, race, disability, sexuality or age;
- A clear written statement from their employer of the key rights provided by their contract of employment;
- Life-long access to education and training;
- Equivalent treatment whether full-time, part-time, temporary, self-employed or working at home;
- Provision to help parents and carers combine work and domestic responsibilities;
- Fair pay, working hours, holidays, pensions and sick pay arrangements;
- Information and consultation on all matters that affect their security of employment;
- Fair treatment when disciplinary action is taken against them;
- Fair treatment in cases of redundancy, including levels of compensation which fully reflect their earnings;
- Proper protection in cases of business transfers, takeovers, mergers and insolvency;
- Join and be represented by an independent trade union with proper facilities and fair treatment for union representatives.

Social partnership

The second element of the alternative approach – social partnership – is seen by some employers as nothing more than rhetoric. This is a fundamental misunderstanding. Social partnership is certainly not about a return to the 1970s or simply a shift in the balance of power in favour of trade unions. Rather, social partnership is a new approach to workplace relationships based on mutual trust and respect. It is founded on a guarantee of job security by the employer, in return for which unions agree to skill flexibility and a positive attitude to change. In a world in which change is inevitable and the pace of change likely to increase, the intention is to ensure that this can be negotiated in an atmosphere free from acrimony.

This model of industrial relations is well established in the European Union. The belief that long-term relationships are essential for competitive success is embodied in both the Social Charter of 1989 and the Social Chapter of the Maastricht Treaty. Our government's rejection of this approach is exemplified by the desire to opt out from as much social legislation as possible and the characterisation of the social dialogue between trade unions and employers as an attempt to resurrect a failed model of corporatism. Nothing could be further from the truth. Dialogue and partnership are important in a pluralistic political culture. Social partnership recognises the rights of major interest groups to participate in decision-making and is rooted in a commitment to secure enduring change through consensus. The Conservative Party's antipathy to social partnership reflects their failure to appreciate the importance of autonomous intermediate institutions like trade unions in a healthy civil society.

In practice, social partnership at the level of the company requires the acceptance of the following common objectives:

- a joint commitment to the success of the enterprise;
- a recognition that there must be a joint effort to build trust in the workplace;
- a joint declaration recognising the legitimacy of the role of each party.

This is not to suggest that conflict will never occur, but there is a world of difference between disagreement in an adversarial relationship and disagreement in a relationship characterised by mutual trust, respect and goodwill.

At the root of this whole argument is the belief that unions are good for business. Unions have an essential role to play in guaranteeing that people are seen as more than simply factors of production. The evidence is clear that unionised workplaces have a better record on investment and are likely to have achieved more on the training front than their non-union counterparts. We know that treating workers as stakeholders has a positive effect on performance and competitiveness. There is therefore a powerful argument that effective trade unionism is necessary to establish the high-trust, stable employment relationships that will enable Britain to succeed in an increasingly competitive world.

A 'stakeholder' model of corporate governance

One of the greatest problems in British corporate governance is that only shareholders are recognised as stakeholders. This is not the case, for example, in Germany, where company law recognises that there is more to success than profitability. Companies are seen as communities of interest, where the concerns of stakeholders have to be balanced and reconciled.

This can be seen in the attitude of German companies to their employees and trade unions. As Heinrich von Pierer, the Chief Executive of Siemens, has commented:

> The hire and fire principle does not exist here and I never want it to.[11]

Perhaps most important, the existence of supervisory boards with worker representation entrenches stakeholder interests in corporate decision-making.

In part, the limited scope of directors' responsibilities in Britain is related to our nineteenth-century framework of company law. However, this is not the only reason for the relative weakness of stakeholder interests in Britain.

It is important to understand that workers are not the only stakeholders requiring a right to be heard. Some consideration must be given to customers, suppliers and the wider community. Consumers have an interest in ensuring that products and services are of a high quality and safe, and there is obviously a community interest that companies adopt environmentally sensitive policies. All of these matters could properly fall within the competence of a supervisory board. No doubt a supervisory board may slow down decision making – a criticism that is often made of the German system – but that may be no bad thing, and may enable managers to proceed by consent rather than coercion. What is needed is an informed public debate about how the functions of the supervisory board might be discharged in the British corporate governance system. Institutions cannot just be transplanted from one system to another, but a great deal can be learned from successful experiences in other countries.

The stakeholder model, when matched with a solid practice of social partnership, can only be good for business. It is also an integral part of any programme to change the culture of British industry and commerce and ensure that the psychological contract is really based on trust and mutual respect.

Making stakeholding a reality has one further ingredient, and that is a legal right to representation at work. In the TUC's view, there should be a right to trade union recognition where there is sufficient support amongst the workforce. There is also a legal requirement for some machinery for collective representation in non-union workplaces following the recent decisions of the European Court of Justice. No doubt, some employers would see this as an unwarranted imposition, but it is wholly consistent with the direction of policy across the EU. The directive on European works councils, for example, emphasises the importance that the EU attaches to information and consultation.[12] It is a clear expression of the belief that unless people are valued by their employers, then the competitiveness of European multinationals will suffer.

What can also be said with some certainty is that the stakeholder model I have outlined, supported by committed shareholding, would have acted as a powerful deterrent to the recent 'distasteful' increases in executive pay, particularly if workers and consumers were represented at board level. It is for this reason that, in the absence of some wider reform of corporate governance, the TUC has proposed that employees should be represented on companies' remuneration committees.

Conclusion

These, then, are some of the TUC's principal concerns and our preferred solutions to ensure that long-term relationships can be rebuilt in the workplace. This approach is an essential element in any programme to improve Britain's competitiveness. The ingredients of an alternative model include the introduction of some minimum labour standards, the development of genuine social partnership, and a recognition that companies are communities of interest with a wide range of stakeholders.

I would emphasise that these are the broad principles, and that the TUC is keen to discuss the proposals with all interested parties. Reaching a consensus on these questions is surely in the interests of all the people of Britain.

References

1   Bischof, R. (1995) *Financial Times*, 18 August.

2 Millward, S. et al. (1992) *Workplace Industrial Relations in Transition*, Dartmouth.
3 Royal Society of Arts (1994) *Towards Tomorrow's Company: The Role of Business in a Changing World*, RSA, p.9.
4 *Industries for People*, TUC (1993), p.5.
5 Eurostat (1995) *Statistics in Focus: Population and Social Conditions*, No.1.
6 *Hard Labour: Britain's Longer Working Week*, TUC, May 1995.
7 LFS data (1994) for full-time employees is used here. The inclusion of part-time employees in the sample reduces the proportion working over 48 hours to 19%, but the rates of increase over time remain high. It has a greater impact on the figures for female employees, nearly half of whom work part-time; for male employees, with only 7% working part-time, including part-time workers in the sample makes very little difference.
8 Employment Department (1994) *New Earnings Survey*, HMSO.
9 Council Directive 93/104/EC of 23/11/93, *Concerning Certain Aspects of the Organisation of Working Time*.
10 *Pay and Perks – Narrowing the Gap*, TUC, April 1995.
11 Cited in Goodhart, D. (1994) *The Reshaping of the German Social Market*, Institute for Public Policy Research, pp.17–18.
12 Council Directive 94/45/EC of 22/9/94.

10 Developing corporate responsibility

Clive Mather

Introduction

The media headlines proclaim that we are either overworked or out of work; that careers are dead and stress is rampant! Everyone with an axe to grind is anxious to blame the government or Brussels or big businesses or any other convenient scapegoat. Even professional commentators would have you believe that in the space of two decades, the UK employment scene has regressed to the values of Scrooge and the regime of the Victorian poorhouse. And why all the hype? Because inexorable forces of change have been steadily reshaping the world of business and the nature of work itself. Change may be exciting for some, but for others it is resented and ruthless: change which is forcing companies to rethink how to build and develop their relational bases across the stakeholder spectrum – with customers, communities and employees.

A world of change

The forces of change are indeed powerful. As the century draws to a close, we see everywhere the practical demonstration of change which has been gaining pace over decades, for the most part unobserved and under-exploited. The technology of semiconductors, satellites and software is now transforming communications and commerce. It links to a world where markets and competition are truly global, the barriers of ideology and sovereignty blown away by the winds of liberalisation. Traditional markets and traditional skills have been overtaken by international competitors who can deliver goods from the Far East to our local store at higher quality and lower price. Today, everyone competes in everyone else's market in search of economies of scale or margin improvement. And because no product or market advantage can be protected, the cycle of competition spins faster and faster. It's a 'copy-cat' world, where information, ideas and efficiency are subject to continuous comparison – the benchmarking phenomenon – and companies are ruthlessly exposed. The best thrive, but for the rest it is transform or disappear.

The impact of this change may seem revolutionary when we first encounter it. The fall of the Berlin Wall, the arrival of the first PC at work and then at home, the firm's merger with a foreign competitor may all represent personal and poignant memories. Worse, the change may seem out of our control, or even out of control altogether. Job insecurity and declining real income are chronic among the less entrepreneurial or less skilled. The gap between the successful and the struggler is growing, so that many people now believe that no matter how hard they work, some unforseeable event on the other side of the world will result in their decline from relative prosperity to real poverty.

Looking back in another two decades, however, we may well conclude that these processes of change evolved quite steadily, delivering sustained long-term economic growth and greater personal freedom. Already, we, the customer, have come to expect and demand better products and performance in every sphere. Already, we, the employee, demand more access to information and decision-making as part of improving productivity and customer service. With better education and valuable skills, each succeeding generation has higher expectations of what their work should provide, be that equality of opportunity, flexibility of working hours or personal skills development. Change may be unwelcome to the human spirit when we are forced to confront it, but it is far from bad for us. Despite all the gloom of relocation, reorganisation and retrenchment, there have been many positive developments across the world of work. The empty rhetoric of collective bargaining is heard less and less, and in its place, informed debate on how, through learning and innovation, individuals can grow and workplaces compete and prosper.

Why relations matter to companies

The health of the relational base is critical to the success of any enterprise. In the first place, companies are dependent on the network of relationships in the communities in which they operate. The social and economic fabric largely determines the size of the market, the level of taxes, the quality of the workforce and the employee relations climate. In areas of high crime, there are increased costs of security and theft. In areas of high unemployment, there will be less spending power but more tension which spills over into the workplace. Good companies – whether big or small – are sensitive to these external relations, and allocate time and resources to help develop them. From major corporate initiatives with national budgets to local school visits, companies are seen to be taking their corporate responsibilities seriously. And so they must. Not only is their self-interest at stake, but their very 'licence to operate'.[1]

Pressure groups, customers, shareholders and governments are all taking an ever keener interest in how companies relate to their societal base. Social action programmes and environmental performance are no longer optional extras for the top 500, but the standard for doing business at all. Not that the interaction with the stakeholders in the community is limited to meeting or even exceeding these standards. The primary role of a business, whether family unit or multinational corporation, is to satisfy consumer demand through the efficient provision of goods and services and thereby generate reward for its various shareholders. It is the only wealth-creation process that has stood the test of time – enabling communities to generate the foundations for individual well-being and community development. Without the vigour and innovation of companies in open competition for capital, markets and efficiency, the relational base in society would erode quickly. The cycle of employment, income, taxation, social infrastructure and wealth turns on the contribution of businesses, great and small.

In the second place, companies are dependent on the network of relationships within their organisations to perform efficiently and to prosper. At its most basic level are the relations between management and workforce, whose relative health was traditionally measured by absenteeism, grievance or industrial action. Nowadays, with the focus on human resource management in a much broader context, it is employee opinion, productivity, quality, ideas for improvement and customer satisfaction which are the key indicators of the workplace. Correspondingly, the issues are so important that they are only effectively dealt with in direct communication with employees.

Attitude surveys, focus groups, toolbox talks, quality improvement teams, one-to-one feedback – these are the techniques which are increasingly used by companies to help understand their employee relations and develop direct communications processes which promote involvement and enterprise. The ability of organisations to learn and regenerate hangs on the contribution and creativity of individuals and teams. The release of this contribution and creativity is a direct function of how well employees feel about themselves, their families, colleagues and the organisation in which they work. It's not new, indeed the Bible offers some interesting examples.[2] What is new is the commitment with which companies treat the subject.

'Employees are our most important asset' has often been said in annual reports, but perhaps little heeded. It is all too easy to think of employees as a cost – a head count to be reduced, an overhead to be rightsized or even out-sourced. 'Lean and mean', 'cost-competitive' and 'fit for purpose' have entered the language of employment, implying that survival, let alone prosperity, is a depressing and ongoing round of job reductions. So it may be for companies which have yet to face the loss of markets to competitors in Taiwan or Korea, or whose income is still protected by public monopoly or regulation. For the majority, however, life has already moved on, and the rest will surely follow in short order. Cost-effectiveness is not at issue; no business can hope to sustain its markets or profits without meeting the challenge of more efficient competitors head on. But much more is needed if companies are to succeed in a world where standards, in every activity, are rising inexorably – be that product quality, product development, time to market or customer care. Not least is creating an employment climate in which able employees give of their best, where professional challenges and teamwork stretch individuals in an environment of mutual support and self-development. This is not a cosy climate, tolerant of the substandard, but one that stimulates everyone to give of their best, thereby attracting the best to join. It is more and more the preoccupation of not just human resource managers, but general managers and chief executives. It is the difference between the companies that continue to grow and those who fall behind.

How companies contribute

As we have seen, companies impact on the relational base of society in many ways. When a company makes a major investment in new capacity or re-locates its head office to a new site away from commuter misery, the impact is dramatic and far-reaching. Much analysis, consultation and even media commentary will precede the decision. Community involvement programmes such as Shell's Better Britain Campaign and Livewire (see Box 10.1) are much less newsworthy, but over time can affect the lives of many more. With perseverance and imagination, they become powerful vehicles for change, linking the company's brand to the very roots of the communities it serves. Everyone involved benefits, although it is hard to prove the strict financial case when times are hard. In the middle of a recession, with market share under attack on all sides, it takes courage and foresight to sustain the level of investment. It is in employment practices, however, that the impact is most direct and immediate. The composition of the workforce, working hours, leave arrangements, childcare provision and other employee welfare programmes each profoundly influence the relational base of the individual and his/her family unit. At what time we come home and in what frame of mind almost certainly dictates the quality of personal relations more than any other factor. It is a sobering thought for any manager.

Work is a principal determinant of each individual's quality of life and achievement. It offers financial, intellectual, physical and social rewards. It also exerts a range of pressures that may produce healthy stimulation at one end of the spectrum and very unhealthy distress at the other. There are pressures in work and pressures out of work. There are also stresses when work changes, be that the hours of work, the place of work, the content of the job, the grade or seniority and the people with whom it is performed. Like it or not, these pressures will grow in line with the competitive challenges facing companies.

Box 10.1 Shell's community relations programme

Many companies view involvement in the communities in which they operate as part of doing business. It cements relationships, shares values and can multiply even a small contribution many times over. The following are some of the ways in which Shell reaches out, with its employees, its expertise and its donations.

Shell Employee Action

Wherever they live, Shell employees and pensioners and their partners are encouraged to play an active role in their local communities. Those who do so can receive up to £350 per year towards the needs of the local organisations with which they are involved.

The Shell Better Britain Campaign

This is a partnership with environmental organisations, which has helped thousands of community groups over the last 25 years to undertake schemes which improve or conserve their local environments. The scheme provides expert guidance and grants to local groups of volunteers, helping to build community spirit while effecting practical improvements.

Livewire

With the opportunities for traditional employment declining, and over 10% of 16-year-olds disconnected from society's institutions, the scheme offers young people practical help with starting their own business and building a future for themselves. It has been running now for some 12 years and has helped 70,000 self-starters so far.

continued

The Shell Technology Enterprise Programme (STEP)

STEP places over 1,000 students each summer in small businesses to undertake key projects for that business. Run since 1986, the scheme helps graduates (who are currently experiencing high levels of unemployment) to appreciate the exciting possibilities of working in the small firm sector. It also gives small firms a subsidised first taste of employing graduates, helping them to look at ways in which they can help their businesses to grow.

In a recently-introduced variation of the scheme, students working with charities, rather than small businesses, have shown that the effectiveness of a voluntary sector organisation can be greatly improved by such help over a short period of time.

The Shell Education Service

Last year, the service received over 20,000 requests for materials. These cover a wide range of subjects, from the oil industry and the teaching of science through to an understanding of enterprise and man's relationship with the environment. Established in 1956, the service helps children to engage in exciting and stimulating ways with the world which awaits them.

School–Education Links Programme

Some of Shell's distribution terminals run visits programmes for their local school children, who can look at how a distribution operation is managed, with particular emphasis on environmental performance. The children are then given a project which involves designing a terminal of the future which meets operational needs while being as environmentally efficient as possible.

A more demanding workforce

The national workforce is changing, both in profile and expectation. The once familiar model of married couples, two children, with father at work and mother at home, now represents a small and diminishing minority of households. Data from various sources shows that:[3]

- women now represent nearly half of the total workforce, many of them part-timers;

- among couples of working age, well over half are now dual bread-winners;
- the divorce rate has risen alarmingly, and with it the number of one-parent families;
- some two-thirds of mothers are now in work;
- these trends coincide with many other developments in society which influence the employment scene, not least the steady improvement in educational attainment. Over two-thirds of the workforce today have some form of qualification, and about one-third of those leaving school go on to higher education before entering the labour market. This may still be structurally lower than our North European competitors, especially Germany, but represents a dramatic improvement since the Robbins report of the early 1960s. As with the employment statistics above, much of the increase can be explained by the higher participation of women.

Whatever the fine detail of the statistics, we may fairly conclude that the workforce today is much more sophisticated than ever before. Better educated and more informed of world events, employees generally have more complicated domestic situations and seek flexibility in their working arrangements. Representative of wider trends in society towards consumerism and individualism, they also look for choice and challenge in their careers. Certainly, employers requiring ever higher quality staff for multi-skilled jobs, often involving computerised processes, have no option but to take notice. The spectre of unemployment may haunt unskilled workers and constrain them to accept jobs whose content and conditions are less than desired – the so-called 'Mac jobs' of the fast-food chains. But for skilled staff of demonstrable worth, their clout in the labour market has never been greater.

How companies respond: The family-friendly agenda

Employers have responded differently to these developments, depending on their own particular imperatives. For some, their employee profile and benefits programmes may look much the same as they always have. For others, the changes may be marked indeed. Across the board, there is certainly growing evidence that employers are taking the needs of their workforce into account in designing working arrangements and conditions of employment. Maternity and paternity leave tend to grab national attention as a result of EU interest, but many employers now offer various arrangements for time off to help staff cope with sickness, childcare or general carer responsibilities.

The variations on working hours are even more disparate, with flexitime, part-time, annualised hours and job-sharing being the most common. Some employees work from home on a routine basis, while others go into the office as and when needed and make use of communal work areas (so-called 'hot-desking'). Sometimes, an employee will team up with two or more colleagues to share a job, or take a career break to give full-time attention to the needs of a young family for a year or so.

Each arrangement has its attractions and drawbacks; it can take considerable effort to make them work well, as shown by the case studies from personal experience described in Boxes 10.2–10.5. With patience and imagination, however, they can have a profound and positive effect on the ability of individuals to manage the interface between home and work, on which so much of the relational base depends.

Box 10.2   Job share – an increasingly successful formula

Susan is a professional administrator and works Monday to Wednesday; her job-share partner works Thursday and Friday. Both have young children and are combining childcare and work. This arrangement has been in place for three-and-a-half years.

After her first maternity leave, Susan returned to work full-time while her mother-in-law and husband's aunt shared the care of the baby in a job-share. After her second child, this arrangement became more difficult, and so she asked whether her job could be done on a job-share basis. Susan's post was being covered on a job-share basis for the duration of her maternity leave, and this allowed her manager the opportunity to consider the option of job-share on a more permanent basis.

By good fortune, one of the people covering her maternity post was a previous incumbent of this post who was also looking for a job-share post at the same time. As a consequence of both having direct experience of the post and complementary skills, Susan and her proposed job-share partner were judged to be the best candidates for the job.

Susan is pleased with the current arrangement, as it allows her additional flexibility to play a larger part in her children's formative years. She envisages working longer hours once both her children are in full-time education. Her manager is delighted that Susan's experience and skills have not been lost. He believes the job-share works well for the department, and thanks to the conscientious approach of both parties, the customers see a seamless service. The main challenge is to find the time to keep abreast of technology. With the additional effort required for partner briefing at handovers, there is less opportunity to gain experience with new software.

Box 10.3 Maternity leave and flexible working – a case of fine tuning

Joan is a qualified solicitor who left private practice to work in Shell. By the time her second child was born, she had risen to a senior position, heading up a syndicate in the company's law firm with responsibility for advising senior management on major policy initiatives. Torn between the professional challenge of her job and the demands of two young children, she at first attempted to work a three-day week with the support of a nanny. This proved insufficient, however, and she found it increasingly difficult to meet her clients' needs. At her request, and after careful consultation with the key clients, she now works a fourth day at home.

So far, the new system is working well, and Joan certainly feels more in control of her work and more relaxed with her family. It will require on-going review to make sure the balance is right.

Box 10.4 Childcare support – a daunting tale

As a first-time mother and professional engineer, Sam relied fairly heavily on Shell's in-house Childcare Advisory Service (CAS). Her case was traumatic in that she had to go through the recruitment process for a nanny on no less than four occasions. The CAS provided practical advice and counselling support throughout.

Nanny No. 1

After four days in post, the nanny did not turn up. Sam phoned the nanny to be answered by an ex-boyfriend, who told her that the nanny no longer lived at this address. He had thrown her out when he discovered she was pregnant, and she had fled back home. When she did show up three days later, Sam decided she was too unstable to be left in charge of her child. All this occurred just before Sam was due to return to work, so she delayed her return by one week and recruited a temp.

Nanny No. 2

The nanny did not show up for handover. Her mother phoned to say she was sick, but it later turned out that the nanny could not cope with the idea of Sam's husband (a shift worker) being in the house during the day.

continued

Nanny No. 3

The nanny was asked to sign a contract which included clauses forbidding smoking in the house and warning that theft would result in disciplinary action. She refused to sign the contract, as she believed it to be too legalistic and implied that she was not trusted. To compound matters, the temporary nanny then went sick and Sam had to call upon the CAS emergency childminder facility for two days.

Nanny No. 4

Sam was desperate and considering giving up work to care for her son. In the end, however, the story has a happy ending, as the fourth nanny, recruited from an agency, has worked out well and remains with the family to date.

This story illustrates the volatile nature of the 'nanny labour market' – it is worse than the typical experience, but the problems it illustrates are common.

Box 10.5 Overseas (mis)adventure – learning from experience

Peter had joined Shell as a career professional and was keen to progress to a management position. After a spell in the London office, he accepted a posting to the tropics with an affiliated company. This offered him exposure to the international side of the business, more direct responsibility as a manager and an expatriate remuneration package.

Indications that his partner was uneasy and ill-equipped to tackle the upheaval were largely ignored in the frenzy of pre-departure activities. Peter himself, preoccupied with work permits and company briefings, felt that she would cope once she had the chance to see her new environment and settle down. Only three weeks after their arrival, it was clear that she could not cope with the culture shock – the language, humidity, bugs and camp life. The assignment was aborted, with recrimination and misery on all sides. For the family, it meant further upheaval and strain. For the company, it meant another four months' wait for a replacement and a second round of travel, freight and expatriation expenses. It was a costly business for everyone.

continued

> Nowadays, much greater attention is given to the family unit, with the objective of providing effective support at every stage. This not only minimises the risk of failure, but helps maintain the supply of staff prepared to undertake expatriate assignments.

The business case is essential

It is important to understand why companies promote these policies, if their application is to be extended and made more useful. For professional firms whose staff represent the only worthwhile assets in the business, it is clearly self-interest. A suite of flexible employment policies helps to attract the best and to get the best out of them. Hard economics will be the driver for others. Hot-desking may be attractive to an employee with home commitments, but it also dramatically reduces office overheads! National initiatives from statutory bodies such as the Equal Opportunities Commission and Commission for Racial Equality raise awareness and reinforce good practice. Employers respond either to the carrot of public regard or the stick of prosecution for discrimination, or more likely to the combination of the two! Sometimes, they seize the initiative themselves, as with Employers for Childcare,[4] evidencing leadership in social responsibility, and self-help through sharing practical experience.

The cynics would counter that it is always the same household names who appear on these various campaign lists – BBC, British Airways, Midland Bank, Shell, etc. Family-friendly policies are the privilege of the major companies, they say, while the mass of smaller businesses offer little more than the law and the market require. Certainly, there can be no argument that for some companies, survival is the only game in town. Caught between recession at home and merciless competition from abroad, sustaining employment itself is the limit of their immediate aspiration. But all cycles turn, and those who do forge a competitive organisation may themselves play a leadership role in the future. As a nation, we need more excellent companies to both generate wealth and lift standards of practice in not just employment, but environmental care, operational efficiency, product development, and so on.

Whatever the size and state of the company, human resource policies that address relational issues at the workplace will only make a telling contribution if they are grounded in the business. Initiatives that derive from the whim of the chairman or a spurious sense of social responsibility will quickly wane. Childcare, employee support programmes and career breaks are tough on the time and patience of managers, and that represents as big a commitment as any impact on the budget. There has to be real value to the organisation in terms of efficiency or quality or service or reputation. In theory, such policies reduce turnover, thus saving the costs of rehiring, retraining and rebuilding work groups. In theory, they save on aborted transfers or relocations. In theory, they lift productivity through improved motivation and reduced stress. In practice, however, it can be very difficult to prove this on a case-by-case basis. The needs of new mothers may be universally acknowledged in principle, but extended maternity leave, in practice, can severely disrupt work schedules, testing the resolve of everyone in the front line.

The answer lies firstly in setting the various programmes in a clear strategic context, introducing flexible benefits in support of the overall human resource plan and not as a specific budget improvement target. Taking all training and turnover costs together, on the one hand, and all service and productivity benefits together on the other, gives a realistic focus as to where initiatives should be targeted and how they should be evaluated. Second, all such initiatives should be formally reviewed at both the top and bottom of the organisation: at the top, to satisfy management that in the round the strategies are effective, and at the bottom, to allow employees and supervisors to tackle practical problems and share learning. It is a process of challenge and continuous improvement that sustains the initiatives within the reality of the business.

Where companies have placed the family-friendly agenda firmly within their business strategies, the claims for reduced absenteeism, turnover and stress do seem to hold up. They are becoming more popular with boardrooms as a result. There has never been any doubt as to their popularity among employees. For both men and women, the flexibility to juggle work and family commitments is a precious benefit. Individuals, families, neighbourhoods and communities all gain, and the relational base is strengthened.

The new contract of employment

The issue of how employers and employees relate goes much deeper than the provision of an appropriate benefits package. The contract of employment is more than just a statement of duties and conditions on one side and a commitment to work on the other. At its core are mutual rights and obligations which will largely determine the health of the enterprise, both in financial and relational terms:

- The employer commitment to make available training and development, and the reciprocal employee obligation to take full advantage of

it. One-way teaching achieves little, but positive learning transforms an organisation. And this is no easy deal for either party. The time and commitment required is substantial, but the rewards can be enormous, for the individual and for the business as a whole.
- The employer commitment to involve, and the employee commitment to participate. Involvement requires both communication and consultation, processes which test the resolve and resources of management. The decision to participate is no less passive, requiring employees to keep informed of developments, to express views and take responsibility for them. How else can the potential of the organisation be realised?
- The mutual commitment to openness and frankness. For companies, this means explaining past performance, plans and prospects in terms which the employees can act upon. For employees, it requires explaining their own ambitions, capacities and constraints in terms which the employer can act upon. A business should be able to expect its workforce to respond, knowing that its financial state is parlous or operational performance has slipped. An employee should equally be able to expect management to respond to difficult personal circumstances or the wish to change career direction or retrain. This may sound a soft option, but it is not. The young executive offered a career move abroad can face an agony of trade-offs with her young child and equally talented husband. It is tough on all the parties to confront the issues and come to a decision without recrimination. Similar stresses confront the lubricants manufacturer who is forced to introduce shift work in order to lift plant utilisation in line with the competition. It is tough on management, production staff and families alike to work out the new arrangements, and even tougher to implement them.

The new contract is truly a balance of trust and responsibility, honesty and commitment. The old values of collective bargaining and formal contracts are an obstacle in the world of free competition. They slow down the processes of change and regeneration necessary to achieve competitive, let alone world-class performance. Neither businesses nor individuals can realise their potential under these rules. By contrast, the new values aren't rules at all. They are the values of learning, involvement and openness which focus squarely on what is best for all the stakeholders in the business. At first sight, they may seem less onerous, but in practice, they carry much heavier responsibilities. It is easier to deliver job performance by the book than for each to accept his or her personal part in meeting standards, making improvements and generating innovation.

In this new culture, relational issues become more, not less, important. Many companies are now adopting '360° appraisal' as a way of helping managers and staff to improve their personal effectiveness. Rather than the boss alone giving feedback to the individual on their performance, style and potential, colleagues and subordinates are asked to contribute as well. In some cases, customers and suppliers are also involved. Handled with confidentiality and sensitivity, the process has been shown to help improve effectiveness across the organisation. By focusing on the network of relationships, it tackles not only the capacity of each employee, but how well that is channelled in delivering results with and through others. In Shell, the ability of managerial and professional staff to 'relate' in this way is now to be one of only three indicators of potential for senior positions. This involves not only the communication and influencing skills required for leadership and team building, but also personal integrity, empathy and cultural awareness. It ranks alongside 'capacity' (the stock of useful experience and personal competences) and 'achievement' (the drive to meet challenges and deliver results). It is a clear signal that success in a changing world will not be linked to the traditional status of hierarchy and professional know-how. In the successful organisations of the future, flexible structures will predominate, with less and less emphasis on formal lines of communication. Small workforces, of higher quality, with stronger information networks and disparate employment conditions are going to require very different management styles to those generally evident today.

Not everyone will feel comfortable in these new, organic organisations, and some will not cope at all. Part of the new contract, therefore, involves providing safety nets, to help individuals adjust. At its simplest, this may entail some retraining, but for others, career counselling and radical reskilling may be needed. Extensive personal and out-placement support to those losing their jobs is already the norm in many companies. But obsolescence of skills or even loss of job altogether are not the only threats. The loss of formality and structure in the new organisations can be deeply disturbing to those who 'know their place' and like it. New technologies, new relationships, new working arrangements can appeal to the young, but make older staff feel insecure and vulnerable. Positive stress can quickly become harmful distress, resulting in expensive rehabilitation. All those who lead organisations through change and regeneration – and that is the vast majority of organisations – bear a heavy personal responsibility to build in the safety nets and make sure that they work well.

What lies ahead?

Whether we like it or not, neither the pace nor impact of change will slacken. The forces of technology, competition and globalism will continue to force enterprises and institutions to adapt or atrophy. For many, the change will offer benefits and opportunities – improved products, slicker services, greater freedom and personal challenge. For others, it will seem only to offer insecurity and isolation.

Relational values inside organisations will be at a premium to release the full talent and energies of their workforce. This will increasingly bring in the new contract of employment, with its emphasis on reciprocal responsibilities and open communications. Measuring the effectiveness of this new contract will be as important as measuring productivity or quality control. The most successful organisations will place it at the core of their human resource strategy, and we may well, in the future, see more comprehensive relational audits than today's opinion surveys offer. Relational values outside the organisation will also be at a premium, with the prospect of greater polarisation in society at large. Social systems will be stretched to cope, and companies as well as public institutions will have to be more imaginative and thorough in maintaining effective safety nets.

Looking into the future, it is easy to imagine a world of complex electronic webs, where information, research, commercial contracts and even corporate finances are freely transacted. Such a world would be largely unseen and difficult to understand, let alone regulate. But I doubt, in practice, the human factor will be so readily displaced. Creativity and ingenuity depend on human interaction, and tomorrow, like today, the big decisions will still be made face-to-face. For companies, the relational agenda will become more, not less important.

References

1 Royal Society of Arts (1995) *Tomorrow's Company: The Role of Business in a Changing World*, RSA.
2 Matthew 20:1–16.
3 Department of Employment Gazette; General Household Survey; Institute for Employment Studies; European Commission; Incomes Data Services; Industrial Relations Review and Report.
4 Employers for Childcare is a forum of many of the UK's major employers who have firsthand experience of trying to implement childcare and family-friendly policies. The initiative seeks the provision of accessible, available, affordable, quality childcare which meets the differing needs and circumstances of parents and children.

11 Employment and caring within households

Shirley Dex

Introduction

In this chapter, I consider the thorny issue of women's employment and its implications for building relationships. There is no doubt that women have been and are doing most of the caring in our society: caring for young children and caring for elderly relatives.[1] Caring is directly related to building relationships. So we need to consider the implications for caring of women participating in the labour market to a greater extent. However, we also need to consider what our ideals might be, in order to evaluate the current trends and suggest public policy options which will work towards these goals.

Far more women have jobs in the 1990s than was the case in the 1950s, although we need to be careful not to over-state the nature of these changes.[2] Many women with children have exchanged time in the home for time in a job. At the same time, men's rates of full-time employment have been falling. Expectations about women's roles have been changing. It would now be unthinkable for a woman to expect to stop work at marriage in order to spend her lifetime in caring work in the home, as happened when the marriage bar operated in some jobs up to the 1950s. Instead, the vast majority of women see themselves as playing dual roles throughout their mid-life years: being a mother and having a job. Public policy has been motivated by a desire to see these expectations recognised and facilitated, for example through the adoption of equal opportunities policies and separate tax treatment.

In the light of these changes, it is important to assess how family and individual relationships are being affected. This chapter focuses mainly on the parent–child caring relationship, since there is only space here to tackle one sphere of caring in any detail, and the care of children has such fundamental implications for the rest of their lives. Policy developments can often appear piecemeal by failing to consider the wider picture. Perhaps this is inherent in the way public policy is formulated, in response to interest group pressures. Certainly, there has been little consideration of these caring implications in the debates over women's equal opportunities, other than to decry the fact that the burden of caring falls largely or solely on women. In this chapter, I want to examine a wider range of issues which are raised by changes in the structure of employment in Britain. After summarising the changes in the patterns of employment, the implications of 1990s employment patterns for caring are examined. I then consider what we should be aiming for, and how we might set about trying to achieve these aims.

Changing patterns of employment

What has been happening to individuals' and, in particular, parents' employment? There has been a general increase in the labour force participation of married women since the 1950s. These women largely returned to part-time employment after having had a break from employment as a result of childbirth and family formation. The gap spent out of work has shrunk progressively, and in the 1980s, there has been a sizeable increase in the women returning, after a short period of maternity leave, to a full-time job. Among women with dependent children, in 1981, 49% of them were employed, compared with 59% in 1992. Half the employment growth over this period was for mothers in full-time work.[3]

While men's rates of employment have gradually been falling and continue to do so, 71% of men over 16 were employed in 1981 and 64% in 1992; the largest falls have been for men aged 50–64. The employment rate for fathers in 1992 was the same level that it was in 1981 (89%). Fathers continue to be employed full-time rather than part-time, the latter having grown considerably among the very young and older men.[4]

Caring and dual-earner employment now characterise a sizeable proportion of British households. Households with two earners were approximately half of British households in 1991. Of all couple households, 28% have both a husband and a wife employed full-time; a further 21% have a husband who is employed full-time and a wife employed part-time. Approximately half of these households contain dependent children. A further 7% of households contained an elderly person in addition to other household members.[5]

On average, in 1991, employed fathers worked 42 basic hours per week in their main job, but this average increased to 46 hours per week when overtime and second jobs were also added into the total. In addition, married men, on average, spent 48 minutes per day travelling to and from work, which, for someone who works every day, adds a further four hours per week to the total.[6] Historically, of course, these represent a fall in men's hours of work, although reliable data across time, based on the same definitions, are difficult to find.[7]

Married women worked, on average, 30 hours per week (including overtime and second jobs) in 1991. If they worked full-time, they added a further four hours per week travel-to-work time, but this was less for part-timers. Also, married women with children worked fewer hours on average: 24 basic hours per week.[8]

The average couple spend 62 hours per week at work between them (including overtime and all jobs). Where the husband works more than 60 hours per week, in 20% of cases, the wife also works more than 40 hours per week. This compares with a figure of 59 hours per week as the average working hours of men in 1881. If we were to compare the average couple of the 1990s with a nineteenth-century couple where the woman was not employed, we could conclude that there has been little change in the household's total working hours over the last century.[9]

British men are working longer hours than anyone else in Europe. While the trend across Europe has been a decrease in men's employment hours and an increase in leisure hours, Britain is alone in spending more time at work and less time with the family.[10]

In addition, there is a growth in insecurity in people's jobs. More jobs are self-employed and temporary than was the case in the 1970s. This applies to both men and women. In 1994, between 22% and 25% of employed men were in flexible jobs, and 50% of employed women were in such jobs.[11] All of the so-called 'flexible' jobs are known to have fewer benefits attached to them: less holiday entitlement, less paid holiday, less entitlement to sick pay and employment protection coverage, and less entitlement to join an occupational pension scheme.[12] The law has recently changed to give part-time employees more rights; they are now entitled to be members of pension schemes, *pro rata*, but it will be a long time before the majority of women see any benefit from this change.

In the long term, these flexible jobs offer a poorer future to employees who hold them, and employed women in such jobs are less likely than men to receive any of these fringe benefits. These jobs imply for women a lack of long-term employment security, a considerable loss of lifetime earnings, and poverty in old age. Given the high proportions of marriage breakdowns, the greater insecurity in men's employment, and the entitlement to statutory maternity leave, it is perhaps not so surprising that far more women are opting for a full-time option in the labour market.

What these figures represent is a growth in full-time/part-time partnerships in families, but also a smaller but significant and growing phenomenon which one commentator has called 'workaholic couples', who put in long hours for high pay and depend heavily on paid domestic help.[13] In terms of household income, there is a growing polarisation between what are being called 'work-rich' and 'work-poor' households in Britain.[14]

We might want to ask who is responsible for these changes. Have people's attitudes changed, or is it the demands of the marketplace which pressure employees to fit in? These sorts of questions are difficult to answer. Influences on both sides of this dichotomy have occurred which have contributed to the changes which have taken place. Similarly, pressure to change these patterns to something different will also need to address the individual or supply side of the labour market as well as the employer or demand side.

Household examples

Family A

We know a couple; they have two children, aged 4 and 6, a recently-purchased Burmese kitten and a garage stuffed with expensive toys. They offer a stereotypical view of the modern, well-to-do lifestyle. The nanny, the third one in less than 12 months, arrives at 7.45 am and leaves at 5.45 pm. Several times a week, a housekeeper arrives at 5.45 pm when nanny is due to go home. She stays until 8.00 pm, when mother comes home late from work. Father goes to work every weekend. The nanny works about one weekend in four, and certainly all bank holidays, as mother works on holidays. The family is taking one week's holiday together this year because they think that they do not have enough money for a longer holiday, after paying the nanny, the housekeeper, the mortgage and private school fees. They think it is necessary to pay for a private school to help the two children get help with their speech problems; also, the children are thought to be too withdrawn to be able to cope with the rough and tumble of a State school. Mother comes home tired and longs for the children's bedtime. They are both academic psychologists with secure jobs but unbounded hours.

Admittedly, this is an extreme case. None the less, there are certain implications to draw out of it which will apply to a lesser degree to many other couples. Certainly, I have felt the pressures in my life pushing towards this scenario, and I know plenty of others who have.

Family B

What happens towards the other end of the income spectrum? There, father works in a manual job getting low basic pay. He is offered overtime to make his pay up to a living wage, but somehow it is not enough to pay all the bills comfortably. He rarely sees the kids. Mother has a part-time cleaning job earning very little, no holiday or sick pay, and no pension contribution; but it is enough to make household income cover the necessities. Her friend, her own mother, and father when he's on the right shift, all provide bits of childcare, while mum does the cleaning. In the school holidays, she takes the children to work with her, and they play outside on the street while she cleans.

The implications of changing employment patterns

It is reasonable to argue that changes in hours of work mean that children see fewer total hours of their parents than they did in earlier generations. In terms of the longer perspective, however, it would be possible in the 1990s for children to be seeing more of their fathers than they would have in the nineteenth century, but probably less of their mother. The more recent changes, increasing women's full-time employment participation, must mean a sizeable reduction, over recent decades, in the time a pre-school child spends with its mother and a less pronounced reduction in the time mothers spend with their school-aged children. Is the father compensating for this reduction in the mother's time with the child? The evidence is mixed but suggests, on the whole, that the answer is 'No.'[15]

Figures from time budget surveys suggest that men are spending more time on childcare than they used to. In 1961, fathers of under-fives spent 12 minutes a day with their children. By the mid-1970s, the figure was 17 minutes. In the mid-1980s, they were spending 43 minutes a day.[16] Other studies in the 1990s have found that fathers prefer spending time on hobbies or playing sport than with their children. More than half of the fathers in one study said that they spent five minutes or less one-to-one with their child, on an average weekday; 15% devoted no time to childcare.[17]

The example of Family A above points up a number of implications. Many jobs expect a commitment to long hours. The long working day can be used in order to justify a living wage, or it can be used as a basis for assessing whether the worker is a suitable candidate for promotion. Men are most affected by this phenomenon.[18] However, the long hours expected by some (men's) jobs has been raised as an issue of equal opportunities; it disadvantages women if they do not wish to work such long hours and if long hours are used as a criteria for promotion.

Submersion in the work culture has a self-perpetuating effect. Men who have been successful then assess the promotion prospects of other men on whether they can survive and neglect their family just like they did. Work becomes all-encompassing and blinds people to the importance of other aspects of life. There may well be societal influences and individual personality traits which bolster these effects.[19] Recent surveys found that many men do not want to reduce their hours of work or spend more time with their children.[20]

People get locked into a lifestyle based on poor relationships: their choice of housing, their level of mortgage, and in the case of Family A, the need for private schooling. Their money is committed to the extent that there is no slack, even for holidays, and certainly not for reducing hours of work. For couples who are desperate for the money, again the pressure is on to take all the overtime going.

Employers are increasingly reducing the non-wage benefits to employees and expecting more efficiencies and flexibility. They have little sense of responsibility for bringing up the next generation of workers. That is someone else's problem.

Finally, children get a raw deal. Their 'significant other' person is often changing, too often for their liking. In Chapter 10, Clive Mather describes another example of the high-turnover nanny scenario (see Box 10.4). Sometimes, the parents are too tired to participate in child-rearing. Perhaps the expensive toys make up for all that? Melanie Phillips raises the possibility, 'the awful truth' as she calls it, that adults may be requiring 'their children to pay a terrible price for their own gratification'.[21]

In looking at the implications of changes, we must avoid nostalgia about a past golden age which very possibly never existed. Linked to this, we need to avoid too much speculation about the past which assumes that things have always got worse. However, we do not need to look much further than our current problems to find justifications for having a rethink about these issues.

What should we be aiming for?

Michael Schluter has outlined the prerequisites for relationship-building in Chapter 1. That directness and continuity are vital elements for building parent–child relationships seems uncontroversial. They are certainly lacking in both our household examples above. The key question, however, is how much time is needed to do this? There are some voices arguing that parent–child relationships can be built with very little time input from parents, so long as it is 'quality time'. Some are arguing that it needs more time. I want to cast my vote for more parenting time being needed, especially in 'workaholic families', and from both parents, if they are to build a lasting parent–child relationship which does not short-change the children. In particular, fathers need to spend more family time in all families.

Why is 'quality time' not enough? Children need both a sense of security and a sense of self-worth. 'Quality time' may well help with the development of self-worth. It will not provide the security which has to be built up through 'quantity time'. Utting, in his review of the evidence about parenting, states that:

> Families are one of the important places where children's behaviour and attitudes are shaped. Through a loving and stable relationship with their parents they can first be introduced to the balance between personal responsibility and interdependence that enables wider society to function. The family is, to adapt a widely-used metaphor, a building block of society.[22]

Can all this be achieved during an hour per day with mother and a half-hour with father? The answer, fairly obviously, is 'No.'

But what about women's equality? Won't this mean just another setback, driving women back into the home to do all the caring and relating? These are valid questions. The answers depend on what is our ideal model of workplace relations and marital or within-family relationships. These issues are often hotly debated. Here, the intention is to discuss these questions from the perspective of relationship-building, being prepared to go against the grain of current fashion, if that is necessary.

There are a number of possible models or ideals we could consider. In terms of workplace positions, do we want workplaces dominated by a single gender group? Do we want to aim for an egalitarian model based on the current structure of jobs, the best jobs being those demanding long hours? Do we want to return to the traditional model, with a one-earner family and the man tending to be the one earner? Not many women would vote for this these days. Or should we think of devising new models? In addition, there is the issue of whether men and women are equally good at caring and equally good at senior management and leadership. People have differing views about these issues. The arguments I want to make in this chapter apply irrespective of the position one adopts on the relative skills of gender groups, so I propose to leave that issue aside.

Household models

To establish the pros and cons of each of these models from this perspective, let us conduct a relationship audit of the options.

The traditional-hours model (one-earner family, man employed in long-hours job)

The benefits of this model are that the children spend a lot of time with their mother. Mother also has more time for other relationships in the community, building traditional community networks. But against all this, it can be quite depressing for her, being confined at home all day with young children and burdened with all the domestic chores. Too much time with young children can seem like a treadmill that women are trapped in. Some women at home all day develop low self-esteem, which can affect the children. Also, husbands think of their stay-at-home wives as having the easy option, and expect them to attend to their needs when they get home from their really hard and stressful day at work. If men work long hours to compensate and produce a living wage, there may be little time for a marriage relationship. Even on average hours, father will see little of the children under this scenario except when he's always tired. This is bad for him and bad for the children.

Over the past few decades, this model has slid into one where the father works full-time, and in many cases long hours, and the mother works part-time and does all the care and domestic work. This is an improvement for her, since it gets her out of the house some of the time and into a wider set of relationships. It still has the problem of the children having little relationship with their father, and he is deprived of experiencing and being responsible for a caring relationship. (He may not see it like that.) Mother also has no independent income in the extreme version, and possibly, will be without a pension, especially if there is a marital break-up.

The egalitarian-hours model (two earners, man and woman both employed in long-hours jobs)

What if we help women to compete more equally for the jobs as they are currently structured? Women could get affirmative action, more training, better childcare provision for long working days. But women would only be able to compete successfully if they do not take time out for caring for their children, since that spells failure and lack of commitment. The main caring for young children would have to be done by someone else. In this scenario, mother still does most of the domestic work.[23] Father would not be available unless he was prepared to sacrifice his career. This is the worst of all worlds for relationships. In the extreme, it is the two full-time workaholic jobs scenario. There is no time for the children, nor any time for building a sustaining marital relationship.

The family-hours model

In this model, there would be a general acceptance that at certain times over the working lifecycle, other responsibilities take on importance. It recognises that shorter working hours are good for women and men. Promotion for both men and women would not rest on a commitment to long hours and family neglect. Both parents might have part-time jobs for a time, while their children were young. This would be good for the children. They would build a better relationship with both their parents. It would not have the negative effects of the traditional model, where one partner feels confined at home. It would be good for the marriage. In the past, it would not have been so good for people's pensions, but recent changes in the law mean that rights to pension scheme membership are now protected for part-timers. But it would mean some reduction in family income. At the top end, this would not be such a problem, but there will be some difficulties for people who are on the poverty line.

Such a model does not require exact equality of men and women in their part-time work. It is compatible with either distinctive gender roles within the family for those who hold the view that there should be equality but not symmetry within the marriage relationship, or with a more egalitarian division of hours.

A very brief audit of these models has shown that, in my view, the family-hours model has by far the most advantages if our aim is to promote the building of parent–child relationships. However, there are several unresolved issues: one is the question of how family finances would be affected. Just at the time when parents need more time to bring up their family, they also meet more financial demands for housing and looking after the children.[24] This is a very major constraint, and not one we can hope to resolve here. Our primary aim here should be to make sure that any policy options which are put forward try not to exacerbate this problem.

Another issue is what should happen to single parents. Single parents suffer the worst from their lack of relationships and from isolation at home if they have young children. Current concerns focus on the single parents who are locked into dependence on State benefits. They cannot afford to take a paid job since it is not economic to come off benefit, take a low-paid job, pay for childcare and face high marginal tax rates. But what will happen to the parent–child relationship if the sole parent takes a full-time job? This leaves the young child with very little quantity or quality time. The ideal for this household would seem to be a part-time job for the single parent to get them out of the house, but with access to State support and subsidised part-time childcare if these are necessary to make this a viable option.

How can we achieve our aims?

A number of policy implications arising from these concerns are described below. I want to be realistic in suggesting ways to implement policy changes which can promote good relationships. At the same time, it is important to recognise that effecting changes is a difficult task, and one which will not be achieved by public policy alone. None the less, when the State adopts policies, it is sending a message to everyone that our society thinks these issues matter enough to set standards and give incentives for this behaviour. Change for those with unbounded hours of work will be the most difficult to effect, and yet possibly the most necessary. Measures that will help to build good relationships are:

1. Introduce measures to limit weekly working hours for all workers who have a child under the age of 10. Hewitt[25] and others have suggested limiting the working hours of all workers, and there is a case to be made for this wider measure. Both the wider measure and the more restricted one adopted here have the added benefit that, if implemented, they would create more jobs, which could be redistributed to those who have none. Introducing changes of this kind would need to be done gradually, of course.
2. Make sure that there are no financial disincentives or penalties for those who wish to look after their own children. Given that those who are employed receive a zero-rated tax allowance, it might be equitable to give carers the equivalent money value of this allowance. This could apply to caring for young children and for the elderly. Young and Halsey suggest there should be a parent wage introduced, targeted on the poorer families, paid either to the mother or the father if s/he stays at home to look after a child under 5.[26]
3. Introduce new parental leave rights, notably: a right to return to work part-time after maternity leave for the mother, even when she had a full-time job before childbirth, and a right to an hours reduction to part-time hours for two years each for a father and mother while their child is aged 7 months to 5 years, with *pro rata* reductions in pay and fringe benefits.[27] Allowing an individual to reduce their hours to 30 per week, for example, could mean in practice, working 8.30 am to 2.30 pm per day and spending most of each afternoon looking after their children. The entitlement might be set for a certain level of hours, but other arrangements might be permitted where individuals and employers agreed.

If a couple had another child within five years, the provisions would not be extended where the period of care overlapped. There might need to be an extension of the part-time right after the first child reached the age of 5, but it could be on a reduced basis. There could also be some reduced right to go part-time for second and subsequent children. Beyond a certain point, employers rights would need to be protected, such that employees might forfeit their rights to return to full-time work if they spend beyond a certain time in part-time employment because of having multiple children.

These schemes could be supported by antenatal education classes informing parents of the importance of building a good foundation of relationships with and for young children to give them self-worth and a sense of security.

One of the main objectives of the parental leave scheme is to signal that it is important and acceptable for men to reduce their hours of work for the purposes of looking after the family. It would also help to remove some of the stigma which currently attaches to part-time work. The parental leave scheme would have another benefit of creating additional working hours. It might be possible to devise innovative employer subsidies to cover these periods of leave. For example, employers might receive a subsidy to take on an unemployed person as a temporary replacement during these periods in order to give them work experience and reduce the debilitating effects of unemployment. But what about the costs?

As it stands, part-time parental leave is costly to the employee, who will lose earnings and pension contributions, the man more than the woman, given the earnings differentials between men and women. The main cost to the employer will be the disruption of filling a part-time position. There will be potential, in some companies, for pairing off people who wish to turn this into job-shares.

To cover the employee loss of earnings, it should be possible to devise what Wilkinson has called a 'life-cycle mortgaging system'.[28] This would make it possible for couples or individuals to either save for this period, through the tax system, before they have the child, being paid back during the period of part-time parenting; or they could take out a loan to give them higher earnings and pension contributions while they are parenting, which would be paid back through their taxes over the rest of their lives; or adopt some combination of the two. Occupational pension scheme contributions will need to be negotiated with the employer (or the State might reimburse employers to some extent during this time). There are ways, therefore, of making this scheme to a large degree self-financing, if it was felt to be necessary.

There may be other reasons which would dissuade some couples from having both partners take up their entitlement. Long travel-to-work journeys might make part-time work seem less attractive, but there would be various ways in which the hours in some jobs might be concentrated into fewer days in order to reduce these problems. However, this solution would be less beneficial for the parenting relationship. Teleworking is also opening up a lot more possibilities for some individuals to work from and at home for some of the time, and that might help where journey times are a problem. At the end of the day, not everyone who is entitled to take up their rights will do so. None the less, it is still important for the State to make a statement that parenting by both mothers and fathers is important. The Scandinavian experience of parental leave suggests that change has been slow, but that it has led to a greater cultural acceptance of men taking time out to parent too, and the numbers of men taking leave have slowly crept up.[29]

Conclusions

Many are realising that our society needs to improve its parenting of children and caring for other dependents. Both fathers and mothers are important in this process. If we get it wrong with our children, and rear children without a sense of security and self-worth, what hope is there for the other spheres of relationship-building which this book examines? Otherwise, we may be producing a generation who do not realise that relationships matter, because they were deprived of experiencing that for themselves. Children are the essential foundation of a society in which relationships matter. We must find ways to put them higher up our list of priorities.

References

1. Recent evidence on carers show that men are equally likely as women to be caring for an elderly relative inside or outside the home, but in terms of the hours spent caring, female carers are doing far more than the male carers; see Corti, L., Laurie, H. and Dex, S. (1994) *Caring and Employment*, Research Series No.39, Employment Department.
2. Many women now work part-time, and full-time women's employment has hardly changed over the post-war period; see Hakim, C. (1993) 'The Myth of Rising Female Employment', in *Work, Employment and Society*, Vol.7, No.1.
3. Evidence of these trends can be found in Dex, S. (1984) *Women's Work Histories: An analysis of the Women and Employment Survey*, Department of Employment Research Paper No. 46; and Brannen, J. et al. (1994) *Employment and Family Life: A review of research in the UK 1980–1994*, Research Series No.41, Employment Department.
4. Brannen et al., op. cit., see also Dex, S. and McCulloch, A. (1995) *Flexible Employment in Britain: A Statistical Analysis*, Research Series No.15, Equal Opportunities Commission.
5. Dex, S., Clark, A. and Taylor, M. (1995) *Household Labour Supply*, Research Series No.43, Employment Department.
6. See Dex et al., op. cit. and Corti et al., op. cit.
7. Hewitt, P. in *About Time: The Revolution in Work and Family Life* (Institute for Public Policy Research/Rivers Oram Press, 1993) cites figures for 1881 where manual men are stated to have worked average weekly hours of 59 per week, compared with 42 in 1981. The problems in these comparisons arise because it is not clear what has been done about overtime, or second job hours, and it is not clear the extent to which overtime or second jobs were prevalent in the nineteenth century.
8. See Dex et al., op. cit. and Corti et al., op. cit.

9   I would argue that this is a reasonable comparison, since there was no formal, part-time paid employment in the nineteenth century. Some wives would have worked full-time, but this proportion appears to be unchanged. So we can presume that a far higher proportion than at present were not in paid jobs. However, these women may have been working in the home or in agriculture and for money, but they are likely to have seen more of their children.
10 Weale, S. (1995) 'Work ethic stunts growth of new man', *The Guardian*, 17 June.
11 Dex and McCulloch, op. cit.
12 Dickens, L. (1992) *Whose flexibility? Discrimination and equality issues in atypical work*, Institute of Employment Rights.
13 See Brannen et al., op. cit., p.7.
14 Gregg, P. (1994) *Work rich and work poor households*, National Institute of Economic and Social Research Discussion Paper No.65.
15 Time budget data is cited in Hewitt, op. cit. to suggest that time spent caring for children has changed very little over time. However, where time budget studies suggest that time spent caring for children has not changed over time for women, it needs to be qualified. It may be the case that the amount of time spent by women, when the primary activity was caring, has not changed, but caring goes on when the primary activity could be any number of other domestic duties. Since women are spending more time out of the home, it is uncontroversial that they must be spending less time with their children, albeit when they might be doing things other than primarily caring for them.
16 The figures are from the work of Professor J. Gershuny and are cited in a quote from him in Weale, op. cit.
17 These results come from a National Opinion Poll (NOP) survey for the charity Care for the Family, cited in Weale, op. cit.
18 Weale, op. cit.
19 For example, the societal stress on achievement and success acts on everyone. It has been suggested that workaholics are those who feel the need for security to make up for the emptiness in their lives and bad relationships.
20 Witherspoon, S. and Prior, G. (1991) 'Working mothers: Free to choose?', in Jowell, R., Brook, L. and Taylor, B. (1991) *British Social Attitudes – The 8th Report*, Social and Community Planning Research, Gower. British Social Attitudes 1991/2 reported that the majority of men are unwilling to work shorter hours for less pay.
21 Phillips, M. (1995) 'Family Planning', in *Search*, No.22, Spring, Joseph Rowntree Foundation.
22 Utting, D. (1995) *Family and Parenthood: Supporting Families, Preventing Breakdown: A Guide to the Debate*, Joseph Rowntree Foundation.
23 Milton, C. (1995) 'Today's woman: still struggling in a man's world', *The Independent*, 9 August.
24 This usually happens relatively early in people's careers, when they are not earning the maximum wages. Later, when they reach maximum earnings, the financial demands on them decline.
25 Hewitt, op. cit.
26 Young, M. and Halsey, A.H. (1995) *Family and Community Socialism*, Institute for Public Policy Research.
27 Statutory maternity leave rights end when a child is approximately 7 months old.
28 Wilkinson, H. (1995) 'Baby I just can't afford you', *The Independent*, 11 August.
29 Wilkinson, op. cit.

Part IV

Sources of pressure on relationships: The wider context

12 Science and technology: Profit or loss?

Andrew Briggs

Introduction

The impact of science and technology on human relationships is enormous. Revolutions in agricultural and industrial technology in earlier centuries changed whole patterns of populations in Europe and the nature of their interactions with one another in their places of work and where they lived. People's attitudes to themselves and to one another were profoundly affected by the work of Charles Darwin in the nineteenth century. Medical science has changed out of all recognition in the past hundred years. The physical sciences tend to affect relationships more through engineering achievements. The nature and scope of human interactions has been changed for ever by developments in transport technology, by rail and ship in the nineteenth century and by car and plane in the twentieth century. Roles and relationships in the home have been affected through labour-saving devices such as central heating and machines for cooking, cleaning and washing, and through the availability and diversity of equipment for communication and entertainment. There is every reason to believe that in the next century, such trends will continue, probably at an accelerating pace, and will spread globally. How will it be decided whether the effects on relationships are positive or negative?

Scientific or technological breakthroughs are often accompanied by lively public debate about their usefulness and their potential to enhance life or to harm it. Bio-genetics, opto-electronics and cybernetics are pushing back the frontiers of human understanding at an ever more rapid rate. New developments such as these enormously enhance the possibilities for caring and communicating, but there is also concern at the pace with which new applications of science and technology become part of our everyday lives and shape – to some extent even determine – human activity. Experience shows that the social dimension of technological change is a key determinant of how technologies come to be used.[1] Differing perspectives about the benefits and limitations of science and technology sometimes appear to rest on the assumption that technology is a neutral artifact which is external to human activity – a product of human endeavour to be used wisely or not – and that only its applications are open to value judgement.

Science and technology have an immediate impact on relationships through industrial employment. The rate of progress in the materials used for industrial manufacturing is now so rapid that significant changes take place in the span of a single employment career. The Iron Age took 500 years to spread throughout the world. The Steel Age took about a hundred years. For the first decade of the Silicon Age (1959–69) the UK had technological leadership; subsequent shifts first to the USA and then to Japan took about ten years each, and reflected the sizes of the electronic equipment markets which were dominant at the time. Silicon materials are at the heart of most electronic products, and although there is no UK-owned industry in the commodity memory market, there is a major 100% British-owned manufacturer of high performance and custom-integrated circuits. Industrial leadership depends crucially on scientific and technological leadership. Discussing UK policy, Professor Humphreys commented:

> Each materials age brings survival benefits. The survival benefits (e.g. improved instruments for farming and fighting) resulting from the Stone, Bronze and Iron Ages are clear. The UK was in the forefront of the Steel Age, and as a consequence derived great benefit from the industrial revolution. This benefit was long-lasting...[2]

Of course, there are other contributing factors, but the historical contribution of science and technology to human prosperity has been very great.

Information and communication technologies can be expected to make substantial changes to the way people relate at work. Professor Shoshana Zuboff has coined a new word to describe how new technologies 'informate' as well as automate; whereas earlier mechanical technologies decreased the complexity of tasks, the information technologies can increase the intellectual content of work at all levels:

> Work comes to depend on an ability to understand, respond to, manage and create value from the information. Thus, efficient operations in the informated workplace require a more equitable distribution of knowledge and authority. The transformation of information into wealth means that more members of the firm must be given opportunities to know more and do more.
>
> To avail themselves of the opportunities, firms must be prepared to drive a stake into the heart of the old division of labor (and the division of love sustaining it). Exploiting the informated environment means opening the information base of the organization to members at every level, assuring that each has the knowledge,

skills and authority to engage with the information productively. This revamped social contract would redefine who people are at work, what they can know and what they can do.[3]

The communications revolution

Central to any relationship is communication, and therefore the impact of science and engineering on human relationships can be seen in particularly sharp focus in information and communication technology (ICT). ICT has great potential to enhance relationships, but there are also dangers. As always, the answer to abuse is not fear and disuse, but discipline and correct use. Some pointers can be identified which may be relevant in public policy to promote the latter.

The advantage that good information gives in business has long been recognised. One of the key factors in the rise of the Rothschild Bank in the eighteenth century was the great attention paid to obtaining accurate and detailed information by the fastest possible route:

> It was a vital lesson ... that information creates wealth ... when [they] set about building up financial operations on an international scale their success owed everything to their incomparable courier service. They prospered because they received before their rivals news of market trends, commodity prices and major political events.[4]

Lord Liverpool first heard of the victory of Waterloo from N.M. Rothschild, though he initially refused to believe what was contrary to his official information. The value of military intelligence is well known, it has been estimated that the appalling failure of information services led to huge suffering in the Second Boer War at the turn of the century.[5]

Developments in ICT are taking place at a faster rate than in any other branch of engineering. Although there have been increases in participation, there has been no increase in the speed of passenger air travel since Concorde, car transport over the same period has been restricted by national speed limits, and yet personal computer power has increased by orders of magnitude within the past ten years. Politicians have waxed eloquent about the possibilities. US Vice-President Al Gore was responsible for popularising the term 'information superhighway' in his election campaign. He wrote of the benefits:

> The linking of the world's people to a vast exchange of information and ideas is a dream that technology is set to deliver ... It will bring economic progress, strong democracies, better environmental management, improved health care and a greater sense of shared stewardship of our small planet.[6]

Much is made of the new and more truly egalitarian world which the Internet, in particular, opens up, where communication and information exchange can take place unhindered by inhibitions of race, class, accent, gender or handicap, or indeed any reservations about pornography. There is parity in participation, all contact is consensual, and geographical location is irrelevant. This assumes, of course, equality of access. The growing inequalities which are, in fact, developing suggest that there may also be other consequences:

> The technological revolution in microelectronics, computers and telecommunication systems has received a great deal of attention over the past two decades. These technologies open opportunities for fundamental changes in information and communication processes. The implications of these changing processes have received far less attention. Yet the consequences for society may be greater because of the close link between information and communication processes and the structure of economic and social institutions.[7]

This is especially true of the enormous growth in the use of interactive communications technologies:

> The routines of everyday life are altered, for instance, when we no longer have to rely on face-to-face relationships in order to communicate. Our social relations become stretched over time and space, connected by tissues of TV signals and fibre-optics cables. More and more, we do things at a distance.[8]

In so far as cyberspace has erased space, it raises questions about the role of space and time in human relationships. David Lyon argues that the accelerating growth of virtual or tertiary 'social' relationships is directly related to a segmenting of primary relations into discrete areas of life. He sees this as both a symptom and a spur to a postmodern world view, where reality is not a unity but a series of fragmented images, where there is no knowledge or truth but only information and 'facts'.[9]

What is beyond doubt is that science and technology will continue to challenge the way we conduct business, academic, social and political relations. If we are to reap the benefits of a more open information society, then we will have to give greater attention to these broader questions of a social and cultural dimension.

The ubiquitous television

Perhaps the most ubiquitous item of ICT in British households is television. Almost every home has a set; by 1991, 46% had more than one. Domestic use has been summarized thus: television is intensely but unevenly used – often constantly on, it is not always watched intensely; it is watched in different ways and at different times by men and women (respectively uninterruptable and constantly interrupted, unless alone); it is the focus of domestic politics, as control over its use follows the political structure of the family (a structure based on both age and gender); it imposes, through its scheduling, a routine for at least certain parts of the household's day, though this is being broken down with certain kinds of narrowcasting; although it has traditionally been the site of whatever domestic togetherness a particular household could manage to generate, this too is changing with multiple televisions; the content of television is still the focus of parental anxiety; television, in its broadcast form, provides an important focus for the expression of national and cultural identities; the consumers of television are subject to heavy persuasion that what they want is more choice (and therefore cable and satellite), yet most of them are quite happy with what they currently have (or cannot imagine being more happy with what they often see as 'more of the same').[10]

The video recorder has done less than might be thought to alter this.[11] It may be used for time-shifting in families with young children or in households of committed television-watchers, but usually, only one member of the household (either the father or a young child) knows how to program it. Local video outlets may determine other uses, which can include repeat viewing of favourite movies by young children or adolescents; 66% of US households rent at least one video per month, while only 22% of Europeans do.[12] Massive investment is going into the future of television broadcasting, and it is certain that large fortunes are there to be won or lost by the media empires:

> The real uncertainties, as ever, relate to issues of control, content and consumption. In short, we can ask how this new media and information environment is to be controlled and regulated, and by whom; we can ask whether such a radical enhancement in the number of delivery channels (500 and more cable channels are being talked about in the US) can possibly be supported; and we can ask does anybody really want or need any of it?[13]

Watching television is essentially a one-way activity. Its contribution to two-way relationships lies, therefore, in its capacity to provide shared experiences – rather as literature can – on the basis of which, common ground can subsequently be established between people ('Did you see . . . ?'). There is a risk that this benefit will be diminished by individual watching patterns and a growing diversity of channels. Many communication technologies are explicitly interactive, providing two-way communication between individuals, with potential for both good and harm.

Beyond the telephone

In the home, the longest-established item of interactive ICT is the telephone. In most homes, it remains unpersonalised (few homes have a different line for each member of the family). It requires privacy in use, yet is often in shared space. It self-evidently plays a key role in developing and maintaining relationships, yet neither incoming nor outgoing calls are always welcome or without frustration or anxiety (the former because of disturbance, the latter because of cost, especially when made by a member of the family who does not pay the bill). Its presence has not always been welcomed. I am told that my grandfather resisted the installation of a telephone in his home and was only eventually persuaded to install one when my teenage aunt pleaded that without one, her social life would suffer irreparably. The upshot was that the telephone was installed in the children's nursery. Since my grandfather generally worked at home, this meant that he suffered the indignity of an expedition from his study to the nursery when he eventually discovered the usefulness of the telephone for making and receiving calls.

The telephone has been described as malleable in its social effects.[14] By and large, the benefits (such as enabling families to keep in touch) far outweigh problems that demand regulation and intervention (such as abusive calls). Much heat has been generated in the debate about caller identification. You may not mind your mother seeing your number identifying an incoming call, but would a woman wish each man she speaks to at a department store to have a record of her number? The issue has raised fundamental questions about the right to privacy, though in fact, both anonymity before caller identification became available and the subsequent loss of anonymity came about for technical reasons that had nothing to do with individual rights. In the UK, every call can be made anonymous by dialling a prefix code to suppress caller identification, though presumably, there are circumstances where this itself could raise suspicions. One of the main uses of numbers revealed by caller identification will be not for malicious or obscene calls, but for commercial use in targeting marketing more accurately. Already in the USA, solicitation by telephone has become a major social nuisance. Some households do not answer the telephone in the early evening on the assumption that it will be a telemarketing call.

The availability of the telephone network has made possible the spread of fax as a means of written communication. The first patent for a fax machine was filed in 1863 by Alexander Bain.[15] Much fax traffic is of a commercial and administrative nature, though even this affects human relationships. Lawyers now claim to be under stress due to the more rapid transmission of documents by fax and the consequent need to respond instantly. Fax can play a major role in human relationships too. I have a cousin who proposed to the woman who is now his wife by fax. He suffered while he was an engineering undergraduate from a disease which left him paralysed except for limited use of one hand, and eventually without speech, so that a keyboard provides his primary means of communication. He and his wife now run a firm which produces communication aids for the disabled, with a multi-million-pound turnover and a Queen's Award to Industry for 1995.

For those who use electronic mail (e-mail), fax seems a quaint technology from the 1980s. The choice between fax and e-mail appears not to be determined by any intrinsic merit of either technology, but rather by the infrastructure which is available to a community. Businesses have access to telephone lines, an infrastructure which was installed for the quite different purpose of voice communication. When fax machines became available which could make use of this infrastructure, they could be adopted at the relatively modest cost of the hardware and an additional line. Most academics have access to local, national and international computer networks. Again, these may have been installed for other purposes, but they have proved invaluable for exchanging messages. In my own experience, e-mail provides high-quality communication between individuals, and in many cases greatly enhances the quality of working relationships. Contrary to popular belief, it does not seem to have the effect of reducing face-to-face contact. Rather, like traditional letter-writing, it enables communication to be maintained when face-to-face contact is not possible, and thus promotes enhanced relationships when it is.

The first reliable accounts of the coup against Mikhail Gorbachev in Moscow in 1991 were e-mailed around the world by Anatoly Voronov, Director of Glasnet. Using Glasnet, which he set up to provide networked information services across the Soviet Republics, he continued to distribute a daily newspaper, *Glasnet-info*, worldwide, giving an independent account of life in Moscow during the dramatic political events.[16] The Association for Progressive Communications provides support for the use of e-mail in support of peace, human rights and environmental protection.[17] Electronic mail is transmitted via the Internet, a rapidly-growing facility for worldwide exchange of every conceivable kind of information.

The infamous Internet

The Internet began life in the early 1970s as an American military defence against nuclear war. The idea was that a diffuse, non-centralised network would be harder to knock out than a single, centralised computer. People then took advantage of the network to send each other messages. Because the network is so diffuse, no one owns it or regulates it. It consists now of a vast number of individual host computers, all interconnected. In 1994, the Internet had an estimated 4 million host computers, with the number approximately doubling annually. Nobody knows how many people are connected. The Internet has become as difficult to control as the air we breathe. The Internet includes the World Wide Web, an arrangement that enables users to set up 'home pages' which can be consulted by any Internet user. More than 8,000 companies had their own home pages in 1995,[18] and the number of other home pages, catering for every interest and none, is growing almost too fast to keep count. Last year, I received a Christmas card which, instead of the usual family newsletter, referred us to the family's personal World Wide Web home page, where we could find up-to-date news and photographs. The Internet provides a superb facility for the availability of information with a huge saving of postage and rainforests, and vastly enhanced access. Much of the key administrative information about university departments and colleges at Oxford is now provided eletronically; it is constantly updated and instantly available within the university and throughout the world. This kind of use of the Internet is well established within academic and research communities and is becoming increasingly so in the world of commerce. All these uses seem to be positive, and yet the Internet often receives bad press. What is the downside?

Concerns about abuse of the Internet include libel, fraud, pornography, and even paedophiles trolling on-line, encouraging children to leave home. Defamation on the Internet is now seen as the next growth area of litigation. Regulation of activities on the Internet is proving elusive. Traditional legislation would regard the distributor as responsible for what is distributed, but this is inappropriate for the Internet. Nor is it a simple matter to control the perpetrators; the Internet is international, and they may be in a country over which there is no effective legislative control. Abuses are causing concern, especially as increasing numbers of schools become connected to the Internet.

Two different approaches are being pursued by policy-makers to tackle this problem. In the US congress, Senator James Exon put down an amendment to the Telecommunications Bill which would have criminalized the creation or solicitation of any indecent material on-line. One response has been that technology exists which can enable parents to determine which parts of the World Wide Web will be allowed access from a given computer, thus shifting responsibility for selection from the State to the individual family: this assumes that all adults are more ICT-fluent than the children for whom they are responsible!

There is little incentive for the companies, such as CompuServe, who run the networks to censor the material distributed by their subscribers, because the more they act as editors, the more likely they are to be served with libel actions. In Britain, a first attempt is being made to regulate e-mail. The

Defamation (Responsibility for Publication) Bill will make the originators of e-mail messages, rather than the service providers, responsible for ensuring they are not being libellous.

Because of its enormous usefulness, the Internet is vulnerable to other impediments to its effectiveness. Distribution and alteration of documents require only a few keystrokes, and there is potential for junk information that could make the present problems of junk paper mail and telemarketing appear trivial:

> As the Internet develops, users could quickly find that: they are faced with huge quantities of junk electronic information they cannot even afford the time to scan; they no longer trust the documents they receive, especially as they see the same spurious information being rapidly recycled and fed back as true; they could lose all feel for who has seen their material and whether comment being offered is valid or not.[19]

The Internet has also provided the means for whole new kinds of human interaction which scarcely existed before. The virtual communities of the Internet consist of people who join because of a common interest, regardless of any accident of their geographical location, and without needing to reveal anything about their gender or racial origin. Participants send messages to the community, and in turn, others respond to these with replies which reach all participants, creating self-perpetuating discussion and interaction:

> On the Internet, human interactions are no longer cluttered with the trivia of our local and bodily identities. Formed not on the worn and crowded terrain of the earth but in the bodiless ether of cyberspace, virtual communities satisfy human needs for communication and belonging without imposing any of the traditional constraints, duties and responsibilities. Virtual community is community at zero cost.[20]

Alas, community at zero cost is also community at zero commitment. There is no need to shoulder the burden of supporting the weak or helping those who are going through a difficult time. A healthy local community is alert to the sickness or absence of a member, but no one will respond to a member of a virtual community who fails to log on.

The most bizarre development is the discussion of 'self' discovery through ICT. Optimism has been expressed about the computer as a 'second self':[21]

> Lastly, then, consider the virtual self. Once again nothing is straightforward, because the self is both central and fragmented. Cybernaughts recognise that identity is in question on-line. One says that 'we who populate cyberspaces deliberately experiment with fracturing traditional notions of identity by living as multiple simultaneous personae in different virtual neighbourhoods'.[22]

There must be implications for relationships in such attitudes. Interaction over the Internet is not a substitute for human relationships (as in computer games) nor for active response (as in television); rather, it has been described as:

> a manifestation of and channel for a broad cultural movement in which all authority is doubted, all hierarchy dismantled and all knowledge reduced to flows of power ... the danger is that whole categories such as 'wisdom' or 'truth' might disappear in the deluge of data and so-called information.[23]

Into the next millennium

There is every expectation that over the next 10–20 years, there will be a major growth in the development and application of communications technology and services. In 1990, they accounted for about 5.6% of the UK Gross Domestic Product. The working assumptions of the recent Foresight Technology Panel were:

- within 10 years it will be normal for commercial transactions other than the delivery of goods to take place over electronic networks (handling an electronic requisition costs only one-tenth of its paper equivalent);[24]
- within 15 years, it will be commonplace for interactive multi-media services to be used from the home for entertainment, shopping and education;
- within 20 years, the majority of these services will be in use from personal mobile units (cellnet phones).[25]

Key recommendations of the Communications Foresight Panel include a substantial increase in the resources devoted to RTD (research and technological development) in ICT, evolution of the UK regulatory regime to maximise benefits, clear technological objectives, dismantling of international barriers to trade, the setting up of at least two virtual centres of excellence, leadership by example from the government in ICT, and:

> By 1998, every school should be connected to public broadband digital networks giving access to high quality interactive educational software, including video-on-demand. The provision of hardware, software and infrastructure should be a Millennium Project.[26]

The educational potential of the information superhighway into the next century is unprecedented. The use of fibre-optic cable transmission dramatically increases both the speed and volume of data which can be carried, including video and audio as well as text. The UK government has expressed a willingness to support the wider use of ICT in schools by funding a study of several new pilot projects in both primary and secondary schools and agreeing to help buy equipment for certain schools, especially in rural areas less likely to be cabled.[27] New models of learning and a 'new literacy' are needed to equip the next generation of computer-dependent workers. If public institutions like schools are to be connected, then so should libraries, hospitals, GPs' surgeries, etc.

Many commentators have recognised that these developments will raise key questions regarding their impact on the quality of life. The description of communication technologies as 'malleable' arose in the context of their social implications. Issues that may be identified include: (1) control and regulation, (2) access and (3) choice.

Control and regulation

If the government, through data protection legislation, has accepted the need to regulate the way information is kept about individuals on databases, it will be forced to consider new methods to set standards or guidelines for the use of the Internet and e-mail. Although the issue of protecting against libel, fraud and pornography dominates public concerns, the business community is very keen to see greater confidentiality and restricted access and secure money transfer mechanisms built into information systems. The academic world uses the superhighway primarily for non-confidential material. As the number of networks proliferate, the Internet's lack of indexing becomes inhibiting: for example, there is no way of distinguishing between the sources of information, whether material emanates from a highly organised and respected institution or a lone fanatic. Issues of control must now be handled at a global level, because the Internet and satellite broadcasting know no national borders.

Access

Although the cost per byte of ICT power is dropping steadily, the increase in the quantity of information may yet lead to a growing divide between the ICT haves and have-nots. Surveys are already highlighting the 'pale, male' dominance of the information superhighway; 73% of all IT training is given to the 16–24 age group, and all training declines with age.[28] Increasingly, as job status becomes linked to computer literacy, older, female and non-English-speaking applicants will find themselves ranked as less skilled. The keys to increasing access are lower costs of connection and equipment, combined with education and training in IT skills. The government, the IT industry, employers and schools all have a part to play.

Choice

ICT will become increasingly user-selected rather than broadcaster-determined. This encourages a highly competitive global market in systems and software which should maintain the trend in reduced costs. Yet governments, as well as the industry, have a responsibility to preserve, on all our behalfs, the key values of universal service and public interest:

> Policy makers must eschew technological imperatives and moderate industrial ones if they are to devise policies which take these social dimensions of technological change into account. At their core, these social dimensions must focus on the issues of universal service and public interest. For, while media change in an increasingly market-led world will almost certainly offer greater choice, it will be choice at a price and only for those who can afford it. The quality of life in our society is threatened by these inequalities as much – indeed more than – any threat that an unregulated video market, for example, might provide.[29]

New technologies can both create and replace jobs; changing employment cannot be left to market forces alone, it must be prepared for by planned education and training.

Quality of life

The UK government has acknowledged the need to parallel scientific development with a renewed grasp of responsibility for ensuring that broader questions of social enhancement are addressed. A White Paper entitled *Realising our potential* set out the policy on science, engineering and technology.[30] This paper signalled various key changes. Previously, after the amount of money available for research had been determined by Parliament, the distribution of the funds through the research councils was decided in principle by members of the academic community themselves, through representatives appointed to administer peer review systems. Under the new proposals, the research councils operate under the direction of the Department of Trade and Industry. The seven research councils have new, explicit mission statements, which differ in detail but which commonly include the overall objective of 'enhancing the United Kingdom's industrial competitiveness and quality of life'. The Particle Physics and Astronomy Research Council (PPARC) alone has this as a subsidiary aim to that of the improved understanding of the concepts and principles underlying physical phenomena and their consequences.

In its response to these proposals, the Council of the Royal Society commented:

> The scientific community fully recognizes that its activities, funded by public money, should serve publicly-determined objectives. We therefore welcome the fact that the White Paper gives a clear statement about these objectives, and have no quarrel with the statement that science should serve 'above all the generation of national prosperity and the improvement of the quality of life'. The difficulties arise when we examine how these objectives are to be delivered. This is partly because of the way individual scientists are motivated at the day-to-day level, and partly because of the way in which scientific research actually contributes to national prosperity and the quality of life. In each case key ingredients are intellectual curiosity and scope for unexpected findings. In the final stages of a development project, major surprises are a problem: in basic research, they are an exciting opportunity. If the White Paper turns out in practice to be saying that basic research should be managed like industrial development, the outcome will not be 'relevant' basic research but second-rate basic research. This would do nothing for national prosperity or quality of life.[31]

If the government's policy is somewhat fuzzy about how the objectives are to be delivered and unwilling to admit the potential for conflict between these two goals, it is utterly obscure on what is meant by the second objective, 'improvement of the quality of life'. One view is that this was meant to embrace the cultural aspect of scientific endeavour, so that increased understanding of the nature of the world in which we live was not excluded from the aims of research, though if that was indeed what was meant, it was expressed more clearly in the aims of the PPARC. A contribution to quality of life might include improved materials for sports equipment, but this would also presumably contribute to the competitiveness of sports equipment manufacturers, not to mention players. Similarly, improvements in transport technology would contribute to competitiveness as well as quality of life.

In reports from a Technology Foresight exercise which followed from the White Paper, the most explicit statements which might refer solely to the quality of life objective have related to the needs of the disabled. The question of what is meant by 'contribution to quality of life' is under discussion in the research councils, and it is to be hoped that they will be willing to make definitions that are not open to ambiguity or doubt; this may require policy choices to be made. It will be interesting to see to what extent a 'quality of life' audit on the results of particular areas of research becomes feasible. If it is accepted that part of the mission of the research councils is to fund research that will enhance the quality of life, then it would seem appropriate to include the impact on human relationships.

Conclusion

Concerns about control, access and choice, about the social dimensions as well as the economic benefits of technological change are leading to a growing awareness of the importance of public debate and public policy on the social impact of ICT.[32] The impact of science and engineering on human relationships has here been illustrated for the case of ICT, because the connections are particularly easy to see. The same kind of reasoning can be applied to other areas of science and technology in which the connection may be less direct but no less significant.

There is an inevitability about technological developments in our days which it would be as futile to try to resist as for King Canute to try to stop the tide coming in. Even if it were possible, that would not be desirable, because rightly used, technology has the capacity to enhance relationships. There is no place, at least in educated debate, for the view that technology is intrinsically against relationships, or even that, on balance, science and technology have done more to harm relationships than to build them up. Text-linking facilities, video conferencing and data analysis need not reduce human interaction or create more superficial relationships. Indeed, technologies enable us to maintain contact with friends across the world, to pursue our areas of specialism with other like minds, and to exchange news and views with others without leaving our chair. So, far from being a substitute for face-to-face contact, information and communication technologies often enhance it.

The rapidity of change calls for careful planning and public policy. In areas as fundamental as communications, information-control, employment, education and training, developments cannot be left to market forces alone. Public policy has a significant role to play in setting guidelines and defining the boundaries of acceptable usage; it has a responsibility to promote universal service and public interest, to invest in education and training and to sponsor research. Any useful policy for the effect of science and technology on relationships should at least:

- consider explicitly the impact of science and technology on human relationships;
- live up to the promise to give weight to contribution to quality of life as well as to UK competitiveness in priorities in research and technological development;
- regulate, using both legislation and technology, abuse of information and communication technologies, to the extent permitted and demanded by the highest commonly accepted standards;
- invest in research and education to equip individuals to cope with and benefit from the social effects of technological changes which they will encounter in their lifetime.

The UK government has given the scientific community a clear mandate to contribute to an enhancement of the quality of life. The response must be to engage in education and research which recognises both commercial applications and social implications. Only then can we ensure that the advances made possible through science and engineering are a blessing and not a curse.

Acknowledgement

I wish to express my thanks for discussions and comments on an early draft to Professor Tony Hoare, Mr Alex Reid, Professor David Lyon, Miss Nicola Baker, Professor Richard Brook and Drs James and Cathy Pain.

References

1. Mulgan, G. (1994) 'Liberation technology?', *Demos Quarterly*, No.4.
2. Humphreys, C.J. (1992) 'Can there be a materials policy in the UK?', Briggs, A. (ed.) *The Science of New Materials*, Blackwell, pp.177–93.
3. Zuboff, S. (1995) 'The Emperor's New Workplace', *Scientific American*, September, pp.162–4.
4. Wilson, D. (1994) *Rothschild*, Deutsch, p.11.
5. Kruger, R. (1959) *Goodbye Dolly Grey*, Pan Books.
6. Quoted in Wilkinson, M. (1995) 'Forget Internet and get a life', *The Financial Times*, 24 September.
7. Melody, W.H. (1988) *The Changing Role of Public Policy in the Information Economy*, PICT Policy Research Paper No. 0, p.2.
8. Lyon, D. (1994) *Postmodernity*, Open University Press, p.21.
9. Ibid.
10. Silverstone, R. (1991) *Beneath the Bottom Line: Households and Information and Communication Technologies in an Age of the Consumer*, PICT Policy Research Paper No.17, pp.16–17.
11. Ibid.
12. *The Guardian*, 26 October 1994.
13. Silverstone, R. (1994) *Future Imperfect: Media, Information and the Millennium*, PICT Policy Research Paper No.27, p.6.
14. Dutton, W.H. (1992) 'The social impact of emerging telephone services', *Telecommunications Policy*, July, pp.377–88.
15. Gomersall, A. (1994) 'Early fax facts', *The Times*, 29 September.
16. Sansom, C. and Baker, A. (1994) 'Liberation technology', *Third Way*, October, pp.18–21.
17. Ibid.
18. Sandberg, J. (1995) 'Regulators try to tame the untamable on-line world', *The Wall Street Journal*, 30 June.
19. OST (1995) *Technology Foresight*, No.8, HMSO, p.44.
20. Gray, J. (1995) 'The sad side of cyberspace', *The Guardian*, 10 April.
21. Lyon, D. (1986) *The Silicon Society*, Lion, p.88.

22 Lyon, D. (1994) 'Hazard warning', *Third Way*, October, pp.22–5.
23 Ibid.
24 *Europe and the Global Information Society. Recommendations to the European Council* (the Bangemann Commission) (1994), European Commission.
25 OST (1995) *Technology Foresight*, No.6, HMSO, p.41.
26 Ibid.
27 Department of Education (1995) *Superhighways for Education: The Way Forward*, HMSO.
28 MORI (1995) *Prepared for the Future? The British and Technology*, quoted in 'Interface', *The Times*, 1 November.
29 Silverstone (1994), op. cit.
30 Chancellor of the Duchy of Lancaster (1993) *Realising our potential: A strategy for science, engineering and technology*, Cm 2250, HMSO.
31 Comment on *Realising our potential*, Supplement to *Royal Society News*, October 1993, p.i.
32 Melody, op. cit.

13 Fiscal and welfare policy: Why families lose out

Gabrielle Cox

> My home life is so difficult because it was disrupted by poverty. My father was unable to work because of illness and he received invalidity benefit, which was not enough to support a family of five on. So my mother got a Saturday job as well as her weekly job. This situation put a great strain on their marriage and finally they divorced.[1]

In the past, both fiscal and welfare policies were seen to have a significant redistributive function: through taxation and social insurance, income could be transferred between individuals and spread across the lifecycle. Over the last 15 years, those principles have been eroded. Fiscal policies have shifted from progressive to regressive forms of taxation, and welfare policies have moved from social insurance and universality principles towards means-testing and targeting. This has happened at the very time that radical changes in employment have led to an increased need for redistribution.

Relationships are not just about what happens within individual household units or how individuals interact with each other. Social relationships are also important, and in many instances, the quality of our social relationships feeds through into the quality of more personal relationships. This chapter will examine the way in which the relationship of care which society should have towards individuals and families has been eroded.

In particular, it will examine three ways in which family life has been affected by an erosion of commitment to social relationships:

1 The cumulative effect of current changes to the tax and benefit systems, particularly within the context of a radically altered employment structure, has been a shift of income from the poorest to the richest, and a massive rise in poverty, particularly for families with children. Thus, for example:

184   *Building a Relational Society*

    (a) the burden of taxation has moved away from direct to indirect taxes, with the poorest in society having to pay an increasing amount in tax while the rich have received tax cuts;
    (b) families with children have seen an increase in the proportion of their income going in direct tax, mainly as a result of the freezing of Child Benefit;
    (c) social security 'reforms' have reduced the value of benefits and excluded young people altogether;
    (d) the benefits system imposes a punitive rate of 'clawback', so that people on means-tested benefits are caught in a poverty trap.

2   The combination of fiscal and welfare changes with trends in employment has led to a polarisation between work-rich and work-poor families. In a family with one person unemployed, there is often no financial benefit for other members of the family to work, unless a job can be found which pays above benefit level altogether.

3   The roles of women and men within households have been changing, for example:

    (a) the shift of employment away from male work means that increasing numbers of men are no longer breadwinners; sometimes this role has been taken by women;
    (b) many young men cannot contemplate marriage and setting up a family because they have no employment prospects;
    (c) because families increasingly survive only by having two parents working, roles within families are either forced to change (to more equal sharing of tasks) or stress is placed upon relationships.

The impact of employment changes

The traditional notion of employment is that men work full-time for a reasonable wage, often in the same firm or the same kind of occupation for a lifetime, with entitlements to holidays, sick pay and pensions, while women have much more varied working patterns, sometimes working full-time, sometimes part-time, and sometimes staying at home to care for dependants, and with lower pay, expectations and entitlements. This traditional notion of employment fits with the traditional notion of the nuclear family, which has father as the main breadwinner and mother as nurturer and possibly provider of extra (but not necessarily essential) income.

However, changes in employment have meant that these traditional notions are increasingly out of step with reality. Between March 1979 and December 1994, male full-time employment fell by nearly a quarter, and there has been a general shift from male to female and from full-time to part-time work, which is largely accounted for by the decline in manufacturing jobs and the rise in service sector jobs.[2] Men and women are now represented equally within the workforce, and 3 out of 10 jobs are part-time, compared with only 2 out of 10 in 1979. The government estimated that by 1993, only 52.2% of men of working age were in full-time employment, compared with 73% in 1979 and 77.2% in 1973.[3]

While the total number of employees in employment, particularly full-time permanent employment, has declined markedly, there has been a significant rise in 'flexible' and 'atypical' work. Temporary work has grown sharply,[4] as has self-employment.[5] This increase in 'flexible' work has meant more job insecurity for many households.

The changes in employment have also had significant consequences for incomes. Many households which used to have their main income from a male full-time earner will now have no earnings, or will have some combination of female and/or part-time earnings. The whole earnings profile has shifted towards lower pay, since average weekly earnings of full-time women workers are over £100 a week less than those of full-time men and represent only 72% of men's average earnings, while average weekly earnings of male part-time workers are only 31.9% and women part-time workers only 27.3% of male full-time earnings.[6] (In fact, since the earnings figures only cover about 60% of part-time workers – those who earn enough to pay tax – the pay of part-time workers is likely to be, on average, considerably lower, and the impact of the shift to part-time work on incomes even greater.)

Nor does self-employment imply a good income. There is increasing concern about the high proportion of self-employed people who appear in the lowest decile of income. There were about 770,000 self-employed people who did not earn enough in 1993–4 to pay income tax (this is 24% of all self-employed at March 1994). Of these, 670,000 (21% of the total) had gross income of under £5,000.[7]

Economic security does not guarantee stable relationships, and insecurity and poverty do not necessarily lead to relationship break-up. None the less, there is little doubt that the problems of unemployment, low income and an uncertain future often place enormous stress on individuals and their families. In a situation where changing employment patterns have exposed more people to poverty either through unemployment or access only to part-time employment, it would be expected that a central element of fiscal and welfare policy would be to mitigate these effects, to ensure an element of redistribution in support of those suffering from economic change, and to give families as much opportunity as possible to participate in such work as is available.

Fiscal policy

One of the key features of recent fiscal policy has been the shift from taxes on income to taxes on expenditure. Thus, there have been cuts in both basic and upper rates of income tax, but rises in VAT rates and extensions of VAT liability.[8] Taxes on expenditure are regressive and have a much greater impact on poor households than on better-off households. The issue of the extension of VAT to domestic fuel, which was widely unpopular just because it was seen to be unfair to the poorest in society, illustrates this point extremely well. Table 13.1 shows how much families on different earnings spend per week on fuel, and how much extra they would have to pay with VAT at 8% on fuel.

Table 13.1   Proportion of household income spent on fuel

Married couple with two children	Spending on fuel	8% VAT
50% average earnings	£13.40	£1.07
Average earnings	£11.70	£0.94
150% average earnings	£13.20	£1.06

Source: Hansard, 26 February 1993, col. 767.

These government figures for spending on domestic fuel show that not only do poorer families spend a higher proportion of their income on fuel, but they actually spend more in money terms.[9] So, although those on half average earnings would have only a third of the income of those on one-and-a-half average earnings, they would actually be paying more tax.

The outcome of the VAT on fuel debate is instructive in relation to the kind of priorities which have underpinned fiscal and welfare policy throughout the 1980s and 1990s. Thus, when public outcry forced the government to introduce a compensation package, it was specifically aimed at pensioners, with virtually no help for families.

There is little doubt that pensioners needed that support, and the compensation package still fell short, on average, by 24p per week for single pensioners and 70p per week for pensioner couples. Non-pensioners on benefits, however, only received an advance Retail Price Index uprating of 0.4% on their benefit. The average unemployed household (comprising 2.8 people, of whom one was a child) would be paying £1.00 extra a week for VAT on fuel but would get only 37p extra in benefit.[10]

These figures underscore the relative lack of priority which has been given to families with children, although it is arguable that the needs of children for adequate warmth are equal to those of pensioners.

The regressive nature of indirect taxes can be seen from government figures for how much of their income different families will pay in tax in 1995/96.[11] Table 13.2 shows clearly how a family on 75% average earnings pay more of their income in indirect tax than a family with twice as much money, while the situation is reversed for direct tax.

Table 13.2 Proportion of household income taken in taxes

Married couple with two children	Indirect tax	Direct tax
75% average earnings	13.5%	18.4%
Average earnings	13.0%	22.5%
150% average earnings	12.8%	25.5%

Source: Hansard, 19 December 1994, cols 947–8.

The progressive nature of direct taxation has also been blunted by the cutting of top rates of tax, giving extra money to the richest, while on different occasions the freezing of tax allowances and the restriction of certain allowances to 15% have brought thousands more low-paid workers into tax liability. National Insurance contributions for workers rose from 6.75% in 1980 to 10% in 1994, but the impact of this was less for higher-paid workers, since NI contributions are not paid on earnings above £440 (1995 levels).

The burden of taxation has swung away from the richest onto the poorest, but it has also affected households with children more than those without, as Table 13.3 shows.[12]

Table 13.3 Proportion of income paid in taxes

Average earnings	Proportion of income paid in income tax and NI		
	1978–9	1994–5	Change
Single person	31.5%	28.6%	–2.9%
Married couples:			
One earner, no children	27.8%	26.8%	–1.0%
One earner, two children	20.9%	21.9%	+1.0%

Source: Hansard, 28 April 1994, cols 257–60.

Thus, at a time when cuts in direct taxation have been a widely-publicised feature of government policy, there have been rises in the proportion of income paid in direct tax by households with children, in contrast to the falls enjoyed by those without children.[13]

The reason for this differing tax experience is because Child Benefit is counted as a negative income tax in the above figures. The freezing of Child Benefit for part of the 1980s contributed to a rising proportion of family income going in tax. Indeed, the whole notion of general support for families with children from the tax system has been under threat.

The integration of child tax allowances and family allowances into Child Benefit at the end of the 1970s was undoubtedly a useful step, since it increased the support given to families who did not earn enough to pay tax, and it also gave income directly into the hands of mothers. With the notion of 'benefit', however, has come a shift of emphasis. No longer is it assumed that all families with children should receive recognition of and support for the cost of bringing up children. Instead, the concept of universal 'benefit' has been under attack on the grounds that it is not needed by the rich. It has been argued that this benefit should be taken away from the rich and targeted on the poor. This seems a not unreasonable notion until it is realised that even at 1995 levels, Child Benefit only produces £540 per year for the eldest child and £439 for subsequent children. Against such small figures needs to be set the fact that in 1995–6, those on incomes over £80,000 a year will pay £16,800 per year less in tax and NI than they would have under the 1987–8 tax regime.[14]

Both the concept and the value of child support have been under attack. While the concept has managed to survive, the value has been eroded. At April 1993 prices, the value of child support (the combined value of Child Tax Allowance after clawback and Family Allowance/Child Benefit) was £10.36 in April 1979, fell to as little as £8.14 in 1990, and stood at £10.00 for the eldest child and £8.10 for subsequent children at April 1993.[15]

Benefit policy

While the erosion of Child Benefit has increased the direct tax burden on families with children, it has been argued that some aspects of benefit policy have been specifically aimed at improving the position of those with children.

A major change in benefits took place in 1988, when Supplementary Benefit was replaced by Income Support, and Family Income Supplement by Family Credit. Income Support was available to the unemployed and to those working for less than 24 hours a week (with the exception of 16 and 17 year-olds, who were given no right to claim Income Support). Family Credit was available to those working 24 or more hours a week who had dependent children. (The working hours threshold was later lowered to 16.)

Family Credit was publicised as a more generous benefit, which would avoid the poverty trap and encourage parents (particularly lone parents) back into work. Before Family Credit was introduced, it was possible for a family's income to go *down* when earnings went up. This was the poverty trap at its worst. The social security changes specifically aimed to remove this anomaly. But the changes also *reduced in total* the amount of money which a family would have at different levels of earnings, as Table 13.4 shows.[16]

Table 13.4   Weekly disposable income of a married couple with two children aged 4 and 6 at different earnings levels

Earnings (£)	Net weekly spending power (£)		
	Before April 1988*	After April 1988†	Change (£)
60	93.23	83.28	−9.95
70	94.68	83.65	−11.03
80	96.11	84.00	−12.11
90	96.06	84.39	−11.67
100	96.01	85.86	−10.15
110	93.34	87.18	−6.16
120	91.31	89.10	−2.21
130	93.11	91.02	−2.09
140	94.91	92.94	−1.97
150	96.11	96.11	—

Notes:
* Pre-April 1988 tax and benefit system, with April 1987 benefits rescaled to April 1988.
† Benefit system from April 1988, before tax changes.
Source: Hansard, 4 February 1988, cols 484–7.

As Table 13.4 demonstrates, before April 1988, a family with earnings of £80 a week would end up with more money than the same family with earnings anywhere between £90 and £140 a week. After April 1988, this would not happen, but the levels of benefits were reduced so that at all earnings levels up to £150, a family would have less money than before April 1988. At the time of the changes, families on the old, higher rates of benefit were given transitional protection at 1987–8 rates, ensuring that their income did not fall. But this meant there was no uprating of benefit until the new rates caught up with the old, so such families had no increase in real disposable income in 1988–9 nor for a period thereafter. It is clear, therefore, that Family Credit was not more generous to families, and the 1988 'uprating' represented a significant downgrading of support.

> **Box 13.1 Life on Family Credit**
>
> Paul and Janet had two children, and Paul worked for 30 hours a week, earning £80. They were able to claim Family Income Supplement, and this meant that after rent had been paid, they had £96.11 to spend.
>
> Paul's brother, Peter, was also married with two children of similar age, and lived on the same housing estate, paying the same rent. Paul told Peter about a job at his factory, and Peter too started work at £80 a week. Peter and his wife were very annoyed to find that because the government had changed the social security system, they were only going to get £84 a week after rent had been paid – over £12 a week less than Paul and Janet. They thought this was very unfair.
>
> Paul and Janet were pleased that the government had 'protected' their money, and that it was not going to fall, but they were less pleased when they realised that they were not going to get any cost of living increases for at least a year, and that their money would not go up until the difference between the new rate 'caught up' with the old rate through inflation.

Even though, after April 1988, no family's income fell as earnings rose, the system still creates a poverty trap, because it is almost impossible to get very much more money, even if earnings go up considerably. As Table 13.4 shows, under the post-April 1988 regime, a family with earnings of £70 a week was only 37p a week better off than a family with earnings of £60 a week, and earnings of £120 only brought in extra disposable income of £5.82.

While there are now no benefits which result in a marginal deduction rate of 100% or more, levels of clawback remain high. A family claiming Family Credit, Council Tax Benefit and Housing Benefit would have 97p clawed back out of every extra £1 earned. A worker claiming Income Support is allowed to keep £5 of earnings only, probably not enough to pay travel-to-work costs.[17]

There is little doubt that many families find this inability to work their way out of poverty a source of enormous stress. The extremely high levels of clawback on earnings mean that it is often not possible for a parent to say: 'By working harder I will be able to provide a better standard of living for my children.' It is frequently not possible to find a job which will take a family out of dependence on benefit. The old notion of parents (particularly men) as providers for the family becomes undermined.

It is true that Family Credit has enabled families with children to enter or continue to participate in the labour market, though the rewards for such participation are low. However, households without 'dependent' children are effectively excluded from the workforce unless they work for less than 16 hours a week or can find work which enables them to earn as much as they would get on benefit.

This distinction between households with and without 'dependent' children creates a number of anomalies, of which the most striking is the effect on family income of a child leaving school and thus no longer counting as 'dependent'. In 1988, the government excluded 16 and 17 year-olds from entitlement to Income Support (except in some extreme situations). The justification for this was that such young people would either be in education (in which case they still count as dependants for benefit purposes), or in work, or on a Youth Training scheme (YT), for which an allowance is paid. Indeed, the government offered a guarantee to provide all young people with a YT place if required. That guarantee has never been honoured. Latest figures show that at any one time, more than 100,000 16 and 17 year-olds have not been in employment, training or full-time education.[18]

Box 13.2 Family Credit and 'dependent' children

Carol and Philip have a son, James, who is 16 and still at school. On Income Support the family would get an income after housing costs of £102.51 a week, but Philip works 20 hours a week for gross earnings of £40 and is thus able to claim Family Credit. This gives the family an income after housing costs of £109.47 a week. This is £7 a week more than they would get on Income Support, but they have to pay for James's school meals, which would be free if they were on Income Support. James leaves school in the summer, and for a while things are all right, because Family Credit is given for 26 weeks at a time. However, when Philip puts in a new claim for Family Credit, he is horrified to find that James is no longer considered a dependant and the family cannot therefore claim Family Credit. Nor can they claim Income Support, because Philip works for more than 16 hours a week. The family's income falls to £37.89 a week. (Philip cannot give up his job and claim Income Support, because if he leaves his job voluntarily, he will be disqualified from benefit for up to 26 weeks.) Eventually, James gets a training place, so family income rises to £67.39, but this is still over £42 less than they got when James was at school.

Source: This case study is taken from a model using 1992 benefit levels, published in *Hansard*, 5 June 1992, cols 657–8.

These extraordinary figures show the severe impact on family income of the policy of refusing Income Support to 16 and 17 year-olds. James is no longer counted as a dependant, but he cannot claim benefit in his own right. Effectively, a 16 or 17 year-old ceases to exist for benefit purposes when s/he leaves school. Neither Income Support nor Family Credit are payable to the family for this child, and if s/he is the only remaining 'dependent' child, then the family loses family premium, if on Income Support, or loses all entitlement to Family Credit.

This particular benefit policy is widely accepted to be the cause of increased homelessness and destitution among young people. Particularly where relationships between teenagers and parents are already strained, the requirement to feed and clothe a child for whom there is no income places intolerable stresses on all concerned. In many cases teenagers walk out or are forced out. Even when they stay at home, the tensions caused by lack of money are likely to lead to greater pressure towards family break-up.

Dependence on means-tested benefits undermines a family's independence and removes its ability to control its own future. Yet dependence on means-tested benefits is an increasing feature of family life, due both to lack of employment which pays enough to support a family and to the erosion of social insurance benefits. (At least a quarter of the population are in households claiming means-tested benefits.)[19]

The importance of social insurance is that it gives people rights to income such as pensions, statutory sick pay and unemployment benefit. While some of these may not produce high levels of income, they give greater flexibility to families because they are not means-tested. If a man who becomes unemployed can claim Unemployment Benefit as of right, whether or not his wife is working, then she can continue in her job. Increasingly, however, the social insurance principle is being undermined.

The most obvious example of this is the new Jobseeker's Allowance (JSA), which is to replace Unemployment Benefit (UB). UB is currently available for 12 months, regardless of savings or other family income, if the unemployed person has paid the relevant NI contributions. From April 1996, the contributory benefit will only be available for six months, after which a claimant (and therefore his/her household) will be means-tested. This means many families will lose the independent income of women claimants, and others will face the situation where the woman may have to give up work because her earnings are below benefit levels. The JSA is also to be aligned with Income Support rates, meaning a loss of over £9 a week for those aged 18–24 (who currently get lower Income Support rates).[20] Since 18–24 year-olds are more likely still to be living at home than older claimants, this cut in income will not only affect them as individuals, but will affect the overall income available to their families.

Other examples of restricting social insurance payments include the freezing of higher-rate Statutory Sick Pay (SSP) and the raising of the threshold for higher-rate SSP, the proposed erosion of State Earnings-Related Pension

Scheme values from the year 2010, and the move from Invalidity to Incapacity Benefit, with more stringent eligibility requirements.

Not only are social insurance benefits being eroded, but increasingly, social insurance costs are not being paid out of the National Insurance fund, but are being moved onto employers. Thus, there has been a progressive shift of the cost of SSP onto employers, with even small employers having to pay the first four weeks of SSP. One consequence of this is that there is an even greater incentive for employers to create part-time jobs which pay below the National Insurance threshold, not merely to avoid paying employers' NI contributions, but also to avoid paying SSP. (This has significant fiscal effects, with less income to the government from employment, leading to increased concerns about the 'affordability' of social security, and thus attempts to cut back benefits.)[21]

The increase in jobs paying below the NI threshold means fewer employees have access to certain benefits as of right. Changes in benefit policies and in employment structures reinforce each other to produce an ever-increasing level of insecurity and lack of control for people in unemployment and in low-paid work. Indeed, this feeling of insecurity is frequently to be found in those who are still in secure, well-paid employment. It is hardly surprising that many families suffer from increased tension and discord.

One particular future benefit change likely to exacerbate insecurity in families is the proposal not to pay mortgage interest for the first nine months after a claimant becomes unemployed (for those who took out mortgages after October 1995). This means that many more families will face the possibility of losing their homes when unemployment strikes, and it will make it much more difficult for young people wanting to become first-time buyers to get onto the housing ladder in the first place (because of the extra costs of private insurance against unemployment, or the inability to get private insurance when in an insecure job). This is not a minor problem: currently, over half a million families rely on Income Support to pay their mortgage interest.[22]

The consequences for families

One major outcome of the complex inter-relationship of employment, fiscal and welfare policies has been a massive growth in poverty, particularly for families with children.

The number of families claiming Family Credit was 572,000 in July 1994, compared with only 78,000 claiming Family Income Supplement in March 1979.[23] 35.2% of all children now live in families which are dependent on either Family Credit or Income Support, compared with only 7.9% in 1979.[24]

A series of studies have demonstrated that Income Support rates are insufficient to provide an adequate diet, proper heating and other generally-accepted necessities.[25] Comparison of a household's income with what it would be entitled to on Income Support is not, therefore, an unreasonable indicator of whether it is in poverty. Using this benchmark, the group with the largest rise in poverty between 1989 and 1992 was families comprised of couples with children. In just three years, 876,000 more people in such families were drawn into poverty, a rise of 30.7%. Poverty in families of lone parents with children rose by 24.6%.[26]

Family poverty is often seen to be a problem which is associated with lone parenthood. It is true that children in families with one parent are still more likely to be living in poverty than children in families with two parents. But increasingly, children in two-parent families are being drawn into poverty. The country is being divided into work-rich and work-poor families, and this is a result of the interaction between employment and benefits.

In a family where the main earner loses employment and moves onto means-tested benefits, it often becomes financially disadvantageous for the second earner to stay in work (unless her/his income is actually sufficient to keep the family out of means-tested benefits altogether).[27] With massive losses of full-time male jobs, more and more families find themselves in this situation. Between 1975 and 1993, the proportion of two-adult households where both worked rose from 51% to 60%, but the proportion with no earner increased from 3% to 11%. The average amount of time a two-adult household could expect to have no earner rose from 18 months to 54 months.[28] In 1979, 82% of children were in households with one or more full-time workers, but by 1992-3, this had dropped to 69%.[29]

While in many instances the loss of full-time male employment makes it not worthwhile for either partner to work, in other cases, the role of breadwinner has shifted to women. Thus, for example, between April 1992 and April 1993, the number of Family Credit cases rose by 26.8%, but the number of cases of a couple where the woman was the main earner rose by 70.7%.[30]

Changes in the labour market, coupled with the effects of benefit policy, have combined to reduce significantly the role of men as breadwinners. In some cases the failure of a man to have full-time employment leads to other members of the family not finding it worthwhile to find or keep a job. In other cases, women have taken over the role of breadwinner. In such households 'traditional' relationships have changed. Growing equality between men and women should be welcomed, but undoubtedly, in many cases, the inability of men to provide for their families is felt by them to undermine their role and status (they become the 'unequal' partner), and leads to severe family stress, particularly when women take alternative views. Nearly half of fathers believe that 'a husband should be the breadwinner and the wife should look after the home and children', compared with less than 1 in 4 mothers.[31]

The increased number of women at work means that women's earnings have generally become more significant, rising from 15.2% of all income of married and cohabiting couples in 1979 to 20.5% in 1991, while male earnings fell from 74.8% to 59.2%. Women working full-time earned 42% of the family income. Without women's earnings, 50% more married or cohabiting couples would have been in poverty in 1991.

The most striking rise in female earnings shares was in couples where there were children. For these couples, the female earnings share rose by over 50% during the 1980s. For all other household types, the female earnings share remained static, or even fell.[32] This is because more and more mothers with children are going out to work. In 1973, only 43% of couples with children had both partners in employment. By 1992, this figure had increased to 60%.[33]

Within the general context of the decline of the male breadwinner, it is worth noting in particular the situation of young men. Unemployment among 18–19 year-old males stands at 19.5% and among 20–24 year-olds at 17.2%, compared with 11.4% for men of all ages.[34] It is this group which has been most disadvantaged by changes in the benefit system, with the 1988 social security changes bringing in a significantly lower rate of Income Support for 18–24 year-olds. Yet without income and prospects of employment, it is increasingly difficult for many young men to contemplate marriage, setting up a home and starting a family. While the growth of lone parenthood is still mainly as a result of divorce and separation, the rise in the numbers of never-married single mothers needs to be put within the context that setting up a 'traditional' family is no longer seen as possible by many young people.

One-parent families still make up only 18.6% of all families. The norm remains a two-parent family. Increasingly, however, the only way for a family with children to keep out of poverty is for there to be two earners. Thus, while over 60% of all two-parent families have both parents at work, less than a quarter of lone parents work. The attitude of policy-makers towards working mothers, whether single or married, remains ambivalent. Lone parents are explicitly urged to take up work. The introduction of Family Credit was aimed particularly at helping lone parents to work, and recently, further attempts have been made to encourage lone parents back into employment by the introduction of a childcare allowance associated with Family Credit.[35] Yet the erosion of the lone parents' tax allowance (which is the same as the married person's tax allowance) and its reduction to 15% both mitigate against helping lone parents to work.

It is unlikely that the married person's tax allowance, the value of which is only £258 a year, has any significant impact on whether couples marry or cohabit. But the erosion in value of this allowance means that less and less support is offered in terms of tax allowances to married couples where one partner is not working. While the retention of the married person's tax allowance may be anomalous where both partners are working, its importance to those couples who have only one earner appears to have been overlooked. This increases the pressure on couples for both partners to work.

While pressure on lone and married parents to work increases, little attempt is made to deal with the crucial issue of childcare. The childcare allowance offered with Family Credit is of only limited value to lone parents and of almost no value to married parents. This failure in the benefit system mirrors the consistent unwillingness within the fiscal system to allow childcare costs to be set against tax. Set alongside the erosion of the value of child support through the freezing of Child Benefit, it is clear that little regard is given to the importance of adequate income for families with children.

Increasingly, families are faced with lack of choice. Decreasing numbers of male full-time jobs, coupled with fiscal policies which increase the tax burden on the poorest and welfare policies which favour means-testing, have led to fewer families being able to evade poverty simply through having one earner. More and more families have to have two earners in order to keep the family out of poverty, and with more 'atypical' work available this often means one partner working unsocial hours (e.g. the twilight shift at the local supermarket). The alternative to the two-earner family is all too often the no-earner family, with both men and women being trapped into unemployment.

The traditional notion of the nuclear family is no longer the norm. It is increasingly rare for men to be the sole breadwinners. In families where there are two earners it may be that this has led to a greater equality in relationships, which is to be welcomed. However, there is much subjective and some objective evidence that suggests that women continue to bear the major load in relation to domestic and caring responsibilities.[36] In families where there is a non-earning male and a female earner, or families where there are no earners, it is clear that the traditional role ascribed to men will have been lost. Not only will this role have disappeared, but for many men this will have resulted in the family being in poverty, with consequent further undermining of self-esteem.

Unemployment and poverty are linked to a whole range of social and personal problems: crime, mental and physical ill-health, suicide, broken relationships. Increasingly, having children is linked to poverty. This is surely one among a whole range of complex reasons for the decline in the number of couples with children, from 54% of all families in 1979/81 to 40% in 1989/91.[37] (There was a corresponding rise in couples without children, from 19% to 29%, and a slight increase in the proportion of single women, both with and without children.)

Conclusions

In the face of a radically altered employment situation, both fiscal and welfare policies have failed to provide security and adequate levels of income for about a quarter of all households. The greatest losers have been families with children. Many families have been forced into choices they would rather not have had to make: both mothers and fathers often taking low-paid, unsatisfactory employment, juggling complex childcare responsibilities, and thus feeling under enormous pressure. The contribution of these pressures to family and relationship break-up cannot be quantified, but they have undoubtedly played a part.

Both fiscal and welfare policy have reflected an increasingly individualistic view of rights and responsibilities. The view that 'There is no such thing as society' may be an extreme one, but it reflects the defining ideology certainly of the 1980s, and probably of the 1990s. Society no longer uses fiscal and benefit policy to smooth out the ups and downs of lifetime experience, nor to cushion its members against the extremities of economic change. Individuals and families are expected to make provision for themselves (e.g. the increasing move to private insurance) with only minimal and grudging 'safety net' support from the State.

The result has been increasing and sometimes excessive pressure upon family units. Relationships have strained or crumbled in the face not only of poverty but of the implications of failure which it carries, particularly for parents. However, not only have relationships within families suffered, but our relationships with each other in community have been eroded. The total failure of society, for example, to provide a means of support for 16 and 17 year-olds at a crucial and vulnerable stage of their development signifies an extraordinary abdication of our responsibilities to each other in community.

Tax and benefit policies must be reformed in order to recover their redistributive function: only in this way will it be possible to give crucial support to people who otherwise find their relationships subverted by grinding poverty. We also need to assert that relationships are not just about what happens within individual household units, but also about the way in which we act together in society.

References

1 'Joanne' (1989) *Decade of Despair*, Campaign Against Poverty, pp.6–7.
2 Official figures show that between March 1979 and December 1994, male full-time employment fell by 2.894 million, female full-time employment rose by 31,000, male part-time employment rose by 433,000 and female part-time employment rose by 1.134 million. (Department of Employment, *Employment*

Gazette Historical Supplement, October 1994; *Employment Gazette*, April 1995).

3   *Hansard*, 3rd March 1994, cols 861–2. The same source shows participation in full-time work also falling for women: from 36.6% of women of working age in 1973, through 35.9% in 1979, to only 33.3% in 1993.
4   1.5 million people are now temporary workers. In the two years to Autumn 1994, temporary work rose by 260,000 while employment as a whole rose by only 143,000, signifying a loss of 117,000 permanent jobs – 94,000 male and 23,000 female (OPCS (December 1994) *Labour Force Survey Quarterly Bulletin No.10*, HMSO).
5   In March 1979, there were estimated to be 1,959,000 people who were self-employed, of whom 208,000 were part-time. By December 1994, this had risen to 3,280,000, of whom 634,000 were part-time (*Employment Gazette*, April 1995).
6   Department of Employment (1994) *New Earnings Survey*, Table A.19. The extent to which changes in employment patterns have of themselves reduced earnings is evident if 1994 average weekly earnings for male and female full-time and part-time workers are applied to the March 1979 and December 1994 employment profiles: this exercise shows an average weekly wage for all workers of £285.20 in March 1979 and £261.29 in December 1994, a fall of £23.91 a week, or 8.4%.
7   *Hansard*, 2 November 1994, col. 1,210.
8   In 1979–80, VAT receipts were £8.2 billion, while Income Tax receipts were £20.6 billion. In 1993–4, VAT receipts were £39.2 billion (a rise of 378%) and Income Tax receipts were £58.4 billion (a rise of 183%). This means that VAT's share of receipts from these two sources rose from 28.5% in 1979–80 to 40.2% in 1993–4 (*Hansard*, 12 July 1994, col. 568).
9   *Hansard*, 26 February 1993, col. 767.
10 Calculations based on Central Statistical Office (1993) *Family Spending: A Report on the 1992 Family Expenditure Survey*, HMSO.
11 *Hansard*, 19 December 1994, cols 947–8.
12 Derived from answer in *Hansard*, 28 April 1994, cols. 257–60.
13 Data across different earnings levels and for two-earner families with and without children show similar patterns, with households without children generally having falls in direct tax liability and those with children generally having rises (though there are some exceptions).
14 *Hansard*, 3 November 1994, col. 1,284.
15 *Hansard*, 25 January 1994, cols 189–90.
16 Derived from *Hansard*, 4 February 1988, cols 484–7.
17 In 1993–4, 230,000 single people and 270,000 couples had marginal deduction rates from wages (including benefit withdrawal) of between 75% and 99%, while the highest earners had a marginal tax rate of only 40% (*Hansard*, 24 February 1994, col. 367).
18 *Hansard*, 15 June 1995, col. 652.
19 In 1992–3, 14.2 million people (25% of the population) were in households claiming means-tested benefits, compared with 17% in 1979 (Department of Social Security (1995) *Households Below Average Income: Statistical Analysis 1979–1992/93*, HMSO). The figures from this survey appear to be an underestimate, since benefit take-up figures from the DSS indicate that 15.5 million people were on means-tested benefits.
20 Cox, G. (1995) *Bagatelle or Benefit: An Analysis of the Government's Jobseeker Proposals*, Greater Manchester Low Pay Unit.
21 For more information on fiscal effects, see: Low Pay Network (1994) *A Case Study*

Fiscal and welfare policy 199

of New Supermarket Vacancies in Stirling Jobcentre, Manchester; Cox, G., in House of Commons Social Security Committee (1994) *Review of Expenditure on Social Security, Minutes of Evidence*, 2 March, HMSO, pp.47–50 and 60–2.

22 In 1993, 555,000 families on Income Support had help with mortgage interest payments, a rise of 97.5% on the figure of 281,000 in 1989 (*Hansard*, 23 January 1995, cols 83–4).
23 *Hansard*, 20 March 1995, cols 3–4.
24 *Hansard*, 16 December 1993, cols 835–6; *Hansard*, 11 January 1994, cols 24–5; *Hansard*, 28 April 1995, cols 714–15.
25 For example: Stitt, S. (1991) *Of Little Benefit: A Study of the Adequacy of Income Support Rates*, Campaign Against Poverty; Family Budget Unit (1992) *Household Budgets and Living Standards*, Social Policy Research Findings, No.31, Joseph Rowntree Foundation.
26 House of Commons Social Security Committee (1995) *Low Income Statistics: Low Income Families 1989–1992*, HMSO.
27 Gregg, P. and Wadsworth, J. (1994) *More Work in Fewer Households?*, Discussion Paper No.72, National Institute of Economic and Social Research.
28 Hills, J. (1995) *Inquiry into Income and Wealth*, Vol.2, Joseph Rowntree Foundation.
29 Department of Social Security (1995) *Households Below Average Income: Statistical Analysis 1979–1992/93*, HMSO.
30 Department of Social Security (1993) *Family Credit Statistics: Final Quarterly Tables, April*, Government Statistical Service.
31 Jowell, R., Brook, L. and Taylor, B. (1991) *British Social Attitudes – The 8th Report*, Social and Community Planning Research, Gower.
32 Harkness, S., Machin, S. and Waldfogel, J. (1994) *Women's Pay and Family Income Inequality*, Joseph Rowntree Foundation. See also: Machin, S. and Waldfogel, J. (1994) *The Decline of the Male Breadwinner: Changing Shares of Husbands' and Wives' Earnings in Family Income*, Joseph Rowntree Foundation.
33 OPCS (1992) *General Household Survey 1992*, HMSO.
34 *Employment Gazette*, June 1995, Table 2.15.
35 Because the childcare allowance operates as an earnings disregard, only those with earnings of £109 or more (1994 rates) would get the maximum benefit, and this would amount to £28 towards childcare costs of £40, leaving the rest to be found from already low income. (For a more detailed analysis of the childcare allowance see 'Lone Parents and the Childcare Allowance', *The Bottom Line*, September 1994, Greater Manchester Low Pay Unit.)
36 In families where both men and women work full-time, women are still mainly responsible for domestic duties in 67% of households (Jowell et al., op. cit.).
37 Harkness et al., op. cit.

14 Banking and finance: The importance of relationships

Timothy M. Green

Introduction

It is difficult to find an industry in which the concepts of trust and relationship are as crucial as they are in the banking industry. The relationships that we have with banks, and the trust we put in them, have important effects on our lives. As customers, good relationships with banks and trust of them are vital, in that our dealings with banks revolve around services that are both long-term and of great importance to us, such as mortgages and the management of day-to-day finances and savings. These qualities are also important to the banks, in that loyalty and reputation, which are components of a good relationship, are tested ways to maintain and attract good business, on which profits depend. My argument in this chapter, however, is that a variety of long- and short-term changes in the banking industry have radically changed the appreciation of the role that relationships play within it. This has had numerous important effects.

In some ways, my family provides me with an interesting perspective on the changes in relationships within the banking industry. My connections with the industry go back three generations. My father and grandfather were both bank managers in the north of England. These three generations, spanning a hundred years, have witnessed huge changes in the way that relationships are conducted in the banking industry, and thus in the impact of the industry upon society.

Banking practice has changed out of all recognition during this period. Developments in technology, the customer base, the structure of the industry and within individual institutions are considered here in more detail, together with the impact that these changes have had on various different sets of relationships in the banking industry, between banks and customers, and those within and between financial institutions.

This chapter then examines the benefits of good relationships from the perspectives of the banks themselves: how often communication engenders loyalty and facilitates a proper exchange of information on which responsible lending and borrowing depend.

Finally, I discuss measures to increase the priority of relationships in the banking industry and argue not for a return to a 'golden age' of banking, but for selective measures to be introduced to best exploit the opportunities inherent in relationship banking.

The nature of relationships in banking

Before examining the effect of changes in the banking industry upon the relationships within and around it, it is important to establish exactly what is meant by a 'good relationship' in terms of banking.

A 'good relationship' has several hallmarks. A central one is trust: that both parties have faith in each other's honesty and good character. Another is loyalty: that both have a commitment to the relationship and to each other's interest through the trade effected through the relationship. These two qualities both address how the two parties feel about each other. Efficiency is also important, in that no matter how well two parties get on, if the trade that they conduct is inefficient, the relationship can hardly be described as 'good'.

There are, no doubt, many opinions as to what constitutes a good banking relationship, but the above qualities seem to be a reasonable starting point. Other important qualities might include sympathy, co-operation, respect and understanding. It is important to note that these qualities are most likely to be engendered by a relationship in which the parties concerned actually know each other (what Schluter and Lee call an 'encounter relationship').[1] Each of us has relationships (of a kind) with people we have not met. I may never have met the directors of my bank, but their decision on lending criteria does affect me. I would argue that the qualities of good relationship mentioned above are more likely to characterise a relationship in which the two parties know each other than one in which they do not. For instance, it would be much easier to keep a £10 note that was mistakenly given to you by a cash machine than one given in your change by your local newsagent, who you know personally.[2]

Changes in the banking industry

Size of the customer base

Today, the adult population of the UK is 45 million. About 10 million (22%)

do not have a bank or building society account. This leaves 35 million (78%) who do. This constitutes the banks' 'customer base'.

In my grandfather's day, the proportion would have been somewhere around 20–25%; in my father's, 40–50%. Today, a major bank such as NatWest or Barclays will have between 6 and 7 million personal customers. This represents a vast increase in the number of accounts held at the banks, and it is simple mathematics to show that with staff levels not growing at the same rate, the amount of time that can be devoted to building a relationship with one individual will have been reduced.

Structure of the banking sector

The change in the structure of the industry has also been substantial. There has been a fitful process of amalgamation and merger in the twentieth century, resulting in centralisation and growth of the major banks. In 1913, there were 37 joint stock banks in the UK, averaging 165 branches each. Now, four clearing banks dominate the industry, with nationwide branch networks. The effect of these amalgamations was to increase the size of the main banks and to centralise them, reducing the importance of their regional origins and identity, which proponents argue has created economies of scale.

My own banking career illustrates this. I began work at the Manchester and Liverpool District Bank, which had a staff of 5,000 and a strong regional identity. This was taken over by the National Provincial, which eventually merged with the Westminster Bank to become NatWest, with its head office in London and employing over 120,000 people worldwide at its peak.

Deregulation in the 1980s led to increased competition, as building societies were empowered to provide more services and to change their status to that of banks. This has coincided with the continuing process of amalgamation and merger, both among banks and building societies, as witnessed by the recent cases of Lloyds and TSB, and the Halifax and the Leeds building societies. Thus, while the number of big players has not fallen, their size has increased. One reason for the recent wave of mergers is that banks, struggling from the high costs inherited from the 1980s, are striving to invest all that they can in new technology to cut costs. The sums involved in such investments are very large, and many banks and building societies feel that the benefits will be best exploited by the largest firms, who have the most capital to invest.

As well as these changes in the domestic arena, the market for financial services has become far more international. Factors like the 'Big Bang', the advent of 24-hour trading, the deregulation of foreign exchange and the growth in the presence of international banks in the City of London have led to a City in which traditions and means of communication have changed enormously.

Structure within banks

While the ownership structure of banks has changed from joint stock to public limited company, the only real change as a result of this was in the public declaration of profits and balance sheets. However, the growth and centralisation of the major clearing banks has altered methods of accountability within them. When banks were smaller and more regional, relationships with prominent local family hierarchies would often be important to them and would enable local interests to be in some measure reflected, as well as allowing the obvious accountability to the bank's owners. An example comes from my time at the Manchester and Liverpool District Bank, where customers included important local families. The bank's board was made up of local industrialists from the North-west, so that the bank was focused on local interests.

However, bank growth has often destroyed this avenue of accountability, leaving banks responsible to shareholders alone, who tend to be institutions rather than individuals. Often, bank ownership is interlocking, in that banks and other institutions own each others' shares.

It is possible that the combination of such ownership patterns in very large institutions can lower the priority of relationships within the whole institution: owners and managers communicate indirectly, through pension funds and investment institutions, and normally only about one issue: profit. It is arguable that some companies that have maintained a measure of individual/family control, such as Sainsburys or the John Lewis Partnership, have a different ethos, and a different view of relationships as a result. Exceptions to the case of size decreasing accountability to local interests include the formation of semi-autonomous regional boards within banks, a phenomenon discussed in the concluding section of this chapter.

Mobility of staff

The growth and centralisation of the banks during the 1980s led to larger branch networks, and thus a greater need for staff to move around. Most staff will probably only move around in one area, for instance around branches in one county, but this is still far more mobility than was asked of managers in the past.

There are inevitable consequences of such increased mobility. While managers do get a broader picture of banking in their region, their knowledge of a local community and the customers within it may well be superficial. This is bound to affect the way that they take lending decisions, making it far more convenient to rely on centrally-produced lending criteria than on personal discretion borne of intimate knowledge of a town and its people.

Previous generations of bankers would have known their customers personally. In my days on the counter in the North, I would be able to greet most customers by name. With the hand-posting of ledgers, bank staff learned a great deal about their customers. When a customer wanted to discuss a loan with his bank manager, the manager's decision would be strongly influenced by his personal knowledge of the customer. While banks hold much information about their customers today, this is clinical computer data about certain 'key' characteristics (e.g. income, postcode, marital status, account history) rather than the kind of information so valued in the past in the making of lending decisions. Thus, mobility, both in society at large and in banking personnel, has diminished reliance on personal relationships in banking.

Diversification

A number of factors have led to banks diversifying their operations in recent years. This diversification is rooted in the long-term growth in bank size, and thus in the potential for branching out, but gained impetus in the climate of financial liberalisation and deregulation of the 1980s. Banks and building societies can now act as stockbrokers, estate agents and providers of pensions. Obviously, the skills required to manage and understand such diverse businesses are very different. As a result, those in a bank's 'executive tier' will often have to be far more mobile and versatile than other managers, not just geographically, but also departmentally, so as to develop as broad a knowledge of all the bank's operations as possible.

As well as making their stay in high street branches even briefer than that of standard managers, the mobile lifestyle will ensure that those who eventually become directors and other executives would probably place less emphasis on building up longer-term relationships in banking.

The credit cycle

The changes in the banking sector in the 1970s and 1980s were not just confined to the breadth of activity. The deregulation and liberalisation came at a time when the banks' surplus 'oil money' deposits coincided with a limited demand for commercial loans. This situation encouraged banks to lend a lot to personal customers, making personal lending and credit a boom sector in financial services, especially as house prices rose sharply (raising wealth) and expectations of future income rose.[3] Commercial lending also soared as recovery set in, and often, bank managers (who were more mobile than their predecessors, and thus less in touch with the locality, as discussed above) were set lending targets, thus increasing incentives to make large numbers of high-risk, high-value loans. Thus, some poor lending decisions were made.

This was the situation in 1988–9, when the rise in inflation triggered a sharp interest rate hike, coinciding with a global downturn, heralding the now familiar story of business collapse, redundancy and home repossession. The multitude of defaults that followed this compounded the banks' earlier losses in speculative ventures abroad (notably, bad debt in the Third World).

As a result of the banks' bad and doubtful losses and provisions, radical strategies had to be adopted to return to acceptable levels of profit. New technology has enabled the banks to introduce 'electronic banking' and to centralise processing. This has led to the reduction in the number of branches throughout the country. The operations of central departments have also been scrutinised, with subsequent downsizing of staff requirements. With computer networks able to analyse lending propositions against centrally-determined criteria, the role of the 'expensive manager' can be undertaken by staff of lesser experience, the result being that many staff and experienced managers have been offered redundancy or early retirement.

These responsive measures have had a major impact on relationships in the industry. Cutbacks have left fewer people to deal with the same customer base. Lending decisions now have little scope for discretion. Thus, the 'credit cycle' seems to have been amplified by these events over the last ten years, going from easy to relatively tight credit, in a way that has eroded the value placed on good relationships.

New technology

Changes in this area have been among the most obvious and widespread. There are now remote telephone banking services, promoted by such organisations as First Direct, and, similarly, insurance from Direct Line. Debit cards like Switch can be used for electronic payment for goods and services; the same card enables people to withdraw cash from any of 6,000 cash dispensers, and bills can be paid by direct debit. The usage of such facilities has risen rapidly recently. The share of electronic means of payment in the total share of non-cash payments rose by 34% between 1987 and 1991 in the UK.[4] In 1985, 1 in 5 transactions were by automated teller machine (ATM) or telephone; by 1992, this had risen to 1 in 3.

The technology change is more widespread than just the personal sector. Banking has become increasingly global, partly because technology has enabled this, with fibre-optics, satellites and the Internet being just some of the communications now used. Companies can now access their bank accounts through their own computer networks, and 'cash management' has revolutionised the way in which they can manage their company's finances on a day-to-day basis, without even having to make any personal contact with their bank. Deregulation and freer trade in financial services has also reinforced these trends, creating 24-hour trading in London, Tokyo and New York.

The impact of banking changes on relationships

Relationships between banks and customers

The changes that I mention above have their most direct impact upon the relationship with customers. While the customer base has grown, staff levels and branch numbers have been cut back. Lending decisions have become centralised, made according to rigid criteria that leave little room for local discretion. All this has been happening at the same time as technological change that allows banks to handle a large number of accounts with very little face-to-face contact.

This combination of circumstances means that bank staff cannot give personal attention to everyone any more, leading to the banks developing *segmentation strategies*. These are strategies to identify segments of the customer base which take priority in terms of direct staff contact time. This may (crudely speaking) take the form of an '80/20' rule, where the most affluent 20% of customers get this special attention, while the rest are left to deal with the bank more impersonally.

An over-simplification of the segmentation strategy and its effects would be along the following lines. While the banks only distinguish between two segments according to the above rule, the 80% not singled out for special attention can be divided into two segments: those who thrive in a banking arena full of products and services but short on personal attention and advice, and those who are bewildered by it. I shall call these three segments: the *affluent*, the *astute*, and the *alienated*.

The *affluent* are the 20% who are high-net worth/high-income customers who are likely to enjoy the services of a personal account manager or even an executive. All their banking needs will be supplied by the manager and his or her team. This is a recent development, replacing the previous 'benign neglect' of customers who generate a high proportion of the bank's income. The objective of such close attention is not only to ensure that the account is retained with that bank, but also that every selling opportunity is pursued. Relationships with this segment of the population are thus strong, which is a positive side-effect of segmentation.

The *astute* comprise a very large segment of the customer base, who will not necessarily be wealthy, but will be financially astute, if not sophisticated. They are financially literate, knowing the meaning of such jargon as 'PEP' and 'APR'. This group are not intimidated by developments in banking that have increased convenience at the price of personal contact. They will make the most of ATMs, remote telephone banking and debit cards, considering them efficient, convenient and cheap services. They will shop carefully for financial services, from TESSAs to mortgages. They will know what criteria they have to satisfy in order to qualify for certain services (e.g. credit). Often, this will be enough for them, and they may consider face-to-face contact with bank employees to be unnecessary. However, without belittling the major convenience and cost benefits produced by new technology and new products, it must be asked whether it would not be a shame if one is compelled to relate to a bank in this way rather than choosing one's own preferred balance of direct relationship and electronic convenience. The case of the third segment of the customer base illustrates this.

This third segment of the customer base, the *alienated*, is the proportion of the population who would appreciate help, advice and human contact in their dealings with a bank. The financial world can seem complex and jargon-ridden to those who have had no reason or opportunity to develop the skills required to map it, and it is this segment of the population who often feel more isolated as banking comes more automated and remote. However, the irony is that as banking becomes more sophisticated, this segment requires more advice and personal contact, just as the changes within the banking industry ensure that such relationships with this segment become a lower priority.

This group may also be intimidated by financial terminology and may not have developed basic money-management skills such as budgeting. They will not always know how best to invest their savings, perhaps failing to exploit the better or more appropriate savings and investments, relying very much on the tradition of their parents. A recent Gallup survey commissioned by the Switch debit card scheme showed that if people need financial help, the majority would turn to their parents for such advice. Only 1 in 5 would ask their bank manager, and the same proportion would consult their spouse or partner. Thus, the survey underlines how mainstream retail banking has failed to meet many people's financial needs, because individuals feel unable to seek their advice.[5]

Relationships within financial institutions

Behind this change of relationships between banks and customers lies another change: major shifts in the internal relationships between bank staff. Over the past four to five years, a major cultural change has taken place in the banking industry, symbolised by the disappearance of the 'job for life' for most employees and by the renaming of personnel departments as 'human resources'. Early retirements and redundancies became commonplace. While it must be said that banks have gone out of their way to make such redundancies and retirements as generous and easy as possible, a permanent change has taken place between the staff and the executive (executive jobs remain secure and increasingly well remunerated). This has all been against the backdrop of banks seeking a harder, more competitive edge, which was necessary, but the question remains whether this has taken place at the expense of the erosion of relationships which have traditionally fostered strong bonds of loyalty.

Another almost accidental dilution of relationships occurred when large companies and financial institutions, in the pursuit of lowering costs, decided to close communal areas like canteens and dining rooms. This has aided the destruction of one of the key activities that helped to develop good relationships within organisations. The reduced staff levels and increased workloads that resulted from the cost-cutting measures combined with these closures in increasing isolation in the workplace, symbolised by the new norm of the M&S sandwich eaten at the desk. This isolation is furthered by changes in communication technology, which, while contributing greatly to efficiency, have had an inevitable impact on relationships. Since it is now easier to communicate remotely, the necessity for face-to-face contact is reduced. The decreasing frequency of such contact means that communication begins to consist merely of facts and words, rather than the largely unquantifiable information and communication that occurs when people meet directly. It is my argument that loyalty, trust, a sense of worth and pride in one's company and other such important qualities are offshoots of such direct contact, which technology has rendered seemingly unnecessary.

Thus, these developments have tended to devalue relationships throughout financial institutions, not just in the 'executive tier', as discussed above. Such low valuation of relationships inevitably creeps into the banks' dealings with customers.

Relationships between financial institutions

I have argued that the City of London has been transformed into a global financial centre. There are now over 500 international banks represented in the square mile. This is a radical departure from the City in my grandfather's day and before, bringing about a major change in the way in which City institutions relate to one another.

Historically, the reputation of the City was developed in the coffee houses in the eighteenth and nineteenth centuries, where financial deals were confirmed by a handshake and the unbreakable principle that 'my word is my bond'. We had a society which was strongly influenced by religious standards and Christian traditions. High standards of morals and ethics were accepted as the norm. However, as the volume of business has mushroomed and broken through national barriers, means and manner of communication between individuals in the institutions have had to adapt and change. People have had to put less time into more relationships, often through the more impersonal means of communication that technology has brought: telephone, fax and e-mail.

It is thus unsurprising that loyalty and trust have been eroded to the extent that they have. There has recently been an unprecedented rash of City disasters and scandals, marring the City's reputation. This erosion of confidence has arguably been brought about by a breakdown in the confidence that we once placed in the relationships we enjoyed with our counterparts in other City organisations. I wonder if the move towards individualism has promoted an atmosphere of personal greed, where 'being economical with the truth' is a means to justify many an end. One hundred years ago, ethical codes of practice were not necessary, since people in the City knew each other, enjoyed their business relationships and trusted each other. However, today, City relationships have broken down. This can again be seen in the fact that the confirmation of even the simplest financial deals now involves teams of lawyers with masses of documentation.

Relationships between banks and the community

This is one area where banks have maintained a good track record, in terms of their involvement in community life. The community I am referring to is that surrounding the bank's local branch – residents, schools and many other local groups. Many banks belong to the '1% club', voluntarily giving 1% of profits to community projects. The level and direction of donations is often based on the involvement and the recommendation of the local branch manager. It is common practice to encourage staff involvement in the community, often by agreeing that the bank will match any funds raised by a local staff member for a local project, such as a new Scout hut. Sadly, these initiatives have been very much unsung, but must nevertheless be applauded.

Many managers and staff have been seconded to community and enterprise projects. To give but one example (that I will develop further in the next section), my involvement with the Jubilee Centre over their Credit Action debt project led to NatWest stepping in to fund a proposed schools' education project, with a budget of over £100,000. It is this sort of initiative that will enhance the banks' reputation in the community, and I do hope that as the banks focus on their bottom lines to satisfy stock market demands, they will not neglect their responsibility to the community, whether locally or nationally.

Relationships between banks and those in debt

My intention in this section is not to apportion blame for the explosive rise in consumer indebtedness in the last few years. Having said that, it does seem that some of the causes are rooted in the declining importance of relationships in financial services. As well as a relational cause, the problem also has major effects on relationships.

The scale of consumer debt amassed in the late 1980s and early 1990s is staggering. Total unpaid debt in Britain (excluding mortgages) has trebled since 1981 to £54 billion (equivalent to £2,400 per household).[6] Over 1,000 houses are repossessed every week, a figure predicted to rise by the Council of Mortgage Lenders. As indicated above, it is difficult not to conclude that easy credit, managerial lending targets and the lower priority given to actually knowing their personal customers in the 1980s contributed to the situation.

Keith Tondeur, drawing on his Credit Action experience, highlights several impacts of debt on relationships, such as loss of friends, despair, suicide and marriage breakdown. He argues that money worries are named as the number one cause of marriage break-up in 70% of cases.[7]

One major role for banks in addressing this crisis of personal sector debt is education. One way that banks have become involved in the community is in projects like the one I described earlier: NatWest not only funded a schools' education programme on debt, but also followed this up by involving 3,000 of their staff in local schools providing financial education programmes to the students. Switch Card Services Ltd have sponsored, for the last two years, a *Better Money Management Guide for Students* in an attempt to reduce the debt that many students face when they leave college.

Benefits of good relationships in banking

It is possible to identify advantages for the banks themselves in making good relationships a higher priority, and crucial to do so, since, unless the banks themselves see the importance of relationships in the industry, there can be no internal impetus for change in the industry.

I do not want to argue that banks should 'turn the clock back' to my grandfather's day by renouncing new technology, slashing their customer lists and de-merging. There are many changes that are irreversible, and some have served to improve efficiency and service. What I do not believe is that these changes must necessarily result in such a low priority being accorded to human relationships in the many areas already examined. I believe that there is long-term self-interest at the heart of the promotion of relationships in banking, which can complement the positive changes in the industry, rather than being their casualty.

There is strong evidence that the cultivation of relationships with customers can lead to valuable marketing opportunities and extra sales. Banks have recent experience of this: NatWest decided, as part of its segmentation strategies, to assign personal account executives to high-net worth or affluent customers. As a result, they were able to sell a wide range of financial products to this group, resulting in a very worthwhile addition to income.

I also suspect that the rigid lending criteria and centralised decision-making rules that are beginning to creep into banking conspire, to some extent, to starve new entrepreneurship of funds. Encouraging good relationships with the top 20% of customers is all very well, but to assume that all new, good business and all entrepreneurship will come from this category and their descendants is dangerous. It is akin to ruling out the possibility of the emergence of able pupils from State schools on the grounds that their parents never showed the aptitude to make money. The other 80% must fit in with the banks' rigid central rules and criteria for borrowing, while it is easy to see from familiar 'rags to riches' stories that entrepreneurship is not necessarily confined to those people whom banks would traditionally consider to be safe lending options. Imaginative business can require imaginative finance, which must rely upon relationship and the character assessment which relationship facilitates.

Businesses, especially small and medium-sized ones, may have financial needs that relate not only to the general state of the economy, which is easily observed, but also to a mass of industry- and location-specific factors that can only properly be understood by banks if they are in regular and direct communication with those running the firms. Many of the banks' business accounts are now conducted from city-centre business units, the relationship having been moved from the local branch. Such a move has mixed effects: the concentration of expertise at 'business centres' enables better and more helpful lending decisions to be made. However, it is doubtful that these 'experts' have the local knowledge and experience enjoyed previously by the local branch manager.

I would never argue that lending criteria are unimportant: the purpose of a loan, the ability to repay, security, income and current financial commitments all have their place in a good lending decision. However, they are not the whole picture. A good lending decision demands information that is unquantifiable. In the past, when an entrepreneur asked for a loan, he or she would expect a visit to his/her work premises from the bank manager, who would probably know him/her well through the time both had lived in the local community.

Default rates have fallen with the recent imposition of centralised lending decisions and criteria, but this is perhaps misleading, in that the comparison is with the irresponsible lending of the 1980s, when lending targets and not relationships determined decisions. It is always possible to reduce default by restricting lending to safer customers, but, as argued above, this is at the expense of missing out on the discovery of tomorrow's entrepreneurs.

It is to bankers' credit that they are starting to realise the shortcomings of centralised and remote lending decisions. A recent newspaper report pointed to much-increased small business satisfaction with banking services, partly because 'instead of simply looking at a company's assets, banks are now prepared to consider the whole business, including its experience, track record and order position'.[8]

I have already highlighted other reasons why the cultivation of relationships might be beneficial to banks. From an internal perspective, good relationships can generate staff loyalty, which has the important effect that banks may not so easily lose employees in whom they have invested tens of thousands of pounds of training to rival institutions. Relationships can also help to secure the loyalty of customers to banks. In terms of the City, better relationships, and a stronger ethical code of practice could help reduce costs such as the legal costs of making documents 'water-tight' and the losses due to fraud and deception. Above all, the credibility of the City as a whole, both nationally and internationally, would be raised.

The future of relationship banking

As I have already suggested, there are many ways in which banking has changed in recent years that should be welcomed, or acknowledged as irreversible. For instance, technology has contributed to a rapid cost reduction, and increased efficiency should be welcomed. However, I wish to conclude by suggesting some ways in which relationships can benefit all parties in the banking industry.

First, I wish to address an issue that is often cited as a solution to the problems in the banking industry that I have been discussing: regional banking. Alan Duncan is a strong advocate, and states, in a recent report:

> if the modern clearing banks were broken up into regional, or even local, suppliers of credit akin to the small partnership banks from which most of them were formed, they would gain a better understanding of their borrowers and adopt a more cautious approach in their lending.[9]

I would argue that most of what such proponents wish for from regional banking is already being achieved by the clearing banks. While their regional links have been reduced, most banks organise themselves regionally: they break down the country into regions (usually eight of them), with each bank appointing regional executive directors, who, with their teams, are responsible for the bank's business in those regions. In effect, these regional departments run like autonomous regional banks, often with the sort of local, industrial representation on regional boards that I mentioned earlier in connection with the Manchester and Liverpool District Bank, and which I consider essential to ensuring adequate, well-directed funding of the regions.

I would thus argue that the current organisation of the clearing banks does not limit the provision of funds to the regions quite so severely as those keen on breaking up the clearing banks believe.

Having said all this, I do concede that good banking in the regions, with a heavy emphasis on regional needs, is vital for the health of the economy as a whole, and banks must be diligent in ensuring that the current good relationships and high priorities put on the regions are not lost as the banks continue to develop and change over the coming years.

I noted how the massive cost-reduction programme of the 1990s followed some poor lending decisions (often by branch managers facing lending targets) during the 1980s. This has led some to argue that managerial discretion over lending decisions should be radically reduced. Martin Taylor of Barclays argued some time ago that the bank manager will be replaced by computers. However, Sir Brian Pearce, previously of the Midland Bank, has announced their commitment to community banking and will be moving senior managers with increased authority to the branch network. Arguably, this latter approach will benefit all parties, in that only managers with a strong local understanding can understand the unquantifiable factors that influence a good lending decision.

While acknowledging the constraints imposed on banks by the mismatch between a shrinking bank payroll and a growing customer base, there is perhaps potential for groups of individuals to play an important role in banking, on both sides of the relationship. A good relationship between groups of individuals is better than a poor relationship between two individuals.

One way to use the concept of groups in banking relationships draws upon the example of the relationships successfully developed by banks with important customers via the assignment of personal account executives discussed in the previous section. If banks are unable to assign much attention to less important customers, they could assign them to a personal account *team*, which would provide relationships conducive to selling other products, providing advice and recognising entrepreneurial potential.

The problems of alienation of many by the complexity of modern banking and of the frustrated potential of such groups to yield future entrepreneurs could, perhaps, be alleviated by banks dealing with groups of customers, such as 'family associations'.[10] Banks could actively promote these, where members of the same extended family could be looked at as one connected relationship. Financial services and products could be offered to such an association, taking account of the combined family resources. The idea needs further thought and development, but it would have the added benefit of binding families together and making them financially responsible to one another. A note of caution is required: it is anticipated that for family associations to take off, some sort of tax-breaks would be necessary. This clearly shows that, unless some existing financial product or institution could be adapted, the group that must be responsible for the furthering of such concepts is not the financial services industry, which must act within the law, but the government.[11]

As far as the City is concerned, I believe that individuals with strong Christian ethical and moral principles and commitments need to 'stand up and be counted'. If dishonesty or deception is observed, then men and women of principle need to speak up. We need to generate and enhance the ethical debate within the City so that the highest of ethical standards is achieved.

Finally, it is worth mentioning some ideas which are outside the mainstream of retail banking but nevertheless worth discussing. Many such ideas revolve around the potential for expansion of bank activities in the community. For instance, while credit unions are outside the banking sector, and while they can only make a small contribution to helping those on low incomes or benefits, it is interesting that some local authorities are now actively promoting them. Perhaps bank involvement in the community could be increased by helping in this promotion. Another, related possibility is to complement bank funding of local projects with the free provision of financial advice and expertise to selected local groups. I also think that there may well be a market niche comprising those people who would choose not to relate to their bank electronically if they could, and that banks should look out for imaginative ways to access this market (referred to above as the 'alienated' customer sector). If not, they risk losing custom to more versatile banks.

It would be a frightening future if banking relationships were rejected in favour of cold, impersonal, clinical data produced by a bank's computer system. I believe that the bank which returns the relationship concept to the top of its agenda will be the one that will receive the applause and support of its staff, its customers, the City and the community. This does not have to be financial suicide: any business enjoying the loyalty of its customer base has long-term financial stability, which will also receive the applause of the stock market.

References

1 Schluter, M. and Lee, D. (1993) *The R Factor*, Hodder and Stoughton.
2 Ibid.
3 *Bank of England Quarterly*, May 1994, p.147.
4 *The Banker*, February 1994, p.33.
5 Gallup (1993) *Family Budget Survey*, Switch Card Services Ltd.
6 Credit Action (1995) *Current Financial Facts*, June.
7 Tondeur, K. (1994), *Say Goodbye to Debt*, Marshall Pickering, p.35.

8 'Easier money as banks fight for customers', *Daily Telegraph*, 2 October 1995.
9 Duncan A. (1993) *An End to Illusions*, Demos, p.36.
10 The concept of family associations is being developed by The Relationships Foundation, see Crook, A. (1996) *Report on Phase One of the 'Savings Syndicate' Project*, The Relationships Foundation.
11 This and other topics are dealt with in more depth in Chapter 18 in this volume.

15 Urban relationships: A challenge in town planning

Dalia and Nathaniel Lichfield

Urbanisation is recent in human history[1]

In their earliest days, human beings had little scope for broadly-based relationships. Hunting and food-gathering sustained less than ten people per square mile, and even less if nomadic. It was only when an ample, reliable food supply became practicable that fixed settlement arose, in hamlet and village, perhaps only around 10,000–12,000 years ago, with the oldest town, Jericho, perhaps only about 9,000 years ago. Thus, the beginning of urbanisation is remarkably recent in the 200,000 or so years history of *Homo sapiens*.

Initially, urbanisation grew quite slowly, there being a predominantly rural economy and a slow population growth. Since then, the escalation has been frenetic. The forecasts are forbidding. Whereas, at mid-1990, 43% of the world's population lived in urban areas (2.3 billion), by the year 2000, it will be half, and by 2030, at 5.2 billion, it will be three-fifths. And this will include many mega-cities of 10–12 million people each, largely in the less-developed countries.[2]

Relationships within urbanisation

The early hamlets and villages enabled families to offer mutual help, perhaps in harvesting and in defence against external enemies. The security gained from collaboration between people of common interest (be it family relations or landlord–farmer relations) was an important factor in the development of towns. These, once established, offered new opportunities. Some were intensely local, as within particular buildings or streets. Some did not depend upon locational proximity, since improvements in transportation and communication generated opportunities on a city-wide basis of common interest, defence, markets for exchange, collective worship and cultural exchange. While such relationships could be less intense than the local, they none the less offered the richness that can only be obtained through conglomeration. As Mumford reminds us:

> Aristotle put into words the nature of this transition from the preparatory urban processes and functions to emergent human purposes, in terms it would be hard to improve: Men come together in the city to live; they remain there in order to live the good life.[3]

Such opportunities for the *good life*, with its opportunity for richness of experience, have in the last half of the twentieth century become available not simply within particular urban areas, but worldwide, with the growth of both air traffic and telecommunications. It is possible to live an urban life in a non-urban setting.[4] Globalisation has increased the possibilities for international conferences, be it the business meeting at the airport or in the city centre, and introduced relationships not based on face-to-face contact. Doubtless, the possibilities of the teleworking information superhighway and the Internet will increase the potential for expanding the breadth, if not the depth, of human relationships.

But as the towns and cities grew, the benefits could be obtained only in association with costs caused by the conglomeration. In medieval days, there were disease, plague and fire, facilitated by the contiguity of buildings and activity. When the towns were rapidly thrown up following the immigration of rural populations to the urban manufacturing centres, the absence of regulation gave rise to insanitary conditions causing disease and early mortality. In this century, it is the accumulation of motor vehicles which has visited all towns and cities with traffic congestion and atmospheric pollution, each with their threat to the standard of living and quality of life. The sheer discomfort of living in the towns can outweigh the rich opportunities that the towns offer for good living. And there are other obstacles. Not all urban people have the capacity to enjoy all the benefits of urban life. Low income is a barrier to pursuing opportunities. Poor health is another. Poor mobility and accessibility is a third. And there is the psychological barrier in modern societies with low social integration, where relationships are limited, functional or fleeting. For this Durkheim, the nineteenth-century sociologist, coined the term 'anomie' in his analysis of the cult of the industrial, the product of an economic order dependent on a rigorous division of labour.[5]

Finally, the *raison d'être* of human settlements – collaboration and mutual protection – is increasingly coming under pressure from a culture of self-interest and competitiveness. Can the comfort of collaboration and security be reinstated within urban society? We shall argue that it can at least be improved upon, and that town planning has a role to play in this respect. We shall explore the ways in which town planning can facilitate relationships and may break down anomie and advance a culture of mutual awareness, respect and collaboration between groups and individuals.

The role of town planning in cities

Towns have been built throughout the ages, by what is today called the 'land market', through the development process.[6] In this, an array of 'factors of production' are assembled by entrepreneurs for consumption services (be it the individual wishing to house his own family, or the Church wishing to build a house of God, or the landowner wishing to sell on to potential occupiers and owners). But there were occasions, even in the early history of urbanisation, and certainly by the Greeks and Romans in opening up new conquests, when towns were centrally *planned* – conceived as a whole, with forethought for their purpose. This approach was adopted throughout the centuries, as, for example, in the *bastides* or medieval fortress towns in France, the Utopian ventures such as Saltaire and Bournville in nineteenth-century Britain, or following the railways which opened up the vast territories of the United States for settlers.

Such city planning has made only a minor contribution to mass urbanisation. There was a growing realisation in the nineteenth century that while the market *could* build towns, it left consequences which undermined the quality of life, in dangers to public health, poor co-ordination in highway and infrastructure programmes and miserable, soul-destroying family environments. As a result, at the beginning of the twentieth century, governments began to take to themselves the powers to remedy this 'market failure' by controlling ongoing urban development, and saw the need to prepare plans for urban areas as a basis for their social control.

Such planning flowered following the Second World War, with a need for rebuilding, but also with a need for the newly-independent countries to begin to shape their own futures free from imperialism. As a result, we are entering the twenty-first century with virtually a hundred years' experience of government-led planning of towns and their regions, and also of learning how difficult and complicated a task it is, particularly in a rapidly changing world. This learning curve has been hugely enriched by the entrance into the planning process of an increasing number of diverse skills to complement that of the generalist town planner. These include the physical (architect, civil engineer, surveyor), the social (sociologist, economist, lawyer) and the environmental (ecologist, hydrologist, acoustic engineer). Of particular interest in our context is the urban sociologist, with his/her concentration on people in planning.[7]

Given the world wide participation in government-led planning, it is difficult to generalise about the planning process which has emerged. In essence, a central but by no means universal practice is for appropriate planning authorities and their advisers to predict what the 'market' would do if it were not controlled by government, and then to put forward plans which are designed in the community or public interest to do better than the market. But however worthy the intent and execution, it does not follow that a government-led plan is an improvement on what the market would otherwise produce. Whereas advocates of planning 30 years ago based their arguments upon the disadvantages of market failure and assumptions that government would do better, they today recognise that while government intervention may seek to remedy 'market failure', government-led planning could lead to other kinds of failure in government, bureaucracy or 'freedom',[8] with equally anti-social consequences.

In brief, the planning road is a hard one to follow. The problems are severe and elusive of solution. They become more so with the ever-increasing tempo of accelerating population growth and migration, apparently insatiable consumer demand, and constraints from limitation of resources and environmental capacity. And perhaps it is not surprising. Since urban living is so comparatively recent in human evolution, this endeavour of planning our urban and regional environments is still relatively immature.

Some boundaries to planning

As set out above, the origins of twentieth-century *government-led planning* in the use and development of land can be traced to the recognition that its *nonplanning* can bring severe disadvantages to the public interest.[9] And while government has achieved dramatic transformation through its planning and related legislation for the use and development of land in the public interest, it is generally recognised that the fundamental reasons for the planning intervention have not disappeared, but have simply persisted at a higher level of inadequacy. For example, while Britain has adequate powers to achieve co-ordination in planning for transportation, it still lacks an integrated, comprehensive transportation system, most notoriously in its metropolis. One reason for this inadequacy lies not in the planning *per se*, but in the 'boundaries of planning' in securing the public interest. This can be probed in relation to various questions:

- Is the substantive content of the planning confined to the physical structure of the urban area, or does it also adequately reflect the socio-economic functions of the urban population in production, consumption, exchange, culture, etc.

- Given that planning is in 'the public interest', is the essence of the socio-economic functions fully understood? Is it just about economic activity (i.e. standard of living), or is it also about a different dimension (i.e. quality of life, which includes relations in terms of human, safe, happy interaction, mutual support, etc.). In the context of this volume, this aspect has particular importance. Is the planning also about relational proximity in its five components of directness, continuity, multiplexity, parity and commonality? (See page 10.)
- Which are the most effective of a possible variety of systems for government-led planning – for example, development planning in Britain, or regulatory zoning in the United States, compared to much of Europe, or indicative planning which has no statutory teeth?
- Is the particular planning system effective in achieving its objectives?
- Is the manpower responsible for the planning sufficiently numerous for the job in hand and sufficiently qualified to undertake it?
- Are sufficient financial resources allocated for the purpose?
- Are there adequate powers in law for implementing the planning decision, or are there important gaps?
- Do the decisions in the planning system rest with professionals (technocracy) or are they made in the last resort by elected representatives (democracy)?
- Does the population being 'planned' have a say in the decision-making and implementation of decisions of the planning system, or are they passive recipients?

From the doubts implied in these questions, it is apparent that there are, in practice, boundaries to the effectiveness of planning, and that these boundaries will vary between countries, and indeed, within particular countries.

Determinism in planning

From the preceding, it is seen that there are many kinds of government-led urban and regional planning aimed at creating a future which will be different from that which would emerge if government intervention were not pursued.

It is also clear, from variations in the boundaries of different kinds of planning, that their influence on the people being 'planned' will not be uniform. This is clearly so in terms of the focus of this book: personal relationships. For example, the British style of development planning clearly influences people's lives, in that there is concern for co-ordinating their diverse interests in home, work, education, culture, and so on. But it cannot be said to be *deterministic*, implying 'a one way process in which the physical environment has a direct and determinate effect on social behaviour'.[10] People and families have freedom within the plan structure to make and lead their own lives. By contrast, the style of planning of the former 'communist bloc', where there was more rigorous intervention from the centre and more political bureaucracy in implementation, could more directly control the people concerned. In some countries, as formerly in China and in North Korea, there could even be direction as to where individuals and families could live and work.

Attempts at determinism in planning can become of particular importance in seeking to influence behaviour. Planning often has a streak of Utopianism in it, and especially so where the creative spirit of architects is involved. One of the images cherished by such Utopians has been the Continental piazza or square, buzzing with people engaged in all manner of friendly relationships. Many a scheme has been designed on that model in the UK, but they have not succeeded to attract – or generate – the same degree of human activity. This is because the activity is a function of many socio-economic forces and is not determined simply by the physical presence of the square. This issue arises also in the attempt to plan urban villages, part of the vision of which is to create within them communities which enjoy the relationship of traditional village life. It is appreciated that the link between the two exists, but is tenuous.[11] The former does not necessarily lead to the latter.

Another striking illustration comes from the attempts in public housing estates to combat crime and vandalism through better design, for example through elimination of the pedestrian tunnel or overpass, which are away from public scrutiny, or through cutting out rear-garden access to houses, which can help thieves in their getaway. While the objectives have been clearly conceived, and the expenditure vast, the results have not been fully successful.[12] And on the debit side of the experiments must be added the loss of certain highly-valued traditional qualities in design which have been eliminated because they were conducive to assisting the criminals. A striking example is the abandonment of the Radburn mode of residential planning, wherein a more pleasant family environment has been achieved by providing cul-de-sacs with vehicular access to the rear of the dwelling and pedestrian access at the front, so protecting the quietness and safety of the frontages onto which the living rooms face and children play.

The examples just presented illustrate that designing for or against certain features of people's lives may not be deterministic, not only in relation to a particular feature in mind (crime), but also in relation to other features (pleasant environment). Thus, there cannot be said to be any clear, deterministic relationship between the planning input and the activity output. But there is certainly, none the less, some influence from planning on the way of life of the people. This could be both 'positive', in the sense of enabling people to live the lives they would choose from among options, or 'negative', in preventing them doing so. A contemporary example is planning policy towards 'out-of-town' or 'edge-of-town' shopping centres, an international phenomenon resulting from greater mobility afforded to people through increasing use of the motor car. A powerful result has been a 'voting with wheels' of shoppers, who have taken to the new one-stop shopping centre, with its plentiful car parking, as opposed to the existing multi-stop town centre, with its inadequate accessibility through an outdated roads system and inadequate car parks. The very success of such relocated shopping activity has had adverse consequences for the established centres in undermining their prosperity, and so leading to a drop in the nature and quality of retailing and business service that the centre as a whole can offer its surrounding residents. In the context of this volume, there is another loss. The central location of the older centre, and the multitude of uses that have congregated there, offer a better relational environment than the out-of-town situation, with its concentration mainly on large-scale shopping.

The possibility of these consequences was not difficult to forecast, since they were obvious in the United States, where planning had less influence than in Britain in reducing the proliferation of the centres and thereby the adverse consequences for town centres and main streets. Despite the confidence in our planning system to control the negative consequences, very recent government planning policy has been to reduce support for the dispersal of shopping centres in favour of the traditional centres, which have lost out.[13] There is a move to reverse the trend and restore some of the 'vitality and viability' to the traditional centres and, by the same token, to reduce the volume of motor car travel to the dispersed centres, so contributing to both energy-saving and diminution of noise from vehicular journeys.

The issue of planning determinism has another dimension. Whatever the deterministic strengths of planning and design, it is clear that the influence is most powerful in the early years of the built environment, when the completed development tends to be used for the purpose for which it was planned and designed. But in the nature of urban society, there evolves a considerable mismatch in the fit between the use of the development in question and the functions for which it was designed. This arises simply because the socio-economic activities of the population, which are the basis for these functions, has, in general, a much more rapid lifecycle than the structures which house them, which are typically built of durable materials which could last from 60 to 100 years. This phenomenon is associated with what has been termed 'urban obsolescence', whereby the urban fabric can become obsolete from a number of causes: structural, functional, environmental, locational and economic.[14]

Thus, there needs to be continuing adaptation between the socio-economic activities and the urban fabric during the latter's life. This leads to a related cycle in determinism. In the early years of the fabric, the development directly influences activity; in later years, the activity outlives the fabric; in the adaptive period, the obsolete fabric then influences a different kind of activity. Thus there is a continuing play, which is described in the adage of Winston Churchill: 'We shape our buildings and then they shape us.'

A complicating factor in this relationship is the other kind of urban dynamics, in the causes for change which are outside the urban entity in question but which nevertheless have a profound influence on it. A decision made in the United States to close down a factory in Britain, for reasons of international company policy or to reflect globalisation in trade, is a case in point. The urban fabric in question becomes functionally obsolete through changes in socio-economic activity or in political systems, which have no relationship to the original planning in question, and so emphasise another kind of boundary to its effectiveness.

How can planning contribute to good relationships?

We have seen that while it is very influential in shaping the good life, planning has limits in its influence on the good life. It is limited by its boundaries and by not being deterministic. How, then, can it contribute to good relationships?

Despite the limits, planning can contribute in both a positive and negative way. On the positive side, it can seek to ensure that the opportunities desired by people to achieve rich and diverse relationships are made available: in brief, the meeting points in work, exchange, culture, recreation, leisure, and also their accessibility to people. On the negative side, it can plan to avoid the disbenefits that urban living can create that undermine the potential of relationships: poor sanitation, congestion, pollution, amenity, overcrowding, noise and separation from nature.

Given this framework, people have greater opportunities to achieve the quantity and quality of relationships they favour. Whether they then achieve the best possible in their relational proximity, and at a cost in time and money they can afford, will depend on their personal attitude and circumstances. It will also depend on their ability to secure beneficial relationships and avoid the less beneficial. It is in this latter connection that urban sociologists have made their contribution in exploring relationships affected by planning.[15]

The costs and benefits of planning decisions

What emerges from the preceding is the reality that the decisions taken under government-led planning systems do have influence on the way of life of people in the community in question. Some will be beneficial (improving mobility and accessibility through better transportation). Some will be adverse (expansion of an airport near a built-up area, with its consequential noise). There will be differences in the potential impacts that will arise either from refusing permission for any particular proposal or granting it; and by the same token, there will be variations in the costs and benefits when refusal to permit change is compared with a number of options in accepting change.

Clearly, the costs and the benefits under any of these scenarios would not be uniform over all people in the impacted community. Some sectors would benefit, and some would gain. In the shopping example above, reversal of out-of-town shopping centre policy could be a cost to frustrated car-borne shoppers wishing to use a new or expanded centre, and a benefit to the elderly and the young shoppers who do not have mobility by cars and find that their benefits from the services of the threatened town centre are protected. This example illustrates that any individual or family in the town will find that certain of their objectives will prosper and some will not from the predicted impacts of any proposal. Any man, woman or child could look at any planning proposal or decision from many viewpoints: of a breadwinner, parent, enjoyer of urban leisure, enjoyer of rural pursuits, motorist or cyclist, of relative wealth or relative poverty. Each is, in a sense, a mirror image of the wider community.

From this, it follows that any analysis in relation to plans or planning decisions must recognise the multiplicity of objectives of the individual, family, and indeed, community. It must also recognise that the community in question cannot be delineated by reference to a single boundary for the geographical entity, and certainly not in relation to any administrative boundary which happens to have grown up. This boundary is certainly important in relation to who will make the administrative planning decisions, but it is often irrelevant in relation to the breadth and significance of the impacts on way of life which will flow from those decisions. In fact, sectors of a community, in this sense, need to be defined in relation to the geographical boundaries of the various impacts in question. These could, for example, be international because of globalisation, or local for a particular group of residents.[16] That defines the 'relevant community'.

The role of community impact evaluation in planning decision-making

Government-led urban and regional plans offer a framework whereby all the multifarious groups in a town can have a coherent, holistic picture of what they might expect for the future of that town as a basis for their individual decisions. As such, it is therefore appropriate that any plan or planning decision be appraised, assessed or evaluated to compare it with other possible ways of planning for that town.

While there could be many approaches to such evaluation, the most suitable approach is that of social cost-benefit analysis, which has evolved over the past half-century for the appraisal of projects from the viewpoint of the public sector. However, traditional, orthodox cost-benefit analysis has been found to be in need of adaptation for the purpose of urban and regional planning, an adaptation achieved via planning balance sheet analysis.[17] In earlier times, the term 'impact' was barely known in this context. Following the explosion in impact assessment after its introduction in the United States around 1970, the planning balance sheet, in turn, was adapted through explicit introduction of impacts of all kinds (physical, social, economic, cultural, natural) as the raw material for the evaluation, and thus became termed 'community impact analysis/evaluation'.[18] This is aimed at aiding choice in decision-making between optional plans, policies, practice, projects and programmes with an eye both to efficiency (surplus of community benefits over costs) and equity (distribution of the costs and benefits among the impacted community sector). The emphasis is on the impacts on people.[19]

The approach has, since the mid-1960s, been used extensively on some 50 actual cases in practice, largely via consultancy commissions. The cases relate to issues of all kinds which are pertinent in urban and regional planning, as diverse as new towns, existing towns, regions, roads, redevelopment, revitalisation, conservation, retailing, leisure, business parks, environment, housing and energy. The method is therefore no longer experimental.

But while the primary purpose is a decision support system, the process of evaluation serves other purposes. One is a means of defining the 'public interest'. Community impact evaluation is built on the following propositions:

- planning is carried out *for* the people;
- it recognises that people are not homogeneous, but must be seen as sectors with possibly conflicting interests in any project proposal or plan;
- the sectors cannot all be net beneficiaries, since some must lose;
- the gains and losses to people must be seen from the viewpoint of *their* objectives, and not those of the planners and politicians.

Planning therefore aims not at a consensus, but at an outcome which does the maximum good or the least harm.

For this purpose, as indicated above, it attempts to define a 'relevant' community on whose behalf the assessment is and should be made, and so side-steps those decisions that might be made by a local planning authority simply in terms of its own administration (to the neglect of others outside) instead of those that are functionally linked to the town in question, or by regional or central government, who tend to think of the national interest without full regard to the local – for example, English interests without full regard to Wales, Scotland or Northern Ireland. Furthermore, the careful distinction can be attempted throughout between the planner/analyst as a technocrat and the political decision-makers/stakeholders as representatives of the values they hold or which they were elected to uphold. The evaluation and its conclusions are seen as statements for discussion, negotiation and bargaining between the sectoral interests that are affected.

In brief, decisions made by use of the community impact evaluation aim to be transparent, accountable, justifiable and defensible.

The community and minority interests

Enough has been said above to show that the purpose of community impact analysis/evaluation and the community-based decisions which are expected to flow from it are not a search for consensus among the people impacted. Adapting the words of Barnum the Great: 'You cannot please all the people all the time.'

Inevitably, therefore, even if the community impact evaluation shows which option is most likely to be in the public interest, the conclusions in favour of particular proposals will attract opposition from those who would be adversely impacted. This will occur even though an individual or family could be shown to have maximum net benefits from the particular proposal to which they are objecting, because their 'gamesmanship' tactic tends to be an attempt to ameliorate *any* features of the proposal which would have adverse impacts on them, and understandably so.

Even though the opposition to the solution preferred in the public interest is sectoral in the way described, it is in the interests of the planning authority and planners to take full note of any objection with a view to trying to overcome it. For one thing, success in this direction could raise the level of net benefit. For another, there is an advantage in reducing or eliminating the 'friction of resistance'.

Another way in which the potential friction can be reduced is to ensure that its possibility is ventilated early in the planning process in question, so that it can be accommodated if at all possible. It is here that practice in the impact assessment leg of the community impact evaluation can play its part. Standard practice in such an assessment is to predict the impacts that would arise, and then to seek ways of mitigating or ameliorating them as much as possible before finalising the study of the proposal giving rise to the impacts. The evaluation is then applied to the impacts in which mitigation and amelioration has been explored and implemented.

Community impact evaluation and relationships

In conclusion, we return to the opening theme of this chapter, which followed Aristotle on cities by suggesting that 'people remain there in order to live the good life'. The resulting kind of urban and regional community carries within it the opportunity for a diverse and rich bundle of relationships, spreading from the immediate neighbours and family (which are also available in the rural areas) to those available from the unique kind of services available in the metropolis (universities, hospitals, culture).

The scope of these possible relationships is brought out by Michael Schluter in his description of mapping the relational base in the 'non-family dimension' (see Chapter 1). It is open to any individual to form relationships in many varied dimensions, such as in the hierarchy of the workplace; in exchange of money for goods and services; in all levels of education; in sport, as spectator or practitioner; in hobbies of the active or passive kind; in religion of various denominations, and in relevant ethnic groups. That is part of the human condition.

But opportunities are one thing, and using the opportunities another. It is here that urban and regional planning of the kind discussed in this chapter can be helpful or unhelpful. The exercise of the opportunities needs a fertile place for setting them up – for example, urban parks for nature lovers or community buildings for meetings on winter evenings. Furthermore, since those sharing relationships of this kind will not all live within walking distance of each other, each focus for non-family relationships needs to be accessible to the potential participants by appropriate methods of transportation, and each of the participants needs mobility to take advantage of the accessibility. The provision of such opportunities, and their exploitation, certainly comes within the province of the urban and regional planning process. In brief, the aim must be to ensure the supply of a maximum range of opportunities for relationships and the maximum array of choice for the diverse tastes and cultures of the residents and workers in the urban area and its dependent sub-region.

It is such attributes of the planned area which must feature in any evaluation of the optional plans and proposals. But because of the nature of such planning, and its boundaries, it is not practicable to carry out the evaluation at the micro-scale necessary to predict implications for individuals or families. In practice, a broader brush is used. But, in principle, it would be practicable, given the time and resources, to carry out the community impact evaluation at the micro-depth needed to predict the impact on individuals and families. In certain kinds of issues, this could well be desirable and needed, as, for example, in a proposal to find solutions for a multi-use street (shopping, residential, parking, passing traffic, etc.). Within such a street, there would be a number of 'sub-communities', each of which would suffer or gain differentially under the various optional solutions chosen. Each would need to consider its own interest within the public interest in that particular street, and in parallel, the total interest and distribution of costs and benefits amongst the sub-sectors.

By the same token, the analysis could be extended from the impact on individuals to the impact on families. The difference is one of degree. Any individual within a family would have his/her own objectives in terms of the attributes just described, which would not necessarily be uniform between the parents and among the children, and would certainly not be uniform between children of different age groups. From the divergence of objectives will arise divergences in preferences for options within the family as a whole, for example in residential locations, mobility for transportation, proximity to the countryside or recreation areas. The glaring example here is the life of unpaid 'chauffeuse' mothers of dependent children, in transportation to school, religion classes, sport activities, etc.

In this sense, the family is also a sub-sub-community, be it the conventional unit of parents and children, the childless couple, the man or woman living alone, the single-parent family, etc. While it might appear far-fetched to think that family attitudes to proposals would benefit from this kind of community impact evaluation, the reality is that the family is a microcosm of the wider community, be it in a street or neighbourhood. There is a diversity of objectives among its members; the bachelor living alone will have different objectives for educational provision, compared to the parents of children. Furthermore, in any decision facing the family, such as, for example, where to have the family holiday, there are divergences of individual objectives (a sea shore for the baby can be compared with a golf course for the father and a comfortable hotel for the mother). There are varying costs and benefits for each of the family members; there is a need to trade off the benefits and costs of particular choices to the individuals in the family as a whole; there is a need to trade off the efficient solution (maximum opportunity for minimum cost) with its equity between the family members (a holiday bungalow on the beach for the working housewife and mother), and there is a need to consider the power struggle within the family in terms of implementation (the father's insistence that he is the breadwinner against the baby's discovery of the power of screaming revolt).

In brief, urban areas provide possibilities for richness in relationships, but they also provide pressures against their fulfilment. The urban planning process can help in the supply and quality of relationships. And evaluation can help in choosing between options with an eye to the prospering of the 'R factor'.

References

1. See Mumford, L. (1961) *The City in History: its origins, its transformation and its prospects*, Secker and Warburg.
2. Data from United Nations, Environment and Development (UNED).
3. Mumford, op. cit., p.111.
4. Webber, M.M. (1964) 'The urban place and the non-place urban realm', in Webber, M.M. et al., *Explorations into Urban Structure*, University of Pennsylvania Press.
5. Durkheim, E. (1893) *The Division of Labour in Society*, transl. by G. Simpson (1965), Free Press.
6. Ratcliff, R.U. (1949) *Urban Land Economics*, McGraw-Hill.
7. For example: Broady, M. (1986) *Planning for People: Essays in the Social Context of Planners*, Bedford Square Press; Pahl, R. (1968) *Readings in Urban Sociology*, Pergamon Press.
8. Buchanan, J.M. et al. (1978) *The Economics of Politics*, Institute of Economic Affairs; Lichfield, N. (1980) 'Land policy: seeking the right balance in government intervention – an overview', in *Urban Law and Policy*, Vol.3, pp.193–203.
9. Ashworth (1954) *The Genesis of British Town Planning*, Routledge and Kegan Paul.
10. Broady, op. cit.
11. Aldous, T. (ed.) (1995) *Economics of Urban Villages: A Report by the Economics Working Party of the Urban Villages Forum*, Urban Villages Forum.
12. Osborne, S. and Sheftoe, H. (1995) *Successes and failures in neighbourhood crime prevention*, Joseph Rowntree Foundation. See also Power, A. and Tunstall, R. (1995) *Swimming Against the Tide: Polarisation or progress on 20 unpopular council estates 1980–1985*, Joseph Rowntree Foundation.
13. Department of the Environment (1994) *Transport Planning Policy Guidance Note No.13*, HMSO.
14. Lichfield, N. (1988) *Economics of Urban Conservation*, Cambridge University Press.
15. For example, see Worsley, P. (1970) *Modern Society: Introductory Readings*, Penguin; Pahl, R.E. (1970) *Whose City? And other essays on sociology and planning*; and Willmott, P. and Young, M. (1957) *Family and Kinship in East London*, Routledge and Kegan Paul.
16. Herbert, P.T. and Raine, J.W. (1976) 'Defining communities within urban areas: an analysis of alternative approaches', *Town Planning Review*, Vol. 47.
17. Lichfield, N. (1960) 'Cost Benefit Analysis in City Planning', *Journal of the American Institute of Planners*, Vol. 26, No.4, pp.273–9.
18. Lichfield, N. (1996) *Community Impact Evaluation*, University College London Press.
19. Lichfield, D. (1994) 'Assessing project impact as though people mattered', *Planning*, No.1058, pp.20–9; Lichfield, D. (1992) 'Making the assessment link', *Planning*, No.975, pp.4–5.

Part V

The way forward

16 The common sense of community

Dick Atkinson

The term 'community' is on many lips today. Across Britain, people are worrying as never before about the state of their streets and communities. There is a feeling that community has been weakened not only by market forces and technological change, but also by the policies of successive governments. Many, including politicians of both Left and Right, are concerned about the lack of sufficiently robust local institutions close at hand for most citizens. Many also fear that the corollary of weak communities is that our belief in common values and our sense of responsibility for each other has atrophied.

This chapter identifies some of the good practices and urges a series of proposals which would result in more confident and coherent communities. It argues in a series of steps, showing how relationships at various levels, starting with families, can be given a greater degree of security and strength, and suggesting how the various institutions of school, housing, policing and public spaces can work in tandem. It describes how, in place of the old model of a local authority as a monopolist of power, we can build networks and clusters of institutions – collaborating groups of self-governing institutions – that can help communities cohere and give them fresh purpose and pride. Above all, it aims to show the common sense of community and its practical relevance to solving everyday problems of city life.

The importance of self-reliance

Attempts to help neighbourhoods, whether in developing countries or the urban neighbourhoods of the industrialised world, will fail, however well funded, if they do not directly involve those they are designed to assist. The point is a simple, common sense one. Yet the recent history of urban policy in the UK has been based on almost contrary principles. Much of the structure of the modern State has been shaped by a steady nationalisation of power. Instead of local or regional health services, we have a National Health Service. Instead of local agencies with some discretion over welfare, we have national, standardised systems that find it easier to distribute resources than to provide the means for self-reliance. And, increasingly, instead of local government, we have agencies working under contract for Whitehall. Meanwhile, at local level, town halls have tended to seek to monopolise their remaining power rather than to share it.

Much the same is true of the multitude of schemes specifically directed to the cities. Successive waves of urban initiatives, Urban Aid, Inner City Partnership, City Challenge even Integrated Regional Offices and Single Regeneration Budgets and City Pride, have all made crucial mistakes. First, they have been primarily aimed at inner-city areas. They have not recognised that it is the very nature and organisation of urban life which has become the problem.

Second, while the aid has helped to finance various new projects, it has not resulted in mainstream budgets being used in fresh ways.

Third, hardware and buildings have been emphasised at the expense of the 'softer' foundations of community identity and relationship. Indeed, the hardware has often destroyed the software, as when new roads have sliced through neighbourhoods.

Finally, while schemes have often given lip service to consultation with local people, their views have not been seriously taken into account. While many useful things have been done 'for' people, much less has been done 'with' or 'by' them. People have rarely been enabled to participate and own decisions affecting their well-being.

These errors would be more understandable if there was evidence that the principles of self-reliance and mutual aid do not work and if the top-down approach had visibly solved the problems of cities. But this has not been the case. Instead, it sometimes seems as if initiatives have multiplied in inverse proportion to their effectiveness.

Historically, it was this belief in self-reliance and self-help which inspired much charitable and voluntary effort, and these human impulses have remained strong in many localities. Even in a predominantly secular culture, there is still a strong base of moral motivation, a desire to be connected and contribute that is not captured by much of the language of modern policy – whether that of 'consumers' or of 'rights'. If it means nothing else, charity today can encompass that sense of being part of and connected to a larger whole, which brings in its wake compassion, responsibility and mutuality, the basic ethical foundations of any community or relationship.

Today, in other areas of life, self-reliance has become a basic principle. Far from being a Utopian, 'soft' option, it has come to be seen as a far more effective way of organising people's energies and their capacity to act as problem-solvers than over-dependence on the wisdom and knowledge of civil servants and elected officials.

One need look no further than the modern business to see this. In recent years, much has been made of the importation of business practices into government and charity. But few policy-makers have quite grasped just how much the principle of self-reliance has become central to modern business, exercised at every level of the modern business organisation, not just at its apex. In his important books, *The Age of Unreason* and *The Empty Raincoat*, Charles Handy describes the industrial business as being shaped like a pyramid, with manual workers at the base of the pyramid, receiving and obeying instructions from a remote head office at the apex of the pyramid.[1] Once, the educated elite who staff head office might have been thrusting and entrepreneurial in spirit and attitude. Over time, however, they became complacent, immune to change, and rule-bound. Compared with their modern equivalents in Japan and America, they became uncompetitive and faced closure, unless they were prepared to undergo dramatic change in form, style and attitude.

From being shaped like a pyramid, those organisations which underwent this change have come to resemble a maypole, with a slim, charismatic head office. The new senior managers devolve much of the day-to-day decision-making process to semi-autonomous units which thus hold the different ribbons of the maypole. Those who hold these ribbons have a similar stake and say in the enterprise to those at the apex.

The maypole is bound by a common set of values: ideas which motivate all who associate together within the company. And within each part of the company, the aim is to foster self-reliance, autonomy and responsibility. The distinction between the pyramid and maypole-like organisation is pictured in Figure 16.1.

Building blocks of community

Community is essentially composed of people in relationships. Geographical communities are formed from a sense of common identity and shared locality. Communities can be broken down into a number of basic building blocks, all of which are seen to be in need of strengthening. The following sections in this chapter suggest how these different building blocks could be refashioned into stronger, more confident and more self-reliant communities – from the 'bottom up'.

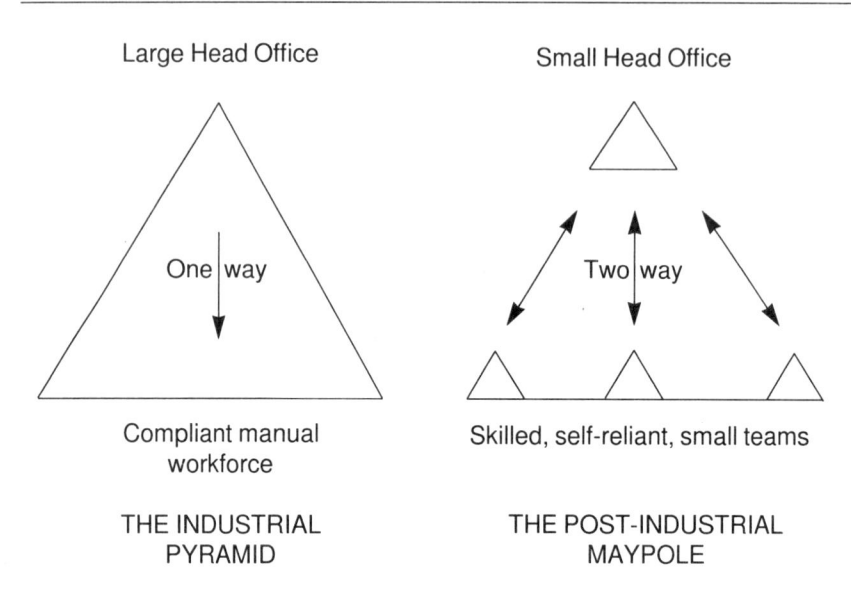

Large Head Office — One way — Compliant manual workforce — THE INDUSTRIAL PYRAMID

Small Head Office — Two way — Skilled, self-reliant, small teams — THE POST-INDUSTRIAL MAYPOLE

Source: Atkinson, D. (1994) *The Common Sense of Community*, Demos.

Figure 16.1   Lines of communication within organisations

The family

Self-reliance starts at home, and the basic building block of community for most people is the family, in all its forms. Every parent wants the very best for their child, even if they do not know how to go about helping it to maximise its life chances, and even if the home circumstances are such that they receive little or no support from relatives or neighbours. Moreover, it is around families that many of the building blocks of community are formed: networks of childminders, voluntary nurseries and playgroups, and the active engagement of an older generation in care for the young in such settings as Scouts, Guides, supplementary schools and leisure activities.

For decades, sociologists have argued that the unfolding logic of modern industrial society implies that the traditional family is in terminal decline and that the role of child-rearing will be increasingly undertaken by the Welfare State in an echo of Plato's *Republic*. They have a point. The extended family of industrial society – two parents, grandparents, uncles and aunts, as well as children – has gradually vanished. First, advances in medical care, family planning and the emancipation of women shrank the family to two parents and a small number of children. More recently, liberal divorce laws and contemporary attitudes have shrunk the two-parent family to a single parent for a rapidly growing minority – a majority in some neighbourhoods.

The Welfare State has supported this shrinking family by ensuring that it receives the financial help it needs to survive. This generosity is justified in the language of choice and social justice. But we now know that this individualistic standpoint is not necessarily beneficial from the young child's point of view or from that of the well-being of society as a whole. These needs require parents and others to exercise restraint, to limit their choices and the range of their goals. There is a need to balance the pursuit of individual goals within the context of the child's need for stability, continuity and the material support which comes from a wage-earner and the role model of two loving adults.

The list of incentives needs to be long and powerful if the trend of decades is to be halted. Amitai Etzioni, founder of the influential Communitarian Network in the USA, believes the problem of individualism goes deeper. His main concern is:

> not with incentives or punishment, but with the need for a change of heart: people need to enter marriage more responsibly and be more committed to making it work ... The long term goal must be to bring up children who are better able to form lasting relationships and participate actively in the life of their community.[2]

Only then can we reduce the false choice between keeping parents together in unhappy marriages and allowing them to break up: both options which guarantee unhappiness for the child.

Sense of place

The second building block is a sense of place. For many decades, this has been in retreat because of a more mobile, disconnected culture. Mobility, whether upward or downward, has been taken for granted as an inevitable consequence of market forces in both the labour market and the housing market. One survey reported that the average British manager moved once every three years.[3] Entire industries have shut down, leaving whole communities with no local employment and only the prospect of uprooting elsewhere to find work.

Mobility can pose a real threat to community. When people move, the connections with friends, family and others which are part of our sense of place are loosened. More time and energy needs to be invested to replace these in a new location. If you never see the same faces down the street or across the landing, where is the incentive to begin making new connections? It is only with the continuity of 'encounter' that community spirit grows and people who live around us become no longer strangers, but 'neighbours' we can trust.

Although, in recent years, evidence does suggest that mobility has been in decline, people are still moving, but less far, usually within a two to three-mile radius. Various factors are tending to root people more in a post-industrial economy. Dual-earner couples (now nearly two-thirds of all households) find it harder to move, as do those suffering from negative equity. New technologies, in theory, are making it easier to find a better balance between work and home. And there is clear evidence of mounting concern for the quality of the local environment, focused on everything from high streets to air quality. However, it is unlikely that these 'rooting' factors will fully reverse the prevailing ethic of economic efficiency which fuels job mobility in particular.

There are many institutions that give expression to this sense of place. Most areas have a residents' association. They are more successful when they have the muscle to achieve modest improvements, say, in street lighting or in gaining a pedestrian crossing on a dangerous road. Some residents' associations have developed into Neighbourhood Watch schemes. There are also few towns which do not have a number of youth and sports clubs. Like playgroups, adventure playgrounds, urban farms and advice bureaux, these take time, skill and finance.

Most towns can boast of one or two significant voluntary agencies which give expression to this sense of place. Birmingham has several. One of the oldest is the Birmingham Settlement, which has made a long-term and significant contribution to the social and economic stability and growth of the Newtown area. The St Peter's Urban Village building in Saltley once housed a large teacher training college. It is now crammed with local enterprises and devolved sections of city departments, and is managed by a local trust which bought the college and runs it as a kind of mini-town hall for the area – an interesting reversal of the voluntary sector's traditional subservience to the local authority.

Another example is St Paul's Community Project, which grew up in the Balsall Heath area of the city. It runs a charitable secondary school, nursery centre, farm, enterprise and community centre, and acts as the village hall, village green and focal point for the surrounding neighbourhood. It is significant for three reasons:

1 It is equal in size to many local authority institutions, yet it is an independent charity which is governed by parents and other residents. The pride which comes from ownership is tangible.
2 Its school takes rejects from the large local authority schools. Without St Paul's, they would roam the streets, take no GCSEs and graduate only with a certificate in failure. In 1993, St Paul's outperformed all but six out of the city's 70 secondary schools in the GCSE league tables.
3 St Paul's has only been able to thrive by linking with all the other agencies, residents and religious associations in the neighbourhood. These links gave rise to a neighbourhood forum which has helped the

whole area to lift itself from the 'bottom up' in a dramatic and compelling way. Five neighbouring 'urban villages' are doing likewise. As we shall see, their implications for a new social order are significant.

The Settlement, St Peter's and St Paul's are development trusts. These trusts are an interesting new way of helping local people to gain greater control over their own lives. A growing number are now scattered in most urban areas of the country. They are self-governing, locally-managed agencies which normally have charitable and limited-company status. Because they respond to local needs, no two development trusts are alike. And because they recognise that to regenerate a community means adopting a comprehensive approach, they are involved in a wide range of activities.

They have a number of basic principles in common:

- They are concerned with the long-term regeneration of their area – with its economy, its environment, its facilities and services and the 'spirit' of its community.
- They seek to be financially self-sufficient and independent.
- They aim to create assets in the community and make a profit to be reinvested in the community.
- They are community-based and accountable.
- They are working in partnerships between the community, voluntary, private and public sectors.

However, even significant ventures like these, let alone the many smaller, voluntary ones, face a huge uphill battle. Most are beset by constant financial or staffing crises. They rely on small donations, voluntary and transient help, have little guaranteed money, no status and virtually none of the authority which could give them leverage over decision-makers.

Schooling for life

For decades, community educators have tried to capture what Henry Morris meant when he said that the best school 'lies athwart its community' and provides it with a mirror which reflects its identity and a dynamo for assisting with its development. There have been many valiant attempts to achieve this aim, and some exceptional successes. However, most have encountered difficulties because, hitherto, State schools have not belonged to their neighbourhood. They have been 'in' it, but not a part 'of' it.

In 1988, the government introduced legislation which enabled all schools to become semi-autonomous and also granted them the right to choose full self-governing status. The new semi-self-governing and fully self-governing schools are now able to bring together the previously separate functions of finance, management, control and delivery under the roof of each individual school. The simple fact that the new semi-self-governing and fully self-governing State schools have at least 15 governors, all elected or co-opted from among the school's parents and neighbourhood, should help each school become more accountable to its neighbourhood. It should ensure that the neighbourhood controls the school through these governors and their head.

Although the government did not necessarily intend to create a situation in which every school could become a community or neighbourhood school, it has none the less done so. Some significant benefits accrue. First, the new situation is educationally beneficial, because it closes the gap between home and school and makes each the extension of the other. Second, it is also potentially much more democratic. Further, it helps to take party politics out of the government of each school and replace it with the real concerns of the catchment area and its parent customers.

Self-governing schools require new administrative posts, which the large secondary schools may be able to afford but the smaller primaries cannot. However, by pooling their resources, smaller schools could provide for a 'cluster' facilitator, or administration officer, and produce a cluster development plan and establish fresh forms of support and new resources.[4]

House and home

Some would argue that the development of the housing co-operative movement is of even greater value to local people in encouraging a shared sense of ownership and involvement. By the same logic, the idea of the housing action trust, which takes responsibility from the town hall to run an entire estate then hands it to the tenants, is a radical and imaginative step. The net outcome is the rapid extension of home-ownership. In place of uniform, drab, remotely-managed, State-provided houses has arisen a combination of privately-owned houses and a range of locally-managed ones. In turn, of course, this has persuaded most town halls to become rather more imaginative in the way they manage those many houses still left under their control.

Street and park

After the home, it is the street and local park with which children identify. If beliefs give a personal identity, place gives a bounded geographical and physical sense of belonging. In real life, identity and belonging merge, and each child's innocent Jerusalem lies within a short radius of home. However, in practice, the street which a generation ago was a safe place to play is now dominated by the passing car and a fear of the unseen stranger. Too many public spaces are uncared for, and the corner pocket park is a 'confused' space. What looked pretty on the architect's map belongs to no one and is thus untended, a site for the accumulation of rubbish, and a hiding place for the petty criminal.

Since the modern town is too large to be administered centrally in every respect, it may be that the neighbourhood would be better at caring for street, park and place if it had a greater degree of ownership and the tools and resources to act. In some places, parks are being handed over to community trusts and being given the freedom to develop in very different ways, linking parks to learning, healthcare or the arts. These ideas are rich with potential. But they are still strongly resisted by most local authorities.

Secure neighbourhoods

As society has become more fractured, crime rates have soared, particularly those for 'petty crimes' – vandalism, car-related theft, robbery from the person and the house. Crime Concern estimates that crime now costs £20 billion per year. Although there is now some evidence that the rise has halted, the debilitating *fear* of crime, the cost of which is incalculable, has risen even more rapidly than *actual* crime. The proportion of children who are allowed to walk to school has fallen from 7 in 10 to 3 in 10 in a decade. Children and women feel afraid to walk the street in the evening. Windows and doors have long been bolted. Insurance companies and investors have virtually deserted some areas.

Poorly-designed schools and houses, dark and dirty streets and confused open spaces do not help. They offer a hiding place and foster low expectations and a disregard for property and person. As Alice Coleman of King's College has shown, a range of simple physical changes to the environment can have dramatic benefits. She suggests reclaiming 'confused' public spaces and giving them to individual families, reducing the number of shared entries and common walkways.[5] Burglaries in Westminster have been cut by 55% by adopting such measures.

But the longer-term solution rests with neither architect nor police, but with the family and the neighbourhood.

First, studies demonstrate that lack of consistent discipline boundaries within the home contributes to anti-social behaviour in children. If a child is allowed to assume that 'anything goes', the seeds are sown of a careless disregard for others. Hard-pressed parents now need help to teach character in the home. Their efforts need to be reinforced at school and in the family centre. For example, it is possible to envisage the nursery and primary school as being not just a 'provider' of education to young children, but also a centre for the whole family. Ideally, the nursery and primary school should combine the functions of education with those of social and healthcare, advice and training in parenting and employment skills. It should help children to learn early about the realities and responsibilities of adult life. The pre-school teacher and colleagues are not so much acting *in loco parentis* as *'in loco grandparentis'*.

Second, neighbours need to acquire the courage of their conviction that it is wrong for children to destroy property, steal, or abuse adults. The Neighbourhood Watch schemes have achieved lift-off. Remarkably, there are now over a million members, 10,000 schemes in the Midlands and over 100,000 schemes in the UK.

The efforts of the St Paul's project and others to 'Build a Better Village' of Balsall Heath so raised residents' expectations and confidence that over 500 people decided to stand on their street corners to eliminate the street prostitution, kerb crawlers and pimps who had blighted the image of their area and held back progress. In addition to solving one problem, others were also resolved. The figures for drug abuse, car theft, burglary and truancy also came down. Residents began to talk of being able to leave their car and front door unlocked.

Today, Balsall Heath claims, with some justification, to have one of the most developed Neighbourhood Watch schemes in the country. Moving from the need to eliminate the negative, these residents have begun to accentuate the positive. They wish to give a face-lift to their local park, employ a park-keeper or sports coach, implement a traffic management scheme to slow speeding traffic, and take ownership of and maintain a range of confused open spaces. The list is endless, as, heartened by the experience of success, large sections of the population have become engaged in an extensive 'community service' programme.

Enterprise and employment

In the last decade, several cities have seen great improvements to their fading industrial centres, achieved by the enlightened combination of public and private money. Birmingham, Leeds, Sheffield and other town centres have become models of enterprise and culture, compared to a few years ago.

Yet, many problems remain. By contrast with countries like the USA or Germany, we still lack sufficiently powerful businesses at the city or neighbourhood level. Despite moves to decentralisation, British industry is one of the most centralised in the world, as is British banking. Progress in city centres has been undermined by run-down residential areas surrounding the centres, which lack education, confidence and cost so much to police. This was the experience of Detroit, where glittering city-centre projects were surrounded by some of the most depressed neighbourhoods in the USA.

But the biggest problem stems from one of the negative consequences of dramatic changes in technology and organisation in both the public and private sectors. Many unskilled manual jobs have disappeared. In his books, Charles Handy has argued with great clarity that if we are not vigilant, this world could be inherited by a new elite, while an increasing number, who have no work, despair. The social divide between the work-rich and work-poor could become a chasm.

On the other hand, the very forces that have sharply reduced the number of stable jobs for male breadwinners are also creating the context for new beginnings.

First, the combination of better teachers and more flexible technologies should make it much easier to produce well-educated, employable young people, and to top up their skills throughout life, whether at home or in the workplace or college.

Second, the enterprise culture is giving rise to a range of smaller businesses, many of them neighbourhood-specific. It is also causing partners to share jobs or undertake part-time ones, and to work from home. Thus, mobility is curtailed and neighbourhood strengthened.

Third, imaginative schemes can solve two problems at once. By creating relatively unskilled jobs for unemployed young and old people, it is possible not only to carry out environmental improvements, but also to repopulate the empty spaces – like parks and railway stations – thus giving people a greater sense of security and place.

It is here that the voluntary (or third) sector can make a dramatic difference. Until very recently, the third sector held little influence, less money and few real jobs. Now, it is growing so rapidly that few recognise the consequences. As it becomes confident in its new role, the third sector will become a major player alongside the public and private sectors. It could use its new-found strength to create a variety of significant jobs in neighbourhoods and be a major resource for any national scheme of voluntary service to communities. Indeed, if the public sector could find as imaginative a way of relating to the third sector in urban neighbourhoods as it has with the private sector in city centres, then even more could be achieved today than Robert Owen and Birmingham's Cadbury family achieved in the past.

Far-reaching schemes are possible. Today, the Birmingham Settlement are building on previous successes with local economic institutions such as credit unions to develop a Community Bank able to support small businesses in the community through difficult times.

Refashioning local democracy

The democratic system is supposed to enable people to freely choose their representatives and government. Yet, at most elections, the resident is confronted with a choice between candidates chosen by the big parties, and others who have no hope of election.

Although there are notable exceptions, almost by definition, politicians are principally concerned with gaining and keeping power in order to implement their policies from the top down. Often, they are not interested in, or suited to, wielding direct influence within the neighbourhood or helping it to build itself up from ground level. Even those who see the point of such action often cannot spare the time to undertake it. As a result, political parties do not do justice to the rich variety of practical circumstances which define real life, and many people in each 'urban village' are, in effect, disenfranchised.

Suited to the pyramids of the industrial world, the political party has become detached from the thrust of today's better-educated, better-informed, more confident citizen. Neither the representative politician nor the resident has yet been schooled in the needs of a post-industrial form of participatory democracy. Before the credibility gap between the politician and today's articulate public becomes unbridgeable, it is important to clarify new roles.

The urban village and the active citizen

It is not sufficient to devolve finances and managerial control to schools and community agencies. Parts of the political process itself must also be devolved. The emergent self-governing urban village needs its own non-party political voice and a degree of control over its own affairs.

Many people might respond far more positively if they had their own urban neighbourhood council or forum, similar to the parish council still found in some rural villages, than to party political councillors. Because most city council wards encompass at least three natural neighbourhoods, in place of one to three local councillors, who must also relate to the whole city, there might emerge three sets of, say, 15 neighbourhood forum representatives. Such neighbourhood representatives would tend to be non-party political and could either be elected on a street-by-street basis or be a mixture of elected representatives and people co-opted from local agencies, such as schools, housing associations, religious groups and development trusts.

Just as parish clerks are funded by a small precept on the rates, so each neighbourhood forum could employ its own neighbourhood officer to act as a social entrepreneur. Just as the private economic sector depends on risk-taking, visionary people to construct new companies, products, services and wealth, so the third sector needs social entrepreneurs. Today, a new breed of determined professional is needed who is employed by the active citizens of the neighbourhood forum to bind together and empower the fractured community.

The new town hall

Together, the active citizen's neighbourhood forum, their entrepreneurial officer and those local voluntary and non-government institutions which relate and are accountable to them should substitute elements of the previously over-intrusive city council machine. As a consequence, the town hall can concentrate its efforts on enabling and resourcing others to achieve excellence.

A fresh, community-sensitive city department is needed which cuts across the city's old bureaucratic specialisms and planning areas. This new department must regard neighbourhoods as the basic building blocks from which towns are constructed. Instead of being organised segmentally and hierarchically, this department would therefore subtend an array of sub-departments, one for each neighbourhood or cluster of neighbourhoods. Although many towns have now developed so-called 'neighbourhood offices' in recent years, they are not always in response to a clear neighbourhood voice.

These new proposals are not fanciful. Hillingdon and Kent have merged several departments to create a new community-oriented one. Tower Hamlets has devolved most of its services. Braintree District Council has already implemented a range of schemes which empower local people to help themselves.[6] Recently, the Department of Environment has challenged Manchester, Birmingham and London to become 'Cities of Pride'. It has asked them to define what they might look like in the third millennium. The winds of change are blowing. As the dust which it stirs settles, it is possible to see what might replace the old pyramid-like town hall (see Figure 16.2).

Democracy has evolved and must continue to keep pace with the times. But if both new and existing agencies are embedded in the area they serve, with clear lines of accountability and clear rights for local communities to remove those that do not perform, they have the potential to be much more responsive and entrepreneurial than when they were locked into the monopoly of local government.

A new paradigm for the third millennium

The rational pyramid of the modern State gives people rights – to free schooling, healthcare, housing and the vote. It gives no place to the equally vital qualities of self-reliance, personal responsibility and mutual aid. Indeed, it has denied them. Dependence on the State has undermined significant ties and obligations – the love of the mother for the child and the duty of the father to protect and care for mother and child are felt as strongly as any objective contract. Consequently, the pyramid has been built on unstable ground.

Figure 16.2 Models of local government

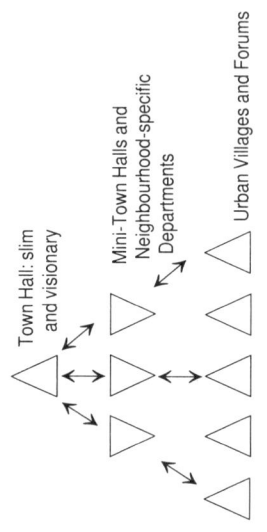

The pendulum has swung so far from traditional authority and obligation towards calculation and rights that their interdependence has been fractured, and serious damage has been caused. But it is not sufficient simply to swing the pendulum back to find a new equilibrium. Instead, we need to move forward to find a new framework which combines the wisdom of maturity with the capacity for change.

Every new generation rebels against some of what it sees as the conservative traditions of its parents, before discovering both how important it is not to reject all the wisdom and maturity of the past and that the wheel of responsibility has to be reinvented in some form. Today, however, while many young people are individualistic and rights-conscious, there is also much evidence that they have a powerful sense of responsibility for the environment into which their children will be born, which their industrial forefathers did little to protect. When entered into deliberately, responsibilities can be exercised with greater effect than when they are simply and unthinkingly inherited. The challenge for those who already appreciate the need for stronger communities is to show how a greater sense of belonging is relevant and attractive, rather than being a nostalgic return to a past which means little to young people today.

In today's less deferential society, authority has to be continually won, justified and remade. It cannot be assumed. If it is to work, then people will need to appreciate and voluntarily accept their responsibilities in each of the areas that communities depend on.

Conclusion

This chapter has set out some of the implications of a positive alternative for communities – how schools, family centres and development trusts could work together in a new framework of clearly defined neighbourhoods with new forms of participatory democracy. It has shown how, once released from the task of delivering services, government can concentrate on the essential strategic and visionary task.

Much has to be done at national level to complement the new spirit of community. New avenues could be opened to enable young people to serve others and contribute to their community, either as part of secondary schooling or afterwards. Imaginative schemes are being considered for mobilising people's moral commitment to help solve problems in the delivery of healthcare and education. In the USA, for example, the simple example of teaching thousands of people how to do emergency cardiac treatment in Seattle, and the mobilising of large numbers of college graduates to help with teaching, have shown the practicality of well-conceived communitarian ideas.

The prospect of the millennium celebrations offers a great opportunity for giving these neighbourhood-level experiments added weight. So far, most of the talk has been about the construction of grand new buildings, the modern equivalent of the Crystal Palace and the Eiffel Tower, as well as festivals, fireworks and street parties. But a great national celebration could also help focus attention on the social innovators. The Millennium Fund could be used, alongside private and public funds, to give new community organisations, development trusts and neighbourhood forums the chance to be at the centre of the planning process in each locality, linking the celebrations to their own initiatives.

The politicians and parties which can demonstrate that they not only recognise the nature of the problems facing modern urban life but also know how to articulate practical solutions will receive widespread acclaim from all those unsung practitioners who are already hard at work rebuilding the torn fabric of social life. If they can tap into this energy of experience, experiment and ideas, and tangibly back the third sector and the social entrepreneur by providing enabling government, they would find that they were not just capturing the decade. They would be setting the agenda for the start of the next millennium. Not just a once-in-a-lifetime chance; not even one which comes once in a hundred years. This chance is an extraordinary one. Who will take it?

Acknowledgement

This chapter is an edited version of a pamphlet of the same title published by Demos (Paper No.11, 1994).

References

1. Handy, C. (1989) *The Age of Unreason*, Hutchinson; Handy, C. (1994) *The Empty Raincoat*, Hutchinson.
2. Etzioni, A. (1993) *The Parenting Deficit*, Demos, pp.49 and 59.
3. Nicholson, N. and West, M. (1988) *Managerial Job Change: Men and Women in Transition*, Cambridge University Press.
4. The concept of neighbourhood school clusters is further developed in Atkinson, D. (1994) *Radical Urban Solutions*, Cassell; and Hargreaves, D. (1994) *The Mosaic of Learning*, Demos.
5. Coleman, A. (1985) *Utopia on Trial: vision and reality in planned housing*, Hilary Shipman.
6. Osborne, D. and Gaebler, T. (1994) *Reinventing Government*, Plume. See also John Stewart and Michael Clark of Birmingham University who have written extensively about other UK examples of good practice.

17 Relational impact statements: Measuring the effect of public policy on personal relationships

Martin Clark

David lived with his wife and three children in a modest, new home on the outskirts of a small southern town. Until recently, he worked as a bank clerk. It was no surprise when he lost his job – people had been expecting the shake-out in the banking world. Nor was it a surprise when he failed to get another job in the same area, and after three months, he resigned himself to the fact that, for the foreseeable future, he would not work in banking again. His claimant adviser at the Job Centre told him to look more widely, but banking was all he had done since leaving school.

The strain of the uncertainty was beginning to tell on the family. His wife could not go out to work because of the young baby. David was at home a lot, busy with endless job applications or skulking around, depressed. After six months, the rows became more frequent and unpleasant. Money was usually at the root of it. Winter was closing in, and the children needed warm clothes. His wife would go back to work, but she did not think David could cope with the children on his own.

Finally, the Employment Service found him a vacancy. But it was little more than part-time, desperately low-paid, started early, and the conditions were terrible. He could not refuse, because it would look as if he were claiming fraudulently. Reluctantly, he took the job on the claimant adviser's assurance that he would soon be eligible for in-work benefits. Not an ideal solution, but at least it was a positive outcome for the claimant adviser: one more off the register and on the stepping stone back to full-time work.

However, the pressure had destroyed David's family. He never saw the children in the morning. The household income had barely changed – in fact, David was sure he ended up with less after travel costs. Separation from his wife followed a few months later.

Was this really a positive outcome?

David's story shows that unemployment – and some policies aiming to address it – can take a heavy toll, not only on the public purse, but personally, on psychological and physical health. Some of these costs can be measured in financial terms – welfare benefits, training and retraining schemes, as well as lost tax revenues. But how do we measure the personal costs? Who else is affected, either directly or indirectly – spouse, children, neighbours – and what about those compounded costs – financial and personal?

This chapter sets out the case for establishing a consistent method of measuring the *relational* costs and benefits of public policies, why these considerations have been neglected to date, and how it might be feasible to include a *relational analysis* as an essential part of future policy formation.

Relational impact: The forgotten dimension

Four principal factors have led to the neglect by policy-makers of a concern for how decisions made at a public level impact on the private world of people's relationships.

First, the overriding ideological motivation for policy reform in almost every corner of government in recent years has been the drive to enhance economic growth and efficiency, in the belief that only when taxes are low and public expenditure cut can the market mechanism be released to eradicate the worst of poverty and create employment opportunity. Many commentators, business people, and even economists – while not necessarily disputing the efficacy of the free market – have come to doubt the fundamental premise underlying this strategy: that economic indicators are the litmus test for measuring national as well as individual success and prosperity. Distinguished Harvard economist Amartya Sen has argued strongly that measures such as disposable income and Gross Domestic Product are wholly inadequate as a guide to human well-being.[1] Rather, indicators should relate to the quality of the social environment, taking account of factors such as social cohesion and mutual aid. Richard Wilkinson, in his compelling analysis of poverty and health, argues that the determining factor for health is not an absolute measure of wealth, but the degree of inequality, and the psycho-social stress related to that relative inequality.[2]

A second obstacle has been the tendency for policy-makers to formulate measures with the individual primarily in view. A relational approach, by contrast, takes a broader perspective and sees the individual in context – surrounded by their network of relationships with family, friends, work colleagues, and so on. The spotlight is shifted away from solitary, individual persons and onto the 'glue' which binds them together and enables them to function.

A symptom of the attention to individuals has been the concern to promote and protect individual 'rights'. Attempts have been made to assess policies for their effects on particularly vulnerable individuals, such as children, elderly people and women. The advantage of a relational emphasis is that it creates a neutral territory for the discussion and resolution of competing individual rights. The term 'relational' is itself neutral and has considerable appeal without necessarily raising the issue of norms.

Third, public policy debate until now has confined any discussion of relationships under the narrowly-defined label of 'family policy'. This has been a debate hijacked by disputes over what is a family, what forms a family should legitimately take, and whether the State should support them. A relational approach sees that all major legislation impacts on relationships. Even such an unlikely candidate as the Jobseeker's Allowance, which will be taken as a case study later in this chapter, can be viewed as having significant relationship implications – and may prove to be counterproductive in terms of its own stated objectives, owing to a failure to take account explicitly of how it will change the relationship between jobseekers and their advisers.

Finally, the most obvious reason for the neglect of relational concerns has been the lack of an effective tool to measure those non-financial, intangible impacts. Although attempts have been made to assess the impact of legislation on families, the results of these family impact statements have been limited. For these reasons, it is time another approach was taken.

Relational impact statements

A relational impact statement (RIS) would aim to assess the relationship consequences of a specific piece of legislation or set of decisions made by a public body. Many different kinds of assessment are now used more or less routinely in public life. Relationship impact assessments fit into the general category of attempts to determine the likely consequences of public decisions, both to make such decisions as effective as possible in meeting their own stated objectives and to anticipate and minimise any unwanted and negative side-effects that a particular policy decision may cause. They could also function as a benchmark to evaluate the direction and rate of change in relationships over time.

Impact assessment is not new. As well as the various assessments made of most new government legislation, which are reviewed below, it is now commonplace that public and private bodies are expected or obliged to conduct environmental impact assessments of new projects and programmes. Some enlightened companies are beginning to conduct 'social audits' which analyse the impact of their activities on their various stakeholders.

However, the idea of a *relational* impact statement is entirely new. The concept has emerged from recent developments in relational thinking by the Relationships Foundation, following the successful piloting of the technique in auditing the quality of human relationships in several institutions.[3] It is the availability of this technique which offers the promise of developing a new approach to impact assessments of public policy proposals.

Relational impact statements have a number of advantages over existing methods of assessment. An RIS could enable a government to be more effective in achieving the goals which it sets for itself in and through specific pieces of legislation. For example, if the Child Support Agency had been examined critically from a relational perspective at an early date, much wastage of public resources, as well as much unnecessary individual trauma and unhappiness, might well have been avoided. If it transpires that fewer fathers are jointly registering their children, then the objective of reinforcing parental responsibility on absentee fathers has failed.

At a time when there is a growing demand for impact assessments from a variety of sources, the RIS may provide an umbrella concept which will allow various interests and lobby groups to express their concerns within a coherent framework. Growing demands for legislative impact assessment by lobbies for women's rights, children's rights and the rights of the elderly would also be better served by a broader framework where the rights of different interests can be put into a wider context and some overall balance of interests be proposed.

For the family lobby, the RIS is more flexible and inclusive than the more familiar family impact statement (FIS), in that indirect sources of pressure on individuals, and hence on families, can be more easily encompassed. Single people or those living alone or without relatives are not excluded. Also, the RIS directly addresses the central goal of concern about family functioning – how to sustain healthy, stable relationships within families – rather than being diverted into a discussion about means to that end, such as a debate about family structure.

More significantly, an RIS would provide a platform for an assessment of public policy which can straddle the departmental divisions of government. One of the major stumbling blocks to achieving a coherent family policy has been the lack of a governmental mechanism with the authority to encompass the whole spectrum of concerns which impact families. As discussed below, committees of Cabinet or inter-departmental working groups can co-ordinate policy, but they cannot create policy: it took the UK government more than a year to decide which ministry would take the lead for the International Year of the Family in 1994 before finally designating the task to the Department of Health.

Family impact assessment: An analysis of past experience

In the USA, attempts to assess the impact of government policies on families emerged early in the 1970s, prompted by a concern that policy-makers should know how their decisions were affecting family functioning. One history starts with a Senate hearing at which several scholars argued that 'family impact statements' should become a requirement in all policy-making.[4] The Family Impact Seminar organisation was established to research and promote this possibility. Over time, it has evolved a sophisticated framework of family impact analysis tools for assessing the past, present and probable future effects of public or private policy on 'family stability, family relationships and responsibilities'.[5] Despite interest by both Presidents Carter and Reagan, their overtures produced no more than a Select Committee initiating a Family Criteria Task Force in 1987. At the time of writing, however, neither the federal administration nor any state or city government has formally adopted family impact statements.

In Britain, the concept was first aired by Patrick Jenkin MP, who, in a speech to the 1977 Conservative Party Conference, stated that ministers in a future Tory government would be asked to accompany new proposals with an 'assessment of the impact on the family'. Once in power, however, the idea disappeared from view – but not until it had been pursued by Frank Field MP in a series of Parliamentary Questions, and then in a paper for the Study Commission on the Family.[6] His concept of a family impact statement focused on the vertical and horizontal distribution of income through tax and benefit systems. Demonstrating that post-war policies had, on balance, acted against families with dependent children, he advocated an FIS to expose and redress this problem. The 1994 International Year of the Family generated some momentum for an FIS,[7] and there have been renewed efforts to generate Europe-wide support for the idea.[8]

The only concrete example of an FIS becoming part of the legislative process is to be found in the state of South Australia. It was introduced there in April 1980 following the election of the Liberal Party (effectively, the Australian conservative party), through a new Family Research Unit in the Department of Community Welfare. It required that all proposals for significant new legislation, projects or administrative operations be assessed for their likely impact on families prior to consideration by Cabinet. Thus, Cabinet should be fully informed of the family implications alongside economic, technical and environmental issues in the decision-making process.

A simple pro-forma is used to assess policy, at the core of which is a rating sheet listing categories of family functioning against different types of family composition and other characteristics. Family functioning is divided into economic well-being, general well-being, family autonomy, family relationships and family structure (each with several sub-categories). Finally, a family impact statement is developed, representing a summary of the whole exercise. Where negative impacts have been predicted, these should be quantified in terms of the numbers of people affected and the extent of the effects together with options for alternative or remedial measures.

However, by 1982, the system was showing signs of strain, with staff complaining that the statements demanded too much time or were difficult to complete adequately. In only 50% of cases was the FIS stipulation even complied with. When the Liberals lost power in 1984, the system was abandoned, but since early 1994, a new and more appropriate version has been operating with greater success.[9]

What lessons can be learnt from these examples? The three key factors in effective assessments are the ease with which an official can conduct the analysis, the clarity of the criteria used, and the existence of political and bureaucratic muscle to act where unsatisfactory conclusions are reached by the assessment. It is also vital that the process carries the implementing agencies with it, engendering confidence that it is both feasible and desirable to conduct it thoroughly. Given that the potential impacts of any policy are invariably complex and contentious, the challenge is to develop a method which offers both simplicity and consensus. In this respect, the South Australian approach is commendable in moving quickly from a general overview to considerable depth when a potential impact is identified.

The FIS approach only became a possibility in South Australia owing to the political support of an explicitly 'pro-family' administration. But in the UK context, the word 'family' has become enmeshed in a stultifying ideological impasse which should make advocates think hard about whether even to use the term. It is this type of issue, as well as the technical problems bedevilling the FIS method, which argues for a new approach.

Measuring relationships

Relationships between individuals can be examined in a variety of different personal and institutional contexts. The individual's relationships can be analysed in the context of his or her 'relational base' or support group, in the context of the household, the extended family or kin group, the local neighbourhood, the town or city, the workplace, the sports facility, or wherever. It is also possible to distinguish relationships which take place in a context of specific roles or tasks which the individuals fulfil, such as between doctor and patient or doctor and nurse, and relationships which occur outside any formalised context.

Probably the main reason why relationships have not been the subject of impact assessment for legislation in the past has been the difficulty of deciding what to measure, as well as the problem of measurement itself. It is not possible to measure easily many aspects of personal relationships such as intimacy, trust, responsibility and obligation.

A new approach to analysing the relational impact of public policy on personal relationships was developed by Schluter and Lee in *The R Factor*.[10] They argued that a sense of mutual responsibility, duty and obligation will only develop generally where there is what they term 'relational proximity', which they define as 'a closeness of relationship between two individuals through which each is able to recognise the other more fully as a complete and unique human being'.[11] Relational proximity does not guarantee a sense of mutual obligation, but mutual obligation will not exist without it. To state it formally, relational proximity is a necessary but not sufficient condition for responsibility and obligation to exist, either between individuals or at the community level.

There are five dimensions of 'relational proximity' – that is, aspects of closeness in personal relationships – which are described below. These may also be seen as preconditions for close relationships to exist. They provide a framework for measuring the impact of public policy on personal relationships on the basis of an objective data source. Hard, factual data can be supplemented by 'soft' opinion data to build up a picture of how a policy impacts on relational proximity.

The five dimensions of relational proximity, and how each of them can be measured, are detailed in Box 17.1.

From analysis of data as to how each of the five dimensions of relational proximity in relationships between individuals will be affected directly or indirectly by a public policy decision, it is possible to build up a picture of the overall relational impact of that decision. As, in some cases, a public policy may have positive effects in one dimension and negative in another, it is impossible to avoid some subjective element in the overall relational assessment. However, the subjective element occurs even in economic analysis, where the long-term effects have to be weighed against the short-term, and economic benefits or disbenefits for one individual or group weighed against those for another group.

Developing a methodology

In assessing the relational impact of legislation or other policy decisions, the primary need is to distinguish the *direct* or *indirect* impact of the legislation. The direct impact of legislation is on those relationships which are relevant to

	Box 17.1　Dimensions of relational proximity
Dimension	*Measurement definition*
Directness	The amount of time spent in contact which is made directly, i.e. face-to-face, rather than through a third party or through an impersonal medium such as by letter or (increasingly) e-mail. It concerns the method of communication as an indicator of closeness of contact.
Continuity	The frequency and regularity of contact, and the period over which contact is maintained. It concerns the reliability or predictability of the relationship, and the capacity of the contact to build mutual respect and trust.
Multiplexity	The extent to which people have contact in more than one role or context. It is a measure of variety of contact in order to develop a more 'rounded' relationship through an appreciation of other dimensions of another person's life, experiences and feelings.
Parity	The extent to which people meet as equals, not necessarily in terms of their role or status, but in terms of their perceived personal worth. It concerns the nature of the power relations between people and their ability to participate equally in decision-making, for example.
Commonality	The extent to which people share common purpose, vision or experience. It highlights the conditions which facilitate mutual understanding and trust between people.

the goals of legislation and which are necessary to make the legislation effective in terms of its own stated objectives.

Taking the Jobseeker's Allowance, for example, the direct relational impact will be on the relationship between claimant adviser and claimant, which is directly relevant to the stated goal of the legislation to encourage claimants back into work as quickly as possible. Also, the adviser is tasked with certain duties towards the claimant under the legislation.

The indirect impact is that part of the relational impact of the legislation which was not a part of its stated intention. Often, legislation can have powerful side-effects, in the same way as medicine. These may be either positive or negative, and may, on occasion, have greater significance than the main, intended effect – just as a medicine's side-effects can, on occasion, outweigh the original purpose for which it was prescribed. Almost always, legislation or other public decisions will have a relational knock-on effect for the families and households of those directly affected. These knock-on effects need to be examined, especially if they are cumulatively negative, as would appear to have been the case with much recent legislation relaxing restrictions in areas such as financial markets and credit controls, Sunday trading, drinking laws, gambling laws and instituting the National Lottery.[12]

For example, to take the case of the deregulation of Sunday trading, the following sets of relationships were impacted and would need to be separately assessed:

Direct

- Sunday retailer–Sunday shopper
- retailer–shopworker
- big retailer–small retailer

Indirect

- shopworker–spouse/child
- Sunday shopper–spouse/child

The first steps, then, are to identify those groups directly and indirectly affected, by studying the mechanisms through which the policy will be implemented. The identification of those individuals and groups most affected is not always straightforward. Second, an assessment of existing research is vital in assessing likely indirect effects on households, families and communities. Again, experience is vital in assessing likely issues to explore, such as the consequences of changed income levels, travel-to-work times, working hours, residential mobility, and other similar factors.

One major research issue here is the limited value of collecting data on how people think they might respond if the legislation were to go through, even if such surveys were politically feasible. Such surveys on likely responses to changes in the law are notoriously unreliable because they can only reflect speculation about a future event. Consumers, for example, found it very difficult to predict if and when they would go shopping on a Sunday if deregulation of shop hours was introduced.[13]

Thus, during the planning stages for legislation, as well as during the period when the proposals pass through the legislative or equivalent process, it might only be possible to indicate the likely direction of change. No accurate assessment of the size or timescale of the change would be possible.

The more research is undertaken into how people relate, and how they respond in their relationships to changes in public policy, the easier it will become to predict the likely relational impact of new proposals. In the early stages, it may be difficult to gather sufficient information prior to the decision being reached to make a detailed assessment. So, *ex post* assessments of legislation are the most promising way to learn the techniques of analysis and likely directions of change resulting from different types of legislative intervention.

No existing data sources adequately capture the complexity of relational issues. Some cover limited aspects of relationships, such as information on divorce/separation, children taken into care and population mobility, but these are often in isolation from other data on the persons concerned.[14]

Thus, available data sources could be used to infer, as far as possible, the direction of relational changes, while specialised measurement techniques will need to be developed which directly address the particular relational issues in question.

In his critique of the South Australian Family Research Unit approach to family impact assessment, Maas argues that it needed to be made more rigorous in a number of ways, one of which was to develop more sophisticated measurement techniques, employing indicators and surveys, for the range of dimensions under scrutiny.[15] Interestingly, he particularly refers to relationships when making this point.

The Relationships Foundation's relational auditing method asks detailed questions designed to elicit an understanding of the five dimensions of relational proximity between parties to a relationship. The Relationships Foundation is developing a track-record in providing quantitative and qualitative information on the state of relationships in arenas as diverse as prisons, companies and elderly people's homes.

Public policy assessment: The UK context

The story of attempts to introduce more 'family-friendly' policy-making in other countries demonstrates both the potential and the problems of such interventions for the UK. In this section, I examine how relational impact assessments might be integrated into our existing policy-development process.

The current assessment process

There is nothing new about assessing the likely effects of new policy during the legislative process at Westminster. Already, three basic forms of assessment are statutory requirements of any bill presented to Parliament. One statement covers the bill's financial effects: its implications for public expenditure. A second predicts its impact on public service manpower. Clearly, these two are related, since savings may be made if staff are cut in affected departments and agencies. The third statement summarises a document called a 'business compliance cost assessment', which measures the likely cost (or savings) to businesses of complying with the legislation.

If it is considered possible and desirable to assess impacts on public spending and employment, and on the private sector, why not extend the process to the wider human environment, given all the benefits which will flow from doing so? It is this argument which has prompted some to claim that the practice of making such predictive statements opens a niche for other impact assessments. For example, Malcolm Wicks MP, formerly Director of the Family Policy Studies Centre, envisaged that an FIS would be conducted alongside the other impact assessments which appear on the face of parliamentary bills. He argued that this would increase the status accorded to a more thorough and consistent consideration of family issues by civil servants, MPs and the media at a stage when any conclusions could be used to modify the proposal.[16]

New legislation comes under two further forms of scrutiny during the policy-development process. These can be divided into those which take place in the preparation of a bill for Parliament and those occurring once that bill has been laid before the House up until the point at which it becomes law. First, in working up policy proposals to the stage at which they are ready to pass to Parliament, government departments customarily subject the ideas to varying levels of internal scrutiny. This ranges from 'subjective' comment, based on the experience of ministers and senior civil servants, to relatively sophisticated application of computer modelling packages.

Secondly, MPs and Lords 'read', debate and refine parliamentary bills in both full session and smaller committees. In the 'Committee Stage', the government is questioned by the opposition in considerable detail on each section of the bill. Evidence for and against the proposals is often heard, and if a sufficient case can be made for change, then the government will sometimes concede to modifications. Once the bill has also been debated by the House of Lords, the revised version becomes law as an Act, subject only to the addition of detailed clarifying regulations.

Is this typical process of predicting the effects of legislation effective in providing government departments, MPs (and the public) with the widest range and highest quality of data available at all appropriate points to enable them to make sound judgements about the impacts of any policy proposals?

While no individual or computer simulation can foresee all possible impacts and eventualities of a new policy, it is legitimate to ask how significant pieces of legislation can be passed, only to receive such criticism that they are quickly withdrawn or modified. One has only to think in recent years of the Poll Tax and the Child Support Agency to recognise that had the full extent of fiscal, relational and ethical dimensions of the proposals been more accurately assessed beforehand, much of the personal suffering and political furore which ensued could have been avoided.

Modes of scrutiny

In addition to these levels of scrutiny, there are other bodies which debate and seek to influence the final formation of new policy.

Select Committees are fast becoming important aspects of the parliamentary machinery, as they have the opportunity to investigate any aspect of policy which falls under their departmental remit. Their weakness is that many issues affecting families and the wider social ecology fall outside their authority or cut across a number of departments where it is unclear which would need to take the lead. Thus, the idea of a Select Committee on the Family has arisen to embrace issues such as parenting support, marriage guidance and juvenile crime. Such a vehicle could also take on broader relational concerns.

Another vehicle used by recent governments has been the Cabinet Committee, set up with the specific task of co-ordinating policy which normally falls across several departments of State. If there is a Cabinet Committee on Women's Issues, then why not one on the family or community, which would have the authority to investigate the relational impacts of all major measures, whether it be in the housing, planning, educational or employment context?

Arguably, it is the extra-parliamentary and governmental lobbies which are even more significant in the UK's process of policy-formation. In recent years, membership of voluntary organisations such as the World Wide Fund for Nature, Greenpeace, Shelter, Age Concern, the National Society for the Prevention of Cruelty to Children and the National Trust has escalated. Political and social commentators talk of a growing disillusionment with the parliamentary democratic process, particularly among young people. Instead, they are placing their desire to see environmental and social change into the hands of pressure groups geared up to fight single-issue campaigns which are calculated to achieve maximum media publicity.

There would be nothing to stop the Relationships Foundation and others joining forces on a relational agenda to compete for media and ministerial attention. This is certainly another avenue to consider. Yet there would then be no need for governments to take responsibility themselves to assess the non-financial aspects of legislation if this process became viewed as just another worthy cause and not fundamental to the business of good government.

A further issue to be addressed if the RIS is to become a standard tool of analysis is where in the civil service the analysis should be performed. If it is primarily within the civil service, should each major ministry have a unit to consider relational impact, or should a special unit in a major ministry such as the Home Office, have responsibility to examine all legislative proposals from a relational perspective? To what extent should government use external consultants, or even rely on lobby groups, to collect information? There are issues here of motivation, cost and reliability.

The Jobseeker's Allowance: A case study

The Jobseeker's Allowance (JSA) is a new benefits regime, sponsored jointly by the Employment Service and the Benefits Agency, which was implemented in April 1996. It is a logical development of government thinking on benefits for unemployed people: the new allowance will be more clearly linked to seeking employment, its level kept low to retain the incentive to enter low-paid jobs. This ties in with the drive to reduce social security expenditure and tackle benefit fraud.

Central features of the new policy are cuts to the level and duration of allowances payable to individuals, a greater degree of pressure exerted on claimants to demonstrate that they are available for and actively seeking employment, and tougher penalties if they are deemed to fail these tests. From April 1996, the old Unemployment Benefit (UB) of one year, which was paid for by National Insurance (NI) contributions, has been reduced to six months' 'contributory JSA'. After that period, or if insufficient NI has been paid, 'income-based JSA' will be paid at the present Income Support level. However, 18–24 year-olds who have paid NI will now receive 20% less than those over 25. New forms require claimants to state the number and type of steps that they will take each week to look for work; and where this is in doubt, they may have their benefit immediately and totally suspended.

The government hopes that these measures will intensify and improve the success of claimants' job-search behaviour, resulting in less time spent unemployed and more time in jobs, with all the relational – as well as financial – benefits which follow. But there could be negative side-effects of the process, particularly since claimants will be expected to look for work in a wider geographical area, at lower rates of pay, and to continue seeking, however many rejections they receive. How much is known about the balance between the JSA's positive and negative impacts?

262   Building a Relational Society

From assessments that have already taken place, the JSA's financial effects are expected to amount to significant reductions in public expenditure on benefits for unemployed people (£140 million in the first year and £270 million in the second). Its compliance cost assessment predicted minor increases in costs to business because of more extensive monitoring of claimants' declarations of earnings, pensions payments and mortgage payments, but offset by the advantages to employers of a more fluid labour market and by the Back To Work Bonus scheme, which offers employers a National Insurance 'holiday' period if they employ a long-term unemployed person. Finally, the JSA's effects on public service manpower are projected to be an overall reduction in staff, resulting from a streamlined administration – ironic that a measure designed to reduce unemployment will be making other people redundant.

However, it appears that there have been no attempts to assess the wider effects that reductions in benefit entitlement will have on individuals and families, nor many of the critical behavioural factors which will determine the degree of success of the new policy. How much was known at various stages of the formulation of the JSA?

The Department of Employment was reluctant to reveal on what data they based their assumptions. So it is a matter of piecing together small clues which arise along the way. One clue was the long delay before examples of family impacts were produced for the Commons Standing Committee. Despite repeated pleas from opposition MPs for 'worked examples' and 'family impact statements' to enable them to scrutinise the legislation thoroughly, it was not until the fifth week – over half-way through proceedings – that material was made available. Even then, it was of a type which appeared to be designed to show only the positive benefits of the JSA. The possibility of the poverty trap continuing to operate, or of other negative effects, was not acknowledged.[17] Furthermore, the fact that the necessary information could not be produced quickly implied that it was not available during the development of the policy. A wider related issue was that, since Parliamentary Questions are responded to in an *ad hoc* fashion, answers given by the departments – as pointed out by one opposition MP – do not always 'mesh together' to provide a helpful picture of the impacts.

The Department of Social Security operates a Policy Simulation Model (PSM) which can be used, at least in principle, to model the effects of major changes in entitlement such as, for example, the change from 12 months' UB to 6 months' contributory JSA. Here, there is enough information in the underlying dataset (the Family Expenditure Survey) to give accurate results. However, this was not the case with other aspects of the JSA. The clearest omission was in the area of behavioural responses, where it was reported that there was insufficient agreement in the academic literature about the nature of such effects to justify building them into the model.[18] Therefore, they were dealt with 'off model' – although it was not stated how.[19]

In particular, it was not known whether the operation of the JSA was likely to create added stresses in the network of relationships surrounding the unemployed claimant. The most direct relationship to be affected is that between the claimant and the Employment Service adviser, where the government has already conceded that the risk of assaults on claimant advisers will increase as a result of the stricter benefit regime and greater incidence of 'unwelcome news'.[20] There are fears that this will undermine the recent efforts by the Employment Service to improve relationships with its clients.

Turning to more indirect relationships, such as those within the claimants' immediate and extended families and their communities, the question is whether stresses will increase or decrease during the claiming period. Obviously, if a claimant is able to find suitable work without uprooting the family, the relational benefits of the JSA 'incentive' are considerable. However, as many family budgets are already at the poverty level, where any financial crisis can prove disastrous, any further downward pressure is likely to cause a knock-on effect on family members' diet, leisure activities, and clothing – all factors which affect physical and mental health, and crucially for JSA claimants, the ability to fulfil the jobseeking criteria.

A further complicating issue is that the type of jobs claimants enter are more likely to be low-paid and/or in a different occupation from their preferred one; this, in turn, may replace the stress of unemployment with the stress of insecure or unfulfilling employment.[21]

The government would argue that these potential down-sides are an unfortunate but necessary corollary of 'targeting assistance more effectively' and of the need to set limits on the growing social security budget. The question any impact study must ask is whether this is an accurate evaluation of the factors being weighed. In other words, the reduction in overall stress from being unemployed for some, plus the national budget savings, have to be weighed against the relational and financial costs for others of lower benefit levels, pressures to move home and neighbourhood, and pressure to take unsuitable jobs. The equation is not an easy one to measure, but measurement must at least be attempted, as otherwise, policy-makers prescribe in the dark.

For the purposes of legislative scrutiny, it is clearly unsatisfactory to allow the debate to polarise between the extreme claims of both sides: from the government, the impression that the new policy will have only positive impacts, while from the opposition and lobbying groups, the most lurid counter-claims.[22] Even though most are aware that the truth lies somewhere in between, this gulf between the opposing 'sides' leaves many participants frustrated and the general public cynical. The availability of consistent impact assessment data could begin to bridge the divide, improve the quality of legislation and restore public confidence. Above all, I believe that the type of impact data which will achieve these goals is relational.

Conclusion

To develop relational impact statements as an effective tool for assessing the likely impact of legislation or other public decisions on those directly and indirectly affected is likely to take a number of years. It will be necessary to carry out such assessments *ex post* as well as *ex ante* on a number of public policy initiatives to develop the techniques of analysis and establish a standardised procedure.

The effort to establish such a procedure is likely to have high returns. It offers the opportunity to make legislation more effective in terms of its own stated objectives, thus saving the public purse substantial sums and preventing the legislative and executive branches of government losing public credibility. In addition, the potential benefits to the public are immense in terms of strong family, community and workplace relationships, or at least not having those relationships subject to a continuous onslaught as the result of unintended negative side-effects of legislation. As strong family and community relationships benefit the public purse in terms of the costs of healthcare, education and crime prevention, even on narrow economic criteria, a strong case can be made for relational impact statements.

However, it would be a tragic irony to conclude a chapter on the method of relational impact statements with an appeal to their economic benefits as the reason for their desirability. If human relationships are the factor of greatest significance in determining individual well-being, as well as the health of wider society, then surely relational impact assessment should take priority even over economic or financial assessment as the primary basis on which legislative proposals and other public policy decisions are evaluated prior to implementation.

Acknowledgements

I would like to thank Michael Schluter, Nicola Baker and John Ashcroft for assistance during the research period on which this chapter is based, and Michael Schluter for material on relational analysis. Nick Bent supplied parliamentary material. Staff of the Department of Social Security and the Employment Service also offered valuable advice.

References

1. Sen, A. (1995) 'Demography and welfare economics', *Empirica*, Vol.22, No.1, pp.1–21.
2. Wilkinson, R. (1994) 'Health, redistribution and growth', in Glyn, A. and Miliband, D. (eds) *Paying for Inequality: the economic costs of social injustice*, Institute for Public Policy Research/Rivers Oram Press.
3. See, for example, Brett, C., Schluter, M. and Wright, M. (1995) *Relational Prison Audits*, Scottish Prison Service, Occasional Paper No.2, for an evaluation of the Relationships Foundation's audit at Greenock Prison.
4. Ooms, T. (1992) 'Appendix to Ford/Casey Proposal', Mimeo, Family Impact Seminar, Washington DC.
5. Priester, S. and Ooms, T. (1988) *A Strategy for Strengthening Families: using family criteria in policymaking and program evaluation*, Report of the Family Criteria Task Force, Family Impact Seminar, p.10.
6. Field, F. (1980) *Fair Shares for Families: the need for a family impact statement*, Study Commission on the Family, Occasional Paper No.3.
7. Henwood, M. (1995) 'Family Policy: retrospect and prospect', *Social Policy and Administration*, Vol.29, No.1, pp.55–65.
8. For example, activities by the Katholieke Universiteit Leuven's Department of Sociology and Prof. Dr W. Dumon.
9. For more detail, see: Stuart, A. (1984) 'Family Impact Statements in South Australia', *Journal of Family Issues*, Vol.5, No.3, pp.383–99; Family Research Unit (1981) *Family Impact Assessment Handbook*, FRU; Family Research Unit (1994) *What is the Family Impact Strategy?*, FRU; Clark, M. (1996) *Tracing the connections: the need for relational impact assessments of government legislation*, the Relationships Foundation.
10. Schluter, M. and Lee, D. (1993) *The R Factor*, Hodder and Stoughton.
11. Ibid., p.276.
12. See various reports from the Jubilee Centre, including Hartropp, A. (ed.) (1988) *Families in Debt: the nature, causes and effects of debt problems and policy proposals for their alleviation*, Jubilee Centre Research Paper No.7, Jubilee Centre; Burton-Jones, S. (1989) *New Facts for Auld*, Jubilee Centre Publications Ltd (on Sunday trading); and Jubilee Policy Group (1993) *All in a Good Cause? The Case Against the National Lottery*, Jubilee Centre.
13. Burton-Jones, ibid.
14. Useful sources include national surveys such as the decennial Census of Population, General Household Survey (GHS), British Household Panel Study (BHPS) and British Social Attitudes Survey (BSAS), and issue-specific surveys such as the Labour Force Survey (LFS), General Health Questionnaire (GHQ), Family Expenditure Survey (FES) and Social Change and Economic Life Initiative (SCELI). These are all large datasets which offer insights into social and economic change.
15. Maas, F. (1982) *Comments on South Australian Family Impact Assessment System*, Mimeograph, Family Policy Studies Centre.
16. Wicks, M. (1988) 'Family Impact – improving the policy process', *Family Policy Bulletin*, Vol.5, p.8.
17. See chapters by Schmitt, J. and Wadsworth, J., 'The rise in economic inactivity', and McLaughlin, E., 'Employment, unemployment and social security', in Glyn, A. and Miliband, D. (eds) (1994) *Paying for Inequality: the economic costs of social injustice*, Institute for Public Policy Research/Rivers Oram Press.

18 DSS (1990) *The Policy Simulation Model in the British Department of Social Security*, Analytical Services Division, Department of Social Security.
19 Informal comments suggest that 'psychological effects are flagged up'.
20 Employment Department (1995) 'Jobseekers Allowance: Risk Assessment on JSA Work Processes in ES Jobcentres (Draft)', 12 January, unpublished paper cited in *Working Brief*, Unemployment Unit, May 1995.
21 Burchell, B. (1994) 'The effects of labour market position, job insecurity and unemployment on psychological health', in Gallie, D., Marsh, C. and Vogler, C. (eds) *Social Change and the Experience of Unemployment*, Oxford University Press. The government has extended the Employment on Trial scheme to compensate for the fact that it anticipates more people entering jobs they cannot stick at.
22 One Peer even went so far as to say that 'people will die because of this bill'.

18 Changed priorities ahead: Rebuilding the relational base

Nicola Baker

Underlying each of the chapters in this volume has been a common theme: that it is the quality of our human relationships which most influences both our personal and our social well-being. For decades, we have taken this as self-evident. But, just as we have been in danger of neglecting the decay and destruction of our physical environment and have only recently recognised the need to restrict the harvesting of fish stocks and rainforests and regulate pollution and green belt development, so must we now take stock of the damage being caused to our social environment.

This is the second theme connecting these chapters: that there are significant external factors operating in the public domain of government and commerce which are having adverse repercussions, not only on our wider social relations, but also on the private domain of inter-personal relationships – in the home, on the streets, at our places of work.

This concluding chapter will attempt to draw together important strands from other chapters and begin to piece together some of the different elements which might characterise a more relational society. It will also present the case for a new approach to public policy analysis which would set in place measures for assessing whether developments in our political, social and economic life were sustaining or undermining our network of personal relationships.

The final section of this chapter will set out an agenda for redirecting our public life. The different contributors to this book are all agreed that we need to review the priorities which underlie public policy and practice in Britain today. How, then, can the balance between economic and material concerns, the tangibles, be redressed in favour of the intangibles, those relational factors which are being eroded and which are in urgent need of protection and positive promotion? Must we necessarily sacrifice the material for the relational and accept a lower standard of living for the sake of spending more time with our children and being there for our elderly relatives and neighbours? Should we think of turning back the clock on the 'Me generation', equal opportunities, individual rights, consumer choice and all our other 'freedoms' to return to the so-called 'golden age' of happy extended families, full employment and open front doors? Even if we should, can we?

To use another analogy, can we redirect the ship of State onto a course which might avoid the consequences of relational neglect? Some of those on board may believe that there is no other place to go but back to more familiar waters; but guided by a different set of priorities which gives preference to relational over economic concerns, it must be possible to find a safer course.

In seeking to chart a new course, or draw up a new political agenda, change must come at many levels of our society. Government cannot hold the tiller alone, even if it wants to. It will take co-ordinated effort at a local level, at a city level, within individual institutions and businesses, as well as nationally, to change course. Thus, four levels of change have been identified and will be expanded on below: (1) legislative and policy formation; (2) organisational structures; (3) institutional ethos, culture and purpose; (4) working practices and procedures.

The centrality of relationships

The opening chapters in this volume demonstrate the weight of empirical research which now exists to affirm the importance of relationships, especially close family relationships, for individual health and happiness. Michael Argyle (Chapter 3) assembles the evidence to make the case positively by reciting the benefits of close relationships in terms of mental and physical health and happiness. He also argues negatively, showing that the consequences of marriage break-up and conflict between spouses and between parents and children can lead to worse outcomes in terms of mental and physical health.

Similarly, A.H. Halsey (Chapter 4) seeks to draw parallels between family fragility and crime rates on the basis of research work by criminologists. One of the strongest variables highlighted by longitudinal studies is the evidence of poor or erratic parenting present in the lives of those young people involved in anti-social behaviour. However, he recognises that to make firm statements of cause and effect in this field of the social sciences, where you are dealing with complex human interactions, is invidious: which is more significant, he asks, poverty or parental breakdown, since poverty can cause breakdown, and breakdown can and usually does cause poverty? What is clear, however, is that there are correlations which enable us to see connections between, for example, secure attachment in childhood and the ability to form co-operative friendships in later life, between the incidence of having divorced parents and an increased likelihood of developing a psychiatric illness. This is a long way from saying categorically that divorce causes psychiatric illness or that the principal way to reduce the need for psychiatric care is to reduce the divorce rate.

Another observation made by a number of authors in this volume is that the critical factor in determining outcomes, especially for children, is the *quality* of relationships which they enjoy. This is more fundamental than, but is also correlated with, the structure of the family. To quote Ceridwen Roberts (Chapter 2): 'Research over the last few years has examined the links between family structure, deprivation, parenting styles and juvenile delinquency and suggested no simple link.' However, it is evident that these 'external' influences exert their effect on the child through the 'direct mechanism' of the parent–child relationship. The amount of time, care and concern available to a child can mitigate the disadvantage or deprivation they might suffer as a consequence of marital discord, divorce or single parenting (see page 25).[1]

Concerning the critical parenting role, Shirley Dex makes a crucial distinction between the benefits of spending 'quality' time with their children and those which flow from 'quantity' time with children. Quality time gives a child a sense of self-worth, but for a child to grow up with a strong sense of security, it needs to know a parent is available for them at any time. The tragedy of divorce and much lone parenting is that children lose touch with their fathers and miss out on a potentially vital source of affirmation and approval. Needless to say, we all know intact families where long working hours deprive children of a bedtime story or a game of football.[2] As Helen Roberts (Chapter 7) cited from a Barnardo's study, children themselves believe that family life suffers more on account of fathers working too long hours than mothers working full-time.[3]

Friendship relationships are a neglected field of social and political study. Yet the few studies which have looked at how friendship networks operate demonstrate how often people look to friends and neighbours, as much as to family members, for emotional and practical support. Job mobility and our dependence on the car have, on the one hand, mitigated against maintaining and deepening friendships, but have facilitated new and diverse social contacts on the other.[4] Elderly people, in particular, rely on friendships for support and for informal caring – a function which might otherwise have to be provided at the taxpayer's expense in the form of home helps (see page 28).

However, it is the marriage or couple relationship which we now take to be the barometer of relationships in our culture. In earlier generations, the prevailing model of marriage was of 'differentiated' and 'complementary' roles suggested by the different economic functions of breadwinning husband and child-rearing wife. Today's model is often described as 'symmetrical' or 'companionate' (see page 22), where the emphasis is less on maintaining a social institution or an economic unit, and where higher expectations are invested in personal happiness and fulfilment.

This shift in perceptions has moved the spotlight onto the nature of the relationship between husband and wife, what cements them together, and how that bonding can be kept strong. A key factor in the survival of many marriages, according to RELATE, is the quality of communication and mutual understanding between marriage partners and the attitude of commitment shown by both partners to work through difficulties rather than escape via divorce (see pages 86–7).

The discussion about causality is thus a central issue for the authors of this volume. This is because a thorough understanding of all the interrelated factors behind social questions must be a prerequisite before effective policy interventions or practices can be implemented. For, without such knowledge, the evidence for what best strengthens relationships – whether within or outside families – remains thin, and our interventions and expectations of what is likely to be effective are going to be based more on conjecture than on a sound basis of wisdom (see page 99).

None can dispute that the relationships we have with family, friends, neighbours, work colleagues and others greatly determine our own individual sense of well-being, self-worth and physical and mental health. What we wish to contend, in addition, is that there are significant connections to be made between the quality of relationship and care within households and neighbourhoods on the one hand, and on the other, the sense of cohesiveness and level of co-operation experienced in the wider context of our social interactions. The stability and security of our intimate relationships with family and friends equips us to take on wider involvements beyond the home environment.

Connecting public and private life

Correlations between the quality of relationships in the household, locality and workplace and the general level of human and societal well-being is a key point of connection brought out in these chapters. But there are other connections.

Politicians and social commentators make much of the accelerated pace of social change we are experiencing, not only in the West, but worldwide. The seemingly distant realms of high finance, global competitiveness and extra-terrestrial technologies each have a huge impact on our 'private' lives. The race to apply new information technologies to previously labour- and paper-intensive processes, such as retail banking and investment transactions, has reduced the reliance on the local retail bank branch network (see page 203). Now, you only need a car to get to a cash point, and you are much less likely to meet your neighbour in the queue. Compliance with centrally-agreed lending criteria will ensure you are granted a loan; assessment of your character and personal integrity is seldom even considered. E-mail, Internet newsgroups and Web sites have eliminated much paper-based transaction and replaced face-to-face communication, even within the same office building.

Perhaps the most obviously neglected connection between the public and the private spheres concerns the impact on the family lives of ordinary people of developments in the labour market and the changing structure of employment in Britain over the last two decades. Overseas competition has rendered large sectors of our manufacturing capacity unprofitable. Companies have restructured, down-sized and out-placed in order to reduce the high costs of full-time manpower. In its place has come a different type of job – typically service sector, part-time, and increasingly female and lower-paid. Now that our economy has adjusted to assume a dual-income household in order to finance a mortgage on a house and other accepted elements of a 'normal lifestyle', couples and family members are having to redefine roles and responsibilities. Many couples are finding that the demands employment makes on both parents, either to earn a basic living or to comply with employer demands to work longer hours, reduces the value placed on children and the time available for them (see page 155).

Whether the trend towards women having a greater role to play in the public arena as breadwinners is more the result of labour market shifts or a consequence of women's own expectations is debatable (see page 151). What is clear is that every household in Britain is engaged in a juggling act to achieve a new balance between breadwinning, child-rearing and wider community involvement. What is not yet clear is how a healthy balance which builds up rather than undermines family life can be achieved. But the connection between employment patterns and family pressures is crystal clear.

Decisions made in company board rooms across the globe and in smoke-filled or smoke-free committees in Brussels or Westminster can have a profound effect on the way individuals in Britain today relate to one another. Work patterns affect the amount of time spouses spend together and with their children; retail developments determine whether individuals rely increasingly on their cars for added convenience, but at the cost of an opportunity to greet their neighbour. The design of housing estates can alter the opportunities for social encounter (see page 222), pensions policies and welfare strategies can affect an elderly person's decision to go into a residential home or remain in their own place (see page 111).

Other chapters in this volume have highlighted disturbing inconsistencies between public policies across the different sectors of government and exposed the lack of connection between the activities of different departments of State.

One major concern has been the knock-on effects of deregulation in the job market. As employers are given greater incentives to create low-paid jobs, and part-time rather than full-time jobs, in order to avoid paying National Insurance, Sick Pay and other employee benefits, so the downstream costs of increased take-up of Family Credit, Income Support and Housing Benefit have had to be met by other departmental budgets. Gabrielle Cox points out in Chapter 13 that the fiscal consequences of increasing numbers of low-paid jobs could mean a reduction in tax revenues to the Treasury and questions raised about the continuing affordability of current levels of social security (see page 193).

Criminal justice policy is another obvious area which has suffered from the lack of a co-ordinated policy across government departments. A concerted strategy to tackle crime prevention would require the Home Office to take a lead responsibility. But it could not be effective without the participation of the Department of Health, Department of Social Security, Department for Education and Employment, the Department of the Environment (who fund closed-circuit television surveillance schemes through the Single Regeneration Budget), as well as the Lord Chancellor's Department, ensuring the involvement of police, probation, schools, local community, the courts and social services. Which single department is going to be willing to fund special support for the families of delinquent children, for respite care or holiday schemes, or for mediation and reparation projects?

It was an administration which purported to espouse family values which deregulated Sunday trading and accelerated the trend towards greater casualisation of the workforce, weaker employment protection provisions and increased numbers working anti-social – i.e. family-hostile – hours.

The present generation has also seen a trend towards the centralisation of political decision-making and a loss of incentive for regions, cities and localities to act on their own initiative to solve local problems of unemployment and urban decay. Although the current encouragement of locally-based partnerships, especially between public and private sector interests, helps to facilitate local relationships and foster co-operation, a continued dependence on central government funding will ultimately stifle local initiative (see page 234).

Thus, a clear-cut distinction between the public domain and the private lives of individuals cannot hold true any longer; each impinges on the other directly and indirectly, advertently and inadvertently. However, although few people would question the responsibility of public agencies to intervene in the private world of families where violence and abuse are destroying relationships, there continues to be a reluctance to see how public policies can be used positively to support personal relationships, whether in the home, neighbourhood or workplace.

Why public policy must address relationship issues

As another general election period looms ahead, both sides of the political spectrum are re-examining their 'family-friendly' credentials. The family ticket may not be fashionable, but it remains a potent force, especially in 'Middle England', a fashionable term among political commentators, which appears to describe the natural – but currently disaffected – Tory voter.

When MPs of the Left and Right acknowledge that family breakdown is the 'no. 1 problem facing our nation', that the family is 'the foundation of any decent society',[5] and that a job and a stable family are the two best crime prevention policies,[6] the electorate may wonder whether, at last, a point of consensus has been reached. However, whatever agreement may now exist on the seriousness of the consequences of family breakdown, there is little sign of a consensus developing within either of the political parties – let alone between them – on identifying and tackling the root causes of family conflict and social fragmentation.

The family policy debate has effectively reached stalemate: the interventionists on the one hand are calling for measures to alleviate poverty and insecure employment and to make provision for specific supports for families in need; in contrast, the *laissez-faire* camp – a curious alliance of 'traditional family values' supporters and libertarians strongly committed to freedom of choice in personal lifestyle – are holding firm to the line that the State must keep out of private family matters.

Several important factors are emerging which will force the body politic to end this impasse. These have all been alluded to elsewhere in this volume.

First, the burgeoning size of the welfare budget. The cost of social security payments in support of pensions, unemployment benefit, child benefit, and so on, now amounts to some £90 billion, or 12.6% of GDP.[7] This figure is set to grow unless welfare payments are cut or demand reduces. The latter appears unlikely at present, while the former, though now firmly on the political agenda of both our mainstream political parties, may well prove politically unacceptable given the level of cuts which might be required in the future.

Demographic trends indicate a significant rise in the elderly population, especially in the numbers of people aged 85 and over: those most likely to need personal support and care. Can we continue to assume that most of the caring will be given, freely, by family members, and more particularly, by married women who are not working full-time outside the home? If not, we may be faced with footing the bill via private insurance schemes. The alternative, as Ceridwen Roberts has pointed out in Chapter 2, is a dramatic increase in taxes to pay for public sector caring which would substitute – to the tune of an estimated £34 billion, equivalent to the NHS annual budget – all the unpaid, informal care currently given by family, friends and neighbours. The strength of family and local networks will determine the size of that bill.

Second, evidence from medical studies shows that relationship breakdown is correlated with poorer outcomes for both physical and mental health. The signficance here is that a decline in the health of the nation will lead to greater demands for public resources to be committed to healthcare, resources which might otherwise have been available to support job creation, urban regeneration or other measures with a potentially preventative effect. Pressure on healthcare funds reaps other tensions which directly impinge on family relationships: hospital patients sent home earlier, care-in-the-community 'customers' left inadequately supervised, and pressure on doctors, nurses and family members to start comtemplating euthanasia.

Third, employers are becoming increasingly concerned that Britain's industrial performance is being constrained by the declining pool of talent and skill of the workforce, relative to international competitors. Unless schools, colleges and retraining schemes are able to provide the level of skills and aptitude required by business today, Britain's ability to compete abroad may well suffer tomorrow. As both John Monks (Chapter 9) and Clive Mather (Chapter 10) argued from their different sides of industry, company performance relies to an increasing extent on the ability of its employees to deliver higher levels of productivity and lower levels of absenteeism. Family troubles and financial stress at home, often leading to alcoholism, addictive gambling and many forms of ill-health, do not help achieve this goal.

Fourth, levels of both crime itself and fear of crime have already led to calls for tougher forms of punishment, longer prison sentences and increased powers for the police. The correlations between inadequate parenting and anti-social behaviour cannot be ignored. This makes criminal justice an issue about relationships: how to prevent crime by improving socialisation at an early age, and how to deter crime by reducing the anonymity of the physical environment of local communities.[8] Although predictions about crime levels vary considerably, it is not inconceivable that Britain will follow the experience of the USA, where the use of imprisonment has quadrupled in 15 years, and 2% of the male workforce is currently in prison.[9] Likewise, there is growing awareness that extreme criminal cases are on the increase and therefore, the pressure on the courts and on the government to be seen to act yet tougher towards the criminal will lead to greater restrictions on civil liberties. It is these concerns which led to the Criminal Procedure and Investigations Bill (1995), which aims to increase the burden of disclosure on the defendant and help gain more successful prosecutions.

Fifth, you do not have to be a 'moral panicker' to accept that while each of these trends above might be successfully solved in isolation, together they represent potentially destabilising forces owing to the numbers of people, families and communities who will reap the whirlwind. It is evident from Dick Atkinson's experience in Balsall Heath in Birmingham (Chapter 16) that those who are 'socially excluded', because they are out of work, dependent on welfare payments, elderly, sick or with a criminal record, also recognise that they are politically excluded and disenfranchised (see page 244).

The law and its limits

It would be naive in the extreme to suggest that all our social ills are the consequence of bad laws or the absence of good laws. Before turning to look at public policy solutions, it is important to emphasise that no edict of the courts or dictate of government can replace the fundamental moral responsibility borne by every citizen to choose attitudes and behaviours which build up our common life rather than destroying it.

Some argue that public policy is powerless to alter social behaviour, and that tax and fiscal measures have little influence in determining people's choices between, for example, marriage or cohabitation, or between staying at home with the children or going out to work. Others believe that politicians and social workers have no right to meddle in such personal affairs. You cannot make people care for one another, or live with each other, when they no longer see the purpose. The law may succeed in modifying behaviour, but the law cannot change men and women's fundamental attitudes. Greed and selfishness warrant another kind of physic. They cannot be cured by changing the economic circumstances. If the roots of relationship breakdown lie in a deeper malaise, as Graham Cray hinted at in his analysis of postmodern thinking (Chapter 5), then public policy may only be able to alleviate its symptoms, but not eradicate its causes.

Yet the evidence presented in this book shows that, in some circumstances at least, the law does act as a deterrent and fiscal measures could operate as incentives to encourage families and communities to stick together. Compassion and self-restraint – the real antidotes to greed and selfishness – can be encouraged by both the content and ethos of our laws.

The law cannot change our hearts of stone into hearts of flesh, but it can act as an important moral signpost, both for good and ill. Fathers should take responsibility for the maintenance of children, says the Child Support Act; young people aged 16 and 17 should still be cared for by their parents if they have left school but not found a job or a training scheme; you need never work again if you play the National Lottery because 'it could be you' who wins the jackpot.

In choosing our political leaders, we can all play a part in choosing what values should be signposted. If we believe that the time has come to change the priorities of government and commerce, then we would call on all our mainstream political parties to respond to a new set of priorities – relational priorities – and make the strengthening of relationships at all levels a central goal of public policy.

Agenda for change

There are no quick-fix solutions to the erosion of relational values. Trust, empathy, commitment, generosity cannot grow again overnight once they have been abused. Therefore, only a long-term strategy, certainly longer than one parliamentary term, and a vision broad enough to motivate not only the 'top-down' but the 'bottom-up' can hope to steer the ship of State onto a sounder course.

This volume has brought together many of the inter-connected strands of our public life and shown how our family, work and social relationships are affected by the external pressures of law and market. They demonstrate the need to review the operations of law and market at four distinct levels of public life:

1 legislative and policy formation;
2 organisational structures;
3 institutional ethos, culture and purpose;
4 working practices and procedures.

Legislative and policy formation

If public policy is to demonstrate a better balance between economic and relational values in its underlying motivation and intention, a new mechanism is required to ensure that relationship well-being becomes one of the 'key performance indicators' of government's activities.

Martin Clark (Chapter 17) has described the potential of relational impact statements and how they might be incorporated into the UK's legislative process (see pages 258–61). Such a process of measurement would provide:

- a means of highlighting the non-financial impact of legislation, and especially its effect on the social ecology;
- an objective assessment of what constitutes the preconditions for healthy relationships using the concept of 'relational proximity'; this framework can be used to establish a benchmark to assess the relationship consequences of a particular piece of legislation;

- a neutral platform to discuss the competing claims of different groups in society – e.g. children, elderly people, ethnic minorities – which focuses not on the individual alone, but on the wider context of the network of relationships surrounding the individual;
- a broader concept than simply 'family impact', which avoids the sterile debate about family structure and concentrates instead on the essence of a healthy family life – the quality of relationships between individuals;
- a coherent basis for conducting assessments of policies which straddle different government departments and which currently require extra *ad hoc* instruments of government to be set up, such as Cabinet Committees or inter-departmental committees.

Thus, relational impact statements could potentially achieve a better co-ordination of policies across different departments of State and address inconsistencies of policy. A number of issues could immediately benefit from such an analysis: what effect would the widespread provision of childcare to enable more mothers to go out to work have on parent–child and couple relationships in the home and wider neighbourhood? Could the operation of Family Credit and Income Support be altered so that families with dependent children are not worse off than other groups? Are recent planning measures to discourage more out-of-town development having the positive effect of encouraging town-centre redevelopment and any cohesive effect on local communities?

Organisational structures

The impact of public policies is mediated by the structures of our public, and now increasingly private, institutions. Some of these structures form a bridge between the State and the delivery of education, health, justice, welfare and other services to the individual. Other structures concern trade and manufacture, business and industry, banking and finance, all of which act as intermediary bodies standing between the realm of government and the citizen.

Are these structures non-relational, and how could they operate more relationally? Is there a need for new structures? Several contributors to this book have highlighted ways in which these intermediary bodies could become instruments for strengthening relationships, facilitating greater co-operation rather than competition, interdependence over independence or dependency.

Taking the world of business, both John Monks (Chapter 9) and Clive Mather (Chapter 10), from their different industry perspectives, referred to the need for a new contract of employment to be at the heart of our industrial life. Both see the future of our economy, and therefore of the labour market, as dependent on deploying human resources most effectively. That cannot happen in a culture of confrontation. The new contract of employment would be based on an exchange of duties and obligations, a commitment to certain working conditions on the one hand, and a commitment to provide labour on the other. John Monks goes further and calls for a 'social partnership' in the workplace, where, in exchange for job security, the employee would commit to flexibility in skills deployment and training and an openness to adjusting working patterns to fit changing market requirements.

Employers and the trade unions are both acknowledging that co-operation and flexibility are the hallmarks of the new 'stakeholder' model of corporate governance, where a successful business seeks to balance the interests of all its stakeholders – employees, customers, suppliers, as well as shareholders – because of the importance of good relationships to achieve higher productivity. The Royal Society of Arts' recent report, *Tomorrow's Company* emphasised the growing importance that business is now placing on good relational skills.[10] This recognition should not be confined to the multinationals with large personnel departments; because of the enormous size of some companies, specific measures may be required to maintain co-operative internal and external relationships. But if it can work on a large scale, it can work in any size of business.

The size of institutions and organisations is a major relational concern. As Timothy Green has described (Chapter 14), global competitive pressures have forced the UK banking sector to merge or perish (see page 203). As a result, financial institutions may reap economies of scale, especially by centralising decision-making, but they are also reaping the consequences of reduced customer interface. Here, there is the potential for new institutions to emerge which may have a regional investment focus, operate on lower margins and expect lower returns on their capital, but are able to engage more with the needs of local business customers because they are able to develop the necessary prerequisite to sound lending: a trusting relationship based on personal knowledge.[11] The concept of family savings syndicates, where banking and insurance services are offered to a group of individuals bound in association at lower risk, is now being developed by the Relationships Foundation. Credit unions, community banks and other co-operative financial institutions and instruments are needed to fill the ground vacated by the mainstream retail banking sector as the local branch network is cut back.

Developments in science and technology will continue to profoundly affect both home and workplace. The new information revolution is already demanding more egalitarian organisational structures within businesses as more people need access to more of the same data and transactions take place electronically, eliminating the need for face-to-face contact or paper transmissions. As e-mail and the Internet become more indispensable, more attention will need to be given to the implications for human relationships, and it will fall to governments to ensure that the key values of universal access and public interest are protected (see pages 177–9).

Local responsiveness and local participation are key components of a relational institution. In the field of local government, Dick Atkinson (Chapter 17) believes that new structures are required to rebuild the sense of communal responsibility in individual neighbourhoods. In his chapter he uses the analogy of pyramids and maypoles to describe his concern that local government and public service structures have lost touch with local people (see page 236). He believes part of the solution is to resurrect the parish council as a model for a new urban 'village' and elect and co-opt neighbourhood representatives to serve in a non-party political capacity. These neighbourhood forums could take on some of the functions currently controlled by the city council and enable local people to 'own' solutions to local problems in housing, employment and welfare.

Community development trusts such as the St Paul's, Balsall Heath Trust (sse page 238) provide another example of an innovative institution set up to restructure local communities which have been by-passed by the existing mechanisms of local government. They enable enthusiasm, enterprise and finance to be channelled into specific projects which directly respond to local needs and provide a platform for disparate interests – public, private, voluntary, religious and secular – to work together towards a shared purpose. Innovative mechanisms are much needed to solve the housing problem, and in particular the lack of supply of social housing. Housing action trusts are one such vehicle, which take the responsibility for running a housing estate out of the hands of the city council and into the hands of the tenants. These trusts have led to a rapid extension of home-ownership and the creation of mixed estates, part private, part locally-managed, in place of drab, uniform, remotely-managed estates.

A neglected area of public policy which impinges in many subtle ways on the structure of our communities concerns the planning system. Although there is evidence to suggest that planners and developers are taking account of local views and relational concerns such as safety, mixed usage and 'encounter' opportunity (for example, the urban village movement), nevertheless, the problems in our inner cities will not be resolved without a determined strategy. One important element must be the widespread application of community impact assessments as an intrinsic part of the planning process to ensure that the social and relational impact of a development has been fully taken into account (see page 226).

Institutional ethos, culture and purpose

Institutions have an ethos and a culture, as well as structure, and it is often at this level of 'values' that an institution or organisation betrays a lack of relational awareness. It is also at the level of a shared commitment to strengthening relationships as a foundational value that conflicting interest groups can unite.

One example where a new attention to the dimension of human relationships has already opened up the potential for a different ethos is within the criminal justice system. The concept of 'relational justice' has been developed by the Relationships Foundation, which has reviewed the operation of criminal justice in the UK from the starting point that crime primarily represents a break in relationship between offender and victim, and only secondly constitutes a breaking of the law of the land.[12] Relational justice offers an alternative ethos for the criminal justice system and a new way of holding in balance its different goals – retribution, deterrence and rehabilitation – by placing the restoration of relationship between victim and offender at the heart of the justice process. Relational justice also provides a useful integrating theme which can bring together the different, sometimes competing, agencies within the criminal justice system and create common ground and a shared purpose.

There is one issue which has served as a touchstone of the ethos in many businesses and which has challenged employers to radically reassess their attitude to staff relations and that is the family-friendly agenda. There are significant costs associated with restructuring work patterns, organising job-sharing schemes, maternity replacements and so on. But there are advantages too, as are pointed out by Shirley Dex (Chapter 11) and Clive Mather (Chapter 10), in having a workforce which is not bringing domestic problems with them to work. This is by no means only a women's issue. Several contributors here have expressed concern that long working hours by fathers place great stress on family life and relationships. Maybe the real test is yet to come, when fathers start seeking paternity leave and request a shorter working week because they want to spend more time with their families!

If Shirley Dex's 'family-hours' household model were ever to be widely adopted, it would provoke a much deeper reassessment of the culture and purposes of economic activity. Much of our economic life and company ethos is still premised on assumptions about gender roles (male main breadwinner, female flexible carer) and on expectations of promotion linked to long hours and a job-first/family-second order of priorities. The family-hours model recognises that at certain times over the working lifecycle, other responsibilities are of special importance. It also acknowledges that shorter working hours would be beneficial for both men and women, and their children, especially while they are young. However, such a model for sharing work/ family responsibilities will mean some reduction in family income, and it would also require employers to give career breaks to both men and women and make other changes, including reviews of pension packages, and so on.

If the State continues to retreat from providing full pensions and sickness benefits, employers may find themselves contributing yet more to the social welfare of their employees, both voluntarily as part of the remuneration package, and involuntarily through the tax system. This would certainly put an employer's family-friendly ethos to the ultimate test. If it works in Germany, John Monks asks, why should it not be possible in the UK (see page 124)?

Another significant indicator of the value being placed on human relationships will be the commitment given by the government and by private bodies to invest in those support services which are known to be beneficial to families under stress or recovering from crisis. To date, we have relied on the voluntary sector to pick up the pieces of damaged relationships, especially in families. However, such is the scale of family tension now that GPs, health visitors, solicitors, clergy, home helps, and even teachers, all find themselves having to give advice on relationship problems. At a basic level, it comes down to the question of resources: should we make a significant investment in preventative measures where these are proven to be helpful, or do we wait for the cost to be borne downstream in numbers of children taken into care, social welfare and housing provision, special needs' education and criminal justice costs, and so on?

David French (Chapter 6) makes four suggestions for supporting family life, based on his experience as Director of RELATE:

1 developing relationship education, primarily as part of the teaching programme in schools, but also elsewhere;
2 developing a labour market which enables men and women to balance the demands of breadwinning and child-rearing;
3 funding adequate marriage guidance, marriage preparation and other family counselling services, family centres, and so on, at a fraction of the current cost of the £332 million matrimonial legal aid bill;
4 reducing the speed at which divorce proceedings can be conducted with a view to allowing time for reflection, mediation and/or reconciliation.

Making sufficient resources available to fund such preventative measures would give a powerful signal of the importance society attaches to strengthening family life.

The success of any preventative programme does, of course, depend on the accuracy of information and research into relationship breakdown. Although we now know more than ever before about the effects of breakdown, the pathway of causation has not been simple to plot. Further research, particularly into what makes for successful, long-term, stable relationships, is still required: we know a good deal about why 4 out of 10 marriages fail, but why do 6 out of 10 succeed?

Working practices and procedures

A fourth level of change could be described as the micro-level, concerning how institutions and organisations operate and how individuals form and sustain relationships on a daily basis. Inevitably, practice and procedures are influenced by the underlying ethos of an organisation and by its structure, so that there would be much to say here which has already been detailed above. However, the authors of this book have highlighted a number of ways in which specific sets of relationships could benefit from a deeper understanding of both their dynamics and the external influences on them.

The couple relationship is probably the most complex and intriguing one. It stands at the heart of family life and provides the framework for the wider web of extended family and friendships which surround it. If greater attention were given to pressures on couples, and particularly those external factors such as long working hours, the cost of housing, media-fuelled expectations of personal fulfilment and consumer choice, there might arise an entirely new set of priorities within workplaces, around the family meal table and in the locality. There could also be a greater acceptance of the value of counselling and other support services such as mediation and relationship education, already mentioned.

Protecting and sustaining the parent–child relationship must also feature as a high priority for public policy involvement. Helen Roberts (Chapter 7) cites three 'protective' factors which are known from the studies into effective parenting to be especially important for the health of the parent–child relationship. First, children whose parents have enthusiasm for and involvement in their education do best. Thus, everything should be done to encourage parental interest in their children's schooling and ensure that home and school influences reinforce each other. Second, significantly higher levels of educational attainment have been reached by children who receive pre-school educational stimulation. For example, graduates of the High/Scope pre-school programme were found to have higher achievement, lower dependence on social services and significantly less contact with the criminal justice system. A third effective aid involves the support of young mothers by other mature mothers, who provide advice on diet and health, and general encouragement. An earlier generation of young mothers could have relied on such support from their own family members; today, this cannot be guaranteed. Thus, the time has come for parenting skills to be taught in schools and special services made more accessible for families struggling with problem children.

In a generation where we are more likely than any other to know our grandparents *and* our great-grandparents, it is ironic that respect for elderly people has seemingly declined. Inter-generational relationships within and outside the family can be priceless. These can be encouraged in small ways by the telephone companies giving family number discounts, or by local authorities providing home aids to enable an elderly person to remain in their own home for longer.

Wally Harbert (Chapter 8) has some further suggestions to enhance inter-generational relationships and ensure that the talents and experience of older people are not wasted. With many newly- or early-retired people looking ahead to as much as 25–30 years of active life, it is important that individuals, employers and local authorities take responsibility to support pre-retirement education and planning to maximise opportunities for further employment, voluntary work, community service, retraining, further education and leisure activities. Certainly, there is a real need for the wisdom of older people to continue to be passed down the generations, especially in the realm of family life.

Relationships in the workplace will be a key indicator of progress towards a more relational society. This must be a concern of government as much as business, because, as Clive Mather argues in Chapter 10, good external and internal relationships are vital to commercial success, especially in a globally competitive market place. A company's capacity to create new employment and to adapt to changing market conditions does impact directly on the government's record on job creation, but also obviously on tax revenues. Fair proceedings for employee relations, greater openness in communication between employers and staff, training and re-training opportunities to improve quality of service, and individual motivation are all recognised as good for the bottom line, even if many companies say they cannot afford to implement them. Both John Monks (Chapter 9) and Clive Mather (Chapter 10) believe the 'new' contract of employment is essential to the future success of British industry, to be based on a new relationship of trust and co-operation between employer and employee and a new emphasis on reciprocal responsibilities and open communications.

Clive Mather outlines three elements to this contract which would create a radically more relational business ethos once the required practices are implemented:

1 the employer commitment to make available training and personal and professional development, with the reciprocal employee obligation to take full advantage of it;
2 the employer commitment to involve, and the employee commitment to participate;
3 the mutual commitment to openness and frankness, for employers to explain the company's performance, plans and prospects, and for employees to explain their own abilities, capacities and constraints – both in terms which the other can act upon.

One way in which the relational benefits of such a new contract could both be implemented and subsequently monitored is by conducting a new kind of audit, a 'relational audit'. The Relationships Foundation has been developing a model for such an audit to be applied, not only to companies, but any institution or organisation concerned to improve relationships, whether between management and staff or with customers, and suppliers. A relational audit has already been completed examining prison officer–prisoner relationships within a Scottish prison.[13]

The audit's function was to measure the structure of relationships using both quantitative and qualitative data and to test for the preconditions for good relationships. Its specific objectives were to provide a benchmark against which to assess the impact of prison policies and relationships, to locate gaps in current working practice, and to help management explain the process of change to both prisoners and officers. In such a highly-charged atmosphere as a prison, it was shown that an objective measure of the nature of the prison officer–prisoner relationship was possible to devise, using a survey framework based on Schluter and Lee's five dimensions of 'relational proximity' (see page 256). This model has also been adapted to audit an elderly people's home where there was concern that the non-material aspects of the home – the quality of care and contact between staff and residents – were not featuring as largely as the material aspects, such as the furniture and facilities, in the assessment of its success as a home.

A further social application of this relational audit methodology has been proposed as a basis for analysing the dynamics of relationships between residents in tower blocks and other inner-city housing.[14] The audit would separate out the effects of architecture, housing policy and estate management on the way relationships develop within housing blocks. Inter-community relations in inner-city situations is another possible area of application.

As we enter a new era in information and communications technologies, the potential for enhanced relationships is enormous. Yet, with more freedom comes a greater responsibility to use our new tools wisely. As Andrew Briggs argues (Chapter 12), public policy has an important role to play in ensuring that the social implications of the new technologies are properly assessed and that quality of life issues are not side-lined in the stampede to achieve a competitive advantage.

Conclusion

Relationships are not private property. They belong just as much to the public domain. If healthy human relationships are central to the individual and society's well-being, and if the decisions of our public servants are now seen to have invaded the 'private' relations of family and neighbourhood, often with the effect of loosening those delicately balanced relationships, the way forward now must be to call on our public servants to make the strengthening of relationships the core goal of public policy.

References

1. For a useful summary of research into family breakdown and outcomes for children, see Cockett, M. and Tripp, J. (1994) *The Exeter Family Study: Family breakdown and its impact on children*, University of Exeter Press, Appendix 1.
2. Parsons, R. (1995) *The Sixty Minute Father*, Hodder and Stoughton.
3. Roberts, H. and Sachdev, D. (1996) *Young People's Social Attitudes*, Dartmouth.
4. Willmott, P. (1987) *Friendship Networks and Social Support*, Policy Studies Institute.
5. 'Divorce reform may be abandoned', *The Times*, 27 October 1995.
6. Rt Hon. Tony Blair MP, Labour Party Conference Speech, October 1995.
7. Spencer, R. (1995) *Daily Telegraph*, 9 June; 12.6% represented the social security proportion in 1994/5 with 4.7% of GDP in 1949/50.
8. Burnside, J. and Baker, N. (1994) *Relational Justice: Repairing the Breach*, Waterside Press.
9. Prison Governors Association (1995) *A Manifesto for Change*.
10. Royal Society of Arts (1995) *Tomorrow's Company: The Role of Business in a Changing World*, RSA.
11. Porteous, D. (1993) *The 'TRUST' Proposals for Regional Banking in the UK*, Jubilee Policy Group.
12. Burnside and Baker, op. cit.
13. Brett, C., Schluter, M. and Wright, M. (1995) *Relational Prison Audits*, Scottish Prison Service, Occasional Paper No.2.
14. The Relationships Foundation (1995) 'A Relationship Appraisal of Council Housing Estates' (draft working paper).

Further reading

Argyle, M. and Henderson, M. (1985) *The Anatomy of Relationships*, Penguin.
Bauman, Z. (1993) *Postmodern Ethics*, Blackwell.
Burnside, J. and Baker, N. (1994) *Relational Justice: Repairing the Breach*, Waterside Press.
Cullingworth, J.B. and Nadin, V. (1993) *Town and Country Planning in Britain*, Routledge.
Dennis, N. and Halsey, A.H. (1988) *English Ethical Socialism: From Thomas More to R. H. Tawney*, OUP.
Duck, S. (ed.) (1988) *Handbook of Personal Relationships*, John Wiley.
Etzioni, A. (1995) *The Spirit of Community*, HarperCollins.
Gill, R. (1992) *Moral Communities*, University of Exeter Press.
Glyn, A. and Miliband, D. (1994) *Paying for Inequality: The Economic Cost of Social Injustice*, Institute for Public Policy Research/Rivers Oram Press.
Gray, J. (1993) *Beyond the New Right: Markets, Government and the Common Environment*, Routledge.
Halsey, A.H. (1995) *Change in British Society*, 4th edn, Oxford University Press.
Halsey, A.H. (1996) *No Discouragement: an autobiography*, Macmillan.
Hernandez, D. (1993) *America's Children: Resources from Family, Government and the Economy*, Russell Sage Foundation.
Hewitt, P. (1993) *About Time: The Revolution in Work and Family Life*, Institute for Public Policy Research/Rivers Oram Press.
Joseph Rowntree Foundation (1995) *Inquiry into Income and Wealth*.
Lichfield, N. (1996) *Community Impact Evaluation*, University College London Press.
Litvinoff, S. (1991) *The RELATE Guide to Better Relationships*, Ebury Press.
McFadyen, A. (1990) *The Call to Personhood*, Cambridge University Press.
Middleton, R. and Walsh, B. (1995) *Truth is Stranger Than it Used to Be*, Society for Promoting Christian Knowledge (SPCK).

O'Neill, J. (1994) *The Missing Child in Liberal Theory*, University of Toronto Press.
Osborne, D. and Gaebler, T. (1994) *Reinventing Government*, AddisonWesley/Penguin.
Pollock, L. (1993) *Forgotten Children: Parent Child Relationships from 1500 to 1900*, Cambridge University Press.
Rapaport, R. and Rapaport, R.N., with Stretlitz, Z. (1975) *Leisure and the Family Life Cycle*, Routledge.
Royal Society of Arts (1995) *Tomorrow's Company: The Role of Business in a Changing World*, RSA.
Sacks, J. (1995) *Faith in the Future*, Darton, Longman and Todd.
Schluter, M. and Lee, D. (1993) *The R Factor*, Hodder and Stoughton.
Squires, J. (ed.) (1993) *Principled Positions: Postmodernism and the Rediscovery of Value*, Lawrence and Wishart.
Utting, D. (1995) *Family and Parenthood: Supporting Families, Preventing Breakdown: A Guide to the Debate*, Joseph Rowntree Foundation.
Utting, D., Bright, J. and Hendricson, C. (1993) *Crime and the Family: Improving Child-rearing and Preventing Delinquency*, Occasional paper No.16, Family Policy Studies Centre.
Walker, J. (1995) *The Cost of Communication Breakdown*, BT Forum.
White, M. (ed.) (1994) *Unemployment and Public Policy in a Changing Labour Market*, Policy Studies Institute.
Wilkinson, R.G. (1994) *Unfair Shares – The effects of widening income differences on the welfare of the young: A report for Barnardo's*, Barnardo's.
Young, M. and Schuller, T. (1991) *Retirement Years – A Burden or an Opportunity?*, HarperCollins.

The Relationships Foundation

The Relationships Foundation provides a platform for people who believe that a new balance needs to be struck between the values of community and hard economic realities. This applies to both public and private life. Its core belief is that public policy should be debated and developed in a way that gives priority to people and their relationships.

The Relationships Foundation exists to research and initiate projects and partnerships which promote relational values in public and private life. It was developed out of the work of the Jubilee Centre in Cambridge in 1993.

Members of the Advisory Board

Viscount Brentford (Chairman)
Sir Fred Catherwood, Former Vice Chairman, European Parliament
Lady Catherwood, Author, Publisher and Speaker
Professor Shirley Dex, Economist and Lecturer in Management Studies, Judge Institute for Management Studies, University of Cambridge
David Faulkner CB, Senior Research Associate, Institute of Criminology, Oxford
Timothy M. Green FCIB, Chief Executive, Switch Card Services Ltd
Professor A.H. Halsey, Emeritus Fellow, Nuffield College, Oxford
Michael Hastings, Chairman of 'Crime Concern', Presenter of political programmes on BBC2
Dr Nick Isbister, Management Consultant, Doctorate in Psychology
Stephen May, Director, John Lewis Partnership
Jill McWilliam MBE, Public Affairs Director, Iceland Frozen Foods plc
Tim Pendry, Public Affairs Consultant
Ceridwen Roberts, Director, Family Policy Studies Centre
Baroness Wilcox, Former Chairman, National Consumer Council

Contact address

Jubilee House
3 Hooper Street
Cambridge CB1 1NZ

Tel: 01223 311596
Fax: 01223 361646
e-mail: RFoundation@cityscape.co.uk